Last One over the Wall

THE MASSACHUSETTS EXPERIMENT IN CLOSING REFORM SCHOOLS

Winner of the 1990
Edward Sagarin Prize in Criminology

Second Edition

JEROME G. MILLER

OHIO STATE UNIVERSITY PRESS
Columbus

Library of Congress Cataloging-in-Publication Data

Miller, Jerome G., 1931–
Last one over the wall : the Massachusetts experiment in closing
reform schools / Jerome G. Miller.
p.   cm.
"Winner of the 1990 Edward Sagarin Prize in Criminology."
Includes bibliographical references and index.
ISBN 0–8142–0758–8 (alk. paper : pbk.)
1. Reformatories—Massachusetts.   2. Juvenile delinquency—
Government policy—Massachusetts.   I. Title.
HV9105.M4M54   1991
365'.42'09744—dc20   90–28677
                                                                    CIP
The paper used in this publication meets the minimum requirements
of the American National Standard for Information Sciences—
Permanence of Paper for Printed Library Materials.
ANSI Z39.48-1992.

9 8 7 6 5 4 3

to Adam

. . . a present death
Had been more merciful. Come on, poor babe:
Some powerful spirit instruct the kites and ravens
to be thy nurses! Wolves and bears, they say,
Casting their savageness aside, have done
Like offices of pity.

Shakespeare

Contents

Preface to the Second Edition

A Vision for the Future or a Memoir?

It has been seven years since I wrote the first edition of *Last One over the Wall*. I wrote it to memorialize a personal journey and a radical experiment in juvenile justice reform from two decades earlier. For whatever reasons, the book has developed a following around the country, and it continues to be read by those interested in alternative approaches to dealing with juvenile offenders.

Ohio State University Press has therefore decided to reissue the book. Aside from this new introduction, I have made no changes or edits. Indeed, the experiences I described cannot be changed, and the policy implications of the reforms are as obvious and valid today as they were then. But really, that doesn't matter much. Results have never driven juvenile justice policy, nor has decency. It is therefore a matter of whether the "Massachusetts Experiment" will be studied and emulated as another way of handling troublesome and troubled youngsters, or whether it will fade into obscurity—an isolated fluke from a time long past.

This year, thirty years will have passed since I was invited by Republican governor Frank Sargent of Massachusetts to join his cabinet as commissioner of the newly created Department of Youth Services. Over the next 3½ years, we closed all of the state's reform schools—scattering the kids and dispersing the budget to an array of humane options, both cautious and quirky, for the truly delinquent.

Nationally, rehabilitation in juvenile justice has now been pretty much replaced by retribution. Whatever vestiges of treatment remain are hidden in the doublespeak of "alternative punishment," "consequences," and "discipline." Winning sound bites shape the facts, and political rhetoric prescribes the solutions.

Lessons

Would I do things differently today were I confronted with a similar juvenile correctional system with its attendant array of reform schools? Definitely. But not in the way the reader might surmise. Given the times, I'd attempt to close the reform schools more quickly and definitively, and I'd shy away from involving many credentialed professionals (particularly M.S.W. social workers) in the process.

In *Last One over the Wall* I noted that as the department became more professionalized, there emerged "the hurtful side effects" that inevitably accompany certain behavioral and medical models when practiced on delinquents. They showed up in the reintroduction of isolation cells in some of the small secure settings (this time in order to "set limits") and the pandemic use of psychotropic drugs to control the recalcitrant. It was a reiteration of the role professional helpers continually play in brutalizing settings: providing a means to avoid dealing with the profound personal, social, or institutional sources of the "unreasonable" demands of the delinquent. Having since run similar agencies in other jurisdictions—Illinois, Pennsylvania, the District of Columbia— I am convinced that the bars to substantive change in these systems grow exponentially with the number of human service professionals involved.

This is not surprising. It has always been the case in agencies with captive (e.g., juvenile corrections) or semicaptive clientele (e.g., child welfare). A dependence upon traditional models of help inevitably dulls the reform impulse, seeing it as a threat to the status quo.

In *Last One over the Wall* I cited Erving Goffman's description of the role of the helping professional in these kinds of agencies as being similar to that of a con artist's confederate. He or she is expected to "cool out the mark." Goffman's analysis has become even more compelling as we have entered a more punitive era. When I wrote *Last One over the Wall* in 1991, the country was already well down this road.

The Punitive Society

In the adult systems, lengthy and mandatory prison sentences have become the rule. The death penalty is being administered more efficiently and liberally. The narrative is increasingly being expelled from our courts—both adult and juvenile. It is now routinely characterized as "the abuse excuse," and its exclusion has robbed lives of meaning and deprived all of us of social instruction. The transfer of thousands of adolescents into the nation's adult courts and prisons is symptomatic of this trend. Most significant, in relation to the thesis of this book, reform schools have made a comeback. Overflowing this time with black and Latino teenagers, they are the vanguard of juvenile justice in America—proudly trumpeting discipline, punishment, and "consequences."

A new sense of one-upmanship drives juvenile justice planners and administrators. Who can label their young charges as the most predatory? Who can be the most detached in administering punishment? How can we disguise viciousness as treatment? How can we couch inhumane policies in moralistic terms? For obvious reasons, the "Massachusetts Experience" stands more isolated today than it did a quarter century ago.

But won't this pass? Criminal justice prescriptions for handling obstreperous or dangerous juvenile offenders have waxed and waned greatly over the years. In the past, however, each new cycle tended toward a certain progressivism. It suggests that if we can wait out this unusually neglectful period, we can anticipate a swing toward more humane and decent juvenile justice policies and practices. Sadly, I think not. I fear that this time things will be different, primarily because of the changed racial makeup of the system's clientele.

A Familiar Dilemma

I wonder not *when* but *whether* we will emerge from this dark period in juvenile justice history. The untamed punitive impulses of those who run American juvenile justice systems stem less from concern over increased crime and violence than from a realization regarding those who are likely to be the beneficiaries of retribution. The juvenile justice system has succeeded in resurrecting that great "American Dilemma" described by the Swedish sociologist Gunnar Myrdal fifty years ago, one that has plagued us for two centuries.[1]

As the destructive "drug war" defined crime and increasingly filled the prisons and reform schools, race came to define the criminal. He is likely to have a black or brown face. We are now at a point where, when we hear predictions of a coming explosion of "superpredator" youths, we all know who they are. We've learned the code.

Fear of the Young

A second contributor to the culture of retribution in juvenile justice is related to a renewed fear of young people in general—a contempt unequaled in recent years. It was reflected in a 1997 national poll that showed that the American public had the lowest opinion of teenagers and children ever measured in national polls.

A symbol for this emerged for a few weeks in 1995 when the nation seemed transfixed by the flogging of an American teenager in Singapore. Most supported the practice, often described in exquisite detail. Although the ostensible purpose of the debate was to consider whether we should use similar corporal punishment for recalcitrant teenagers, sadistic titillation was never far from the agenda, the kind Emile Durkheim no doubt had in mind when he described "moral indignation" as a kind of "disguised envy." The prospect of publicly flogging our teenagers tapped a flood of previously unexpressed possibilities—whippings, stocks, solitary lockups, shackles, handcuffs, and assorted paramilitary rituals—largely indistinguishable from sadomasochistic fantasy.

How Many Kid Killers?

Perhaps the most controversial chapter of *Last One over the Wall* was chapter 14, "The Myth of 'Violent' Teenagers." I wrote, "Of the 20,000 persons arrested for [homicide], approximately 2,000 were juveniles. Even this figure is inflated, however, since juveniles tend to get involved in such incidents in groups and with peers. A single offense often yields multiple arrests of teenagers. In addition, due to police overcharging, charges made at the time of arrest are often lowered later, if not completely dismissed. That leaves something like 1,200 juveniles across the United States who are tried annually for murder or manslaughter. Of these probably no more than 500 will be convicted of murder in a court of law" (192–93). The reviewer in the *New York Times* found these comments informative and recommended the chapter to his readers. Conversely, a reviewer for the conservative journal *The Public Interest* saw my comments as wrongheaded and certainly inaccurate.

I wrote this chapter to address the inflated fears of the public and the media over the numbers of homicidal juveniles abroad in the nation. In 1990 I had written an op-ed piece for *USA Today* on violent juveniles for a "point/counterpoint" column. The opposing view was put forth by a representative of the Washington Legal Foundation—a conservative "think tank" in the District of Columbia. His lead screamed that juveniles kill 20,000 Americans each year. This outrageous and inaccurate number passed editorial muster with no questions asked. It gives some indication as to how easily otherwise intelligent and informed persons can be misled on a major issue of crucial importance.

I tried to address this issue as best I could in "The Myth of 'Violent' Teenagers," using what I could glean from the studies then available on juvenile homicide. I concluded that there were about 1,200 arrests annually of juveniles who were accused of killing another human being. Of these, about 500 would eventually be convicted in a court of law.

Since then, researcher Eric Lotke has looked more closely at the issue.[2] He sought out figures on the number of youthful perpetrators of homicide in 1992. His purpose was to identify exactly how many teenagers under the age of eighteen were convicted for personally killing another human being that year. Lotke concluded that across the nation 940 youngsters fit that category. Of these, nearly 100 killed their parents, often in the context of abusive relationships. Half of the original 940 killed acquaintances, including abusive parental substitutes (e.g., a mother's boyfriend). *Less than one-third killed strangers.* Lotke summarized his findings by noting that across the United States in 1992, only about 290 children personally killed a stranger.

Though we hear that the times have changed dramatically with regard to juvenile violence and that we are seeing a previously unknown psychopathic "breed" of juvenile offenders, the facts indicate otherwise. Whatever rises there were in juvenile homicide rates in the late 1980s and early 1990s, they had less to do with a "new breed" than with the epidemic availability of handguns in four major cities—Los Angeles, Chicago, Detroit, and New York.

Prospects

It is my view that the model outlined in the Massachusetts Experiment is probably more appropriate than ever for dealing with contemporary delinquents. Despite its demonstrated success, however, it has not grown or developed as a philosophy of correctional treatment and practice. This is hardly surprising in an era when we must hide any intention of treating young offenders with compassion or understanding. In this situation, the Massachusetts Experiment stands as both a beacon and an irritant. If matters continue along their present path, it seems likely that the life will surely be sucked from the Massachusetts Experiment. In the final analysis, however, the survival of any model in this politicized field will not be based on results. It will, as I stated in the final chapter of this book, be "a matter of chance, of happenstance, of politics and mood." The same can be said of the current destructive juvenile justice system.

Notes

1. Gunnar Myrdal, *An American Dilemma: The Negro Problem and Modern Democracy* (New York: Harper and Brothers, 1944).
2. Eric Lotke, "Youth Homicide: Keeping Perspective on How Many Children Kill," *Valparaiso University Law Review* 31, no. 2 (1996): 395–418.

Preface

It's easy to recall what doesn't heal,
more difficult to call back what leaves no mark.

Carl Dennis

The failed products of a century and a half's dependence on the custodial institution haunt us daily. The homeless person who embarrasses, the mental patient who shocks, the chronic offender who threatens, the teenage delinquent who elicits both fear and pity—each reflects our society's bizarre skills in sequestering marginal members of our communities.

There are some who say that we routinely institutionalize a given percentage of the population in our society. Inmates of tuberculosis sanatoria are replaced by mental patients, by prisoners, and by youthful offenders. As we close one type of institution, we fill another. Studies suggest we fill prisons to occupy empty cells, regardless of crime rates.[1] Those states that build more prisons have more prisoners, those that do not have fewer. Hard on the heels of a massive "dumping" of mental patients into the general society, we began incarcerating the largest number of prisoners in our history. This is not to suggest that former mental patients filled the prisons (though some patients did end up in prison). Other social and political dynamics were at work.

Most of those who seriously jar, bother, confront, or threaten us are the alumni of our systems of exile—mental hospitals, prisons, jails, and children's institutions. The institution has been the exemplar of treatment, asylum, or supervision for certain groups from among the mentally ill, offenders, neglected children, and delinquents. We have labeled such groups with any handy legal or psychiatric nosology as falling at the "deep end" of the mental health, corrections, or child welfare bureaucracies—the most "psychotic" patient, the most "violent" offender, the most "serious" delinquent, the most "emotionally damaged" youngster. The institution was created to deal—albeit neglectfully, incompetently, and often violently—with these categories of persons. For these, the institution is likely to be the first, as it is the last, resort.

Our misplaced reliance on institutions has served only to sap our imagination. The political and the professional relationships it has engendered ensure that alternative programs are seldom considered. We cannot conceive of certain groups of our fellow citizens being safely dealt with in anything other than institutions or quasi-institutions. As a result, alternatives are seldom what they claim to be. They are quasi-institutional additions to an unassailable institutional tradition.

Alternative programs are not meant for those who would otherwise fill our mental hospitals, prisons, reform schools, and children's institutions. Alternatives are for whole new populations—the tractable mental patient, the interesting offender, the verbal neurotic, the compliant homeless person, the white middle-class delinquent—those who promise unusual rates of success in treatment and probably would not be otherwise institutionalized. We allow these alternatives only so long as they don't threaten institutions. In the disastrous dumping of mental patients over the past two decades, for example, patients left the institutions, but the staff, resources, and monies stayed on the hospital grounds. Resources were never allowed to follow the patients to the community. In New York and Pennsylvania, even as thousands of patients were methodically and massively dumped into the streets or crammed into welfare hotels, budgets for the depopulated state hospitals actually increased.[2]

What follows is about a different kind of deinstitutionalization—different in two crucial ways: (1) the resources followed the inmates to the community, and (2) the alternatives were reserved for the most difficult inmates in the system. Though this is the story of a distinct group of inmates (youthful offenders) in a particular kind of institution (reform schools), the issues differ only slightly from those involved in dealing with mental patients, dependent children, retarded clients, and adult offenders. The parameters of debate may shift, but the same dilemmas remain. Successful deinstitutionalization has more to do with manipulating labels than with diagnosis; more to do with deflating stereotypes than with management techniques; more to do with mitigating immediate harm than with proper rehabilitative models; more to do with smarmy politics than with human service planning. The real world of deinstitutionalization is seldom discussed in the polite literature of social work, psychiatry, and psychology.

Fifteen years ago, as commissioner of the Massachusetts Department of Youth Services, I closed that state's "training schools" for delinquents, beginning with the maximum-security walled institutions for violent juveniles, and sent the inmates home or into alternative programs. My action was more than just another reform in a traditionally unreformable system. Rumors abounded—the inmates had been dumped; we would set off an explosion of crime in the state; the inmates had been shipped out of the state; the reform schools had quietly reopened; juveniles were being sent to adult prisons in record numbers; other juveniles were committing violent crimes in equally record numbers; juvenile corrections in Massachusetts was in chaos; deaths among the juveniles in state care had increased dramatically; funds had been misused; I had been run out of the state—and too many more to list here. Toward the end, someone showed up in my office with a gun, apparently to kill me. A mélange of fantastic tales, distortions, and death threats suggested we had touched something complex.

Young offenders in the reform schools were considered the most recalcitrant and dangerous in the state. As a Boston juvenile court judge told me, "Forget the alternatives. These are the bottom of the barrel." Reform schools (an old-fashioned but honest name) had dominated youth corrections in Massachusetts for 140 years. Although reform schools now come disguised as youth development centers or learning centers, they remain the backbone of youth corrections throughout the United States.

The "Massachusetts Experiment," as it came to be called, is completing its second decade. One would presume that by now, if it had not been dismissed as a wild experiment that failed, it would be on the cutting edge of correctional reform. Neither has happened. The reforms have been successful, but in the inane world of corrections, nothing fails like success or succeeds like failure. The United States has just gone on locking up ever greater percentages of its young offenders— with no evidence of success.[3] The deinstitutionalized Massachusetts youth corrections system has stayed in place even as its rationale is slowly worn away by current political rhetoric. The fact that it might be effective to treat young offenders with individual concern and decency is, sadly, beside the point. We seem forever mired in the sticky policies born of our worst impulses.

Rumors about Massachusetts youth corrections have never ceased,[4] and they won't while the most serious delinquents in Massachusetts remain outside state institutions. That fact is an abiding irritant to a field grounded in mythology. It's not that those troubled and troubling teenagers present a greater risk to the community. Rather, their presence challenges not only our perception of them, but of ourselves. I've come to the view of the American criminal justice researcher Eugene Doleshal—"There is a dynamic equilibrium in criminal justice which prevents those attempting to reform criminal justice by reducing penalties or incarceration rates from succeeding."[5]

The Massachusetts Experiment was neither the "chaotic sixties countercultural event" portrayed by some nor the management-focused "planned change" we've come to expect of state human service agencies. It was anathema to most of my fellow human service professionals (at one point the publicist for my alma mater requested that I not list the university on my résumé). It fit even less easily into the neat models of contemporary consensus liberal politics.

Since 1975, the Kennedy School of Government and Politics at Harvard University has used the Massachusetts deinstitutionalization experiment as a teaching case for its graduate students—an amalgam of bright academics, temporarily out-of-work politicians, and government bureaucrats.[6] Ten years after I left Massachusetts, I was invited to sit in on a class in which the Massachusetts Experiment was being dissected. I was afforded an opportunity few have—of hearing an intensely personal time of one's life laid out in the rationalizing argot of management, tinged ever so slightly with neoconservative ideology. The professor (ironically, a protégé of the conservative criminologist James Q. Wilson, who opposed virtually everything I did) did his best within the narrow constraints academics allow themselves when approaching the workings of government. In the classroom exposition of our battling for deinstitutionalization, I recognized very little. In the translation, reality had left Harvard Yard.

As I listened to the seminar students assiduously culling the experiment for models, tools, and methods, I knew why change is so elusive in human services. These would-be managers and their proctors were neither attuned to nor interested in the factors that must mark every authentic reform in this field: a commitment to individual clientele, personal responsibility, case-by-case involvement, the ability to rebound from unanticipated crises and to exploit vulnerabilities while adhering to values beyond smoothness. For this class effective reform lay in modern management techniques.

The Massachusetts experiment was something quite different. It was as well planned and executed as any reform in state-operated human service. But it was also a human passage—raucous, fitful, threatening, exhilarating, at times impulsive, often unpredictable, changing direction as we took advantage of unexpected opportunities—and always difficult. We lived for a time on the edge of bureaucracy, professional ethics, legality, and politics. But our small deinstitutionalization challenged many of the preconceptions that sustain most state institutions and provide the rationale for the mishandling of many of the mentally ill, the homeless, the delinquent, and the criminal.

In writing this book, I have had to pluck discrete experiences from among memories and images that jogged loose in conversation or jumped out at me from yellowed news clippings. Finally, I chose the most personal, those that shook or changed me and cling to me still, too often intruding into my dreams and reveries. In the process, I am sure I have overlooked important events and slighted friends, associates, and others who were integral to what happened. For this I apologize.

It has been unusually hard for me to find the words which best express the personal aspects of those years. Suffice it to say that the experience does not lend itself easily to the discourse of management. The reader will perhaps forgive me for an analogy from music. From time to time when listening to Bach's *St. Matthew Passion,* the *Four Last Songs* of Richard Strauss, or perhaps Mahler's Second Symphony, I have occasionally found myself unable to absorb the experience. I remember blacking out, while I was seated in the Royal Albert Hall, at the thunderous C-major chord in the "Libera me" near the end of Benjamin Britten's *War Requiem.* Similar things had happened two or three times before, though it was a rare accident to lose hold of time and place. Perhaps this all has to do with some unresolved adolescent repression I find impossible to relinquish. I mention these experiences because in a sense, they come closest to describing those that overtook me during particularly difficult times in trying to deal with a relatively insignificant state youth corrections agency. They rose in my consciousness tied to a face, a family, a particular youngster, or a haunting story that made forgetfulness fitful, demanded attention beyond my capacity, occasionally transported me, and always gave matters meaning.

Acknowledgments

I cannot possibly acknowledge all those who were part of this book. For that, I apologize.

The opportunity to take some time away from a busy schedule was afforded me through a grant from the Edna McConnell Clark Foundation.

I appreciate the support of my colleagues at the National Center on Institutions and Alternatives, particularly Herb Hoelter, Tim Roche, and Jim Sprowls. The patience of Alice Boring, who typed and retyped the manuscript through its reincarnations, was heroic.

My thanks to Simon Dinitz, Ivan Illich, John McKnight, David Rothman, Andrew Rutherford, Seymour Sarason, and Wolf Wolfensberger for their critiques and suggestions.

Thanks also to Lynne Bonenberger for her patience, and to Nancy Woodington for putting some structure to my ramblings.

Finally, I must acknowledge my best and most honest critic, my wife, Charlene, who shared the events in this book, helping me keep my equilibrium and ensuring some perspective in their narration.

I

Going to Massachusetts

A man's work is nothing but this slow trek to rediscover, through the detours of art, those two or three great and simple images in whose presence his heart first opened.

Albert Camus

1 *Juvenile Justice Rhetoric*

The comment (variously attributed to Dostoevsky or Churchill) that the degree of civilization of a society can be judged by the condition of its prisons applies a fortiori to juvenile justice. Youths, by their youthfulness, tend to offend us most. One might surmise that a system designed to correct errant adolescents would be characterized by care and concern. Not so. In this respect we are not unlike some disturbed families. When problems arise, all fault comes to rest on that member most visible through his or her aberrant behavior and least able to raise a credible defense. When law supports this ritual, the possibilities for harming the adolescent multiply.

Juvenile justice reform has always been more rhetoric than anything else. Some think we are caught up in cycles. The pendulum swings from toughness to permissiveness, from rehabilitation to incapacitation, and back again. In reality, however, the cycles exist only in the rhetoric. We have never had a period of permissiveness or authentic rehabilitation in juvenile justice in the United States. Juvenile justice has always been, and continues to be, neglectful, demeaning, frequently violent, and largely ineffective. Permissive treatment of delinquents is reserved for middle- and upper-class adolescents who are not likely to enter the juvenile justice system, which is reserved for the children of the poor. Nearly 90 percent of the inmates of juvenile detention homes and reform schools come from fragmented and damaged

3

families which live at or below the poverty line. Even the meager rehabilitative efforts directed at these youngsters have been twisted to meet the demands of political expediency.

Twenty years ago, the Supreme Court recognized this and held in *In re* Gault that the juvenile justice system actually subjected offenders to more severe punishment while depriving them of the minimum legal protections given adult offenders.[1] Despite the plethora of lawyers in juvenile courts joined with the myriad of helping professionals, little has changed. A recent study showed that a larger percentage of juveniles was being institutionalized than ever before. Recidivism rates remain high, and institutional abuse is rampant.

Community-based programs sprout up occasionally but are seldom what they claim to be. They are ersatz alternatives unwilling to take youngsters who would otherwise be institutionalized. In this sense, they are not so much alternative as they are additional. This kind of community-based program extends the net of social control by whisking more youngsters away from their families into residential care.

New language emerges to cover old realities. Youth prisons have changed from reform schools to industrial schools, youth guidance institutes, youth development centers, learning centers, and therapeutic communities. More recently they've moved proudly back to juvenile jails and engines of deterrence. To use Ivan Illich's term, a kind of "uniquack" pervades the field, giving validity to authoritarian, psychological bullying techniques aimed at conformity and blind obedience. I have seen professionally designed programs where at the beginning the youngsters have had to earn the right to wear clothes or be let out of isolation, where the floors of the "intensive care" cells (formerly called "holes") must be washed to flush away fecal waste left by teenagers locked in with no toilet, where "psychotherapeutic" sessions are conducted with polygraphs, where delinquents are hog-tied and left to rock on their stomachs for "calming" or because of "attitude" problems (and who, while trussed, are interviewed by a psychiatrist to assess suicidal potential).

Why is juvenile justice so impervious to reform? Is it because the clientele is so intractable? Hardly. It's something much deeper—an abiding need to see some offenders as qualitatively different from the rest of us. This compulsion colors, distorts, and eventually undermines all reform. I say "some offenders" because destructive labels are restricted to those who come into the juvenile justice system. The offense is of relatively minor importance in this process. The overriding determinants are class, race, and family composition.

An invariable theme in detention centers and reform schools is that the inmates cannot conceivably be our own. Few middle- or upper-class youngsters enter such places. When they do, they are truly the exceptions that prove the rule. In the heyday of the youth counterculture of the sixties a few middle-class juveniles briefly ran afoul of the juvenile justice system. But they were quickly diverted into the mental health system or other systems of less extreme social control (private counseling, outpatient therapy, private military schools, or prep schools). With the current national hysteria about drugs, one might have anticipated a few more middle-class youths' appearance in the youth corrections system, but it has not happened.

A two-tiered system of residential care has grown up across the country with a dramatic surge in short-term hospitalizations in private psychiatric hospitals for recalcitrant, disobedient, or drug-abusing suburban adolescents. Whether or not this approach works, the effect is to spare these youngsters the correctional diagnoses and the labels which undermine hope—"psychopath," "sociopath," "unsocialized aggressive." Such terms apply only to the children of the poor and of the racial minorities who populate our youth correctional institutions.[2]

A Brief History of Reform

The establishment of the juvenile court in 1899 obscured the fact that another revolution in juvenile justice had occurred in the early 1800s. The earlier movement had resulted in increased institutionalization of juveniles, albeit in facilities different from adult jails and prisons. The practice was firmly entrenched fifty years before the creation of juvenile courts. Long before Dorothea Dix sought better institutional care for the mentally ill, Samuel Howe of Massachusetts was pointing out the unconscionable conditions which had already arisen in these new juvenile institutions.[3]

In their report to the French government on the corrections system in the United States, de Tocqueville and Beaumont approvingly described these juvenile institutions, with their inmate self-government and exclusion of corporal punishment.

In Boston, corporal chastisements are excluded from the House of Refuge; the discipline of this establishment is entirely of a moral character and rests on principles which belong to the highest philosophy.

Everything there tends to elevate the soul of the young prisoners, and to render them jealous of their own esteem and that of their comrades; to arrive at this end they are treated as if they were men and members of a free society. . . .

The early use of liberty contribute[s], perhaps, at a later period, to make the young delinquents more obedient to the laws. And without considering this possible political result, it is certain that such a system is powerful as a means of moral education.[4]

The founder of the Boston House of Reformation, the Reverend E. M. P. Wells, had ideas about "juvenile wickedness" which differed considerably from those accepted at the time.

Wells believed that bad boys were no worse by nature than others and was convinced that a boy "can always be reformed while he is under 15 years old, and very often after that age." He became superintendent in 1828 and first drew attention to himself by introducing an educational curriculum that was wholly unlike anything that the staid overseers of delinquents at that time had ever seen. Regulated play and gymnastics figured prominently in the program and Wells frankly admitted that the "mechanical" parts of education such as arithmetic, writing and spelling, held a low place in his opinion.[5]

Contrast this description of a Massachusetts training school in 1828 with a report made on the St. Charles School for Boys by the Illinois Crime Commission in 1928, a century later.

All whippings were administered by a disciplinary officer who went . . . to each cottage each evening after supper and whipped any boys who had been reported earlier by the house father, or for whom the house father requested punishment at that time. Some boys were punished by being locked up in the "hole" for up to thirty-two days with no shoes and no mattress. They slept on wooden boards nailed to the concrete floor. Some were handcuffed to iron pipes and kept manacled day and night.[6]

Juvenile Court Reform

The invention of the juvenile court was hailed as signaling a new era in the treatment of children. Separate juvenile courts were established in all but three states by 1917. In Massachusetts Julian Mack, citing two centuries of *parens patriae* philosophy in English law, saw the juvenile court as a logical outgrowth of that tradition. Pointing to the inadequacies of criminal procedure in the handling of youth, Mack noted:

> It did not aim to find out what the accused's history was, what his heredity, his environment, his associations, it did not ask how he had come to do the particular act which had brought him before the court. It put but one question, "Has he committed this crime?" It did not inquire, "What is the best thing to do for this lad?" It did not even punish him in a manner that would tend to improve him; the punishment was visited in proportion to the degree of wrongdoing evidenced by the single act; not by the needs of the boy, not by the needs of the state.
>
> Today, however, the thinking public is putting another sort of question. Why is it not just and proper to treat these juvenile offenders, as we deal with the neglected children, as a wise and merciful father handles his own child whose errors are not discovered by the authorities?[7]

By 1932 there were more than six hundred independent juvenile courts across the land. Yet from the outset they failed to change the pattern of confining juveniles in unspeakable institutions. Rather, they added to their numbers.

In 1925 the reformer Louise Bowen noted that the Cook County Juvenile Detention Home had "every appearance of being a jail, with its barred windows and locked doors—the children have fewer comforts than do criminals confined in the county jail. They are not kept sufficiently occupied and have very little fresh air." These comments were made seven years after a report to the Cook County Civil Service Commission on the juvenile detention home. That commission called upon people like Mrs. Bowen, Jane Addams, Amelia Sears, Dr. William Healey, Judge Franklin Chase Hoyt of the Children's Court of New York, Judge Edward F. Waite of Minneapolis, and others of the "child-saver" movement to assess matters and make recommendations for reform. Its report concluded:

> Children are not now detained in jail with criminal adults. . . . . Neither is our juvenile detention home a home. For the dependents and the minor delinquents it has some of the qualities of a jail.
>
> Can the County protect its children by a better separation of the dependents and the tractable from the incorrigible, the immoral, the

confirmed juvenile delinquents? Can the Home give to its children or a deserving portion thereof a little more of a real home during their detention period?[8]

The commission recommended reclassification so that some juveniles could be placed in more homelike surroundings.

The report, however, ended on an ambivalent note: "For the remaining children, the immoral girls, the incorrigible and unruly boys and girls, the present juvenile detention home and the present custodial care are none too severe. In Detroit individual separation rooms are installed to be occupied by the incorrigibles who deserve complete isolation, which we also recommend."[9] The distinction was clear. Humane reforms were for the "deserving," while the "undeserving" should receive stringent discipline. This was the hallmark of progressive reform thought: reforms were not meant for the undeserving.

Roscoe Pound's famous statement that the juvenile court represented the most significant advance in the administration of justice since Magna Charta reflected his awareness of the gravity of the issues facing the juvenile justice system.[10] As George Herbert Mead in his classic 1918 article "The Psychology of Punitive Justice" saw it, the juvenile court forced a breach in the wall of the criminal justice system.[11] The question was whether to treat or to punish. The dilemma was complicated by the existence of reform schools, which had been around for most of the century before the juvenile court was invented. Their presence ensured that juvenile offenders would receive the worst the system could offer—punishment labeled as treatment.

Rather than putting an end to questionable child-care institutions, the juvenile court nourished them. Labels were broadened in meaning to justify a proliferation of programs by which the juvenile court could increase its power. Under banners like "delinquency prevention," the juvenile justice system involved itself with ever-larger numbers of "deserving" offenders. Progressive reforms were reserved for these. The undeserving went off to reform schools or adult prisons.

The Growth of the Helping Professions

The helping professions developed and grew through ties to institutions—prisons, reform schools and state schools for the retarded, and state mental hospitals. After the turn of the twentieth century, however, professionalism became increasingly academic and gained a measure of independence from such institutions through its ties to universities. Take social work, for example—the preeminent profession in juvenile corrections. The consequences of developments in professionalism are dramatically demonstrated by comparing the themes around which social workers' 1893 and 1928 national conferences were organized. There was a marked shift from a concern for administering institutions to a concern with a broader set of issues.[12]

National Conference of Charities and Corrections 1893	National Conference of Social Work 1928
1. State Boards of Charities	1. Children
2. Charity Organizations	2. Delinquents and Correction
3. Indoor and Outdoor Relief	3. Health
4. Immigration	4. The Family
5. Child-Saving	5. Industrial and Economic Problems
6. Reformatories	6. Neighborhood and Community Life
7. The Prison Question	7. Mental Hygiene
8. The Feeble-Minded	8. Organization of Social Forces
9. The Insane	9. Public Officials and Administration
	10. The Immigrant
	11. Professional Standards in Education
	12. Educational Publicity

Concomitant with the change in focus was the development of standardized professional methodologies such as those put forward in Mary Richmond's book *Social Diagnosis,* first published in 1917.[13] And as Willard stated in 1925: "Social work no longer attends chiefly to the confinement and management of state wards, but derives its problems from community processes far beyond state institutions. . . . On account of the necessary reference to social ends involved in social work thus broadly conceived, those ends must be fixed through appreciation of the social processes themselves in any state, and their merits defined in terms of social values."[14] Though social work joined psychiatry and clinical psychology in fostering the rehabilitative ethic, institutional bureaucracies heavily influenced the on-the-job training of professionals. The theories, categories, labels, and techniques all dovetailed with the traditions of institutionalization.

Because most of the clients were, in a sense, captive, a seductive tendency to justify the coercion grew. In an essay written in 1947, Lionel Trilling argued, "Some paradox in our nature leads us, once we have made our fellow men the objects of our enlightened interest, to go on to make them the objects of our pity, then of our wisdom, ultimately of our coercion."[15] Although the helping professions these days enthusiastically embrace coercive methods, they have developed rather complex ways to diminish the conflict between their progressive goals and their coercive practice. Diagnostic labels are readjusted so as to remove the need for the professional to coerce clients personally. Less deserving clients are defined as being outside professional expertise and responsibility. These are left to nonprofessionals—primarily lower-level staff in mental hospitals, prisons, and reform schools. To justify receiving treatment, one must show some promise. It is a world in which professionals characteristically treat only those who are likely to succeed and leave the difficult clients, who aren't expected to succeed anyway, to nonprofessionals.

This tradition dominates current professional practice with offenders. Psychiatrists, psychologists, and social workers get involved with serious delinquents only when clients with lesser problems are unavailable. It is a system in which captives are redefined and reassigned by those who, having failed, persistently claim the expertise for dealing with the problem. But if helping professionals won't deal with serious offenders, will they leave the field (and the budget) to others willing to try? Hardly. Rather than engaging in self-appraisal, they switch focus and identify more felicitous targets—"status" offenders, "pre-delinquents," or youngsters with the kinds of angst available only to the privileged. The major effect has been the creation of an inverse system whereby those most likely to present major problems to society in terms of violence or repeated crimes are systematically excluded from professional care. Conversely, those least likely to be involved in serious crimes are the most likely to receive the care of professional helpers.

Later Reforms in Juvenile Justice

Later reforms concentrated on such things as prevention, diversion, and deinstitutionalization. With millions of federal dollars from the Law Enforcement Assistance Administration (LEAA) available, programs proliferated in the 1970s and into the 1980s.

Prevention.   Richard J. Lundman and Frank R. Scarpitti estimated that, between 1965 and 1978, more than sixty-five hundred different attempts at delinquency prevention had been launched. The authors found a thousand citations in the literature about delinquency prevention programs and examined 127 of them in careful detail. They concluded: "Most projects reported in the professional literature did not permit reliable assessment of results. And those projects with experimental designs and objective measurement of delinquent behavior had not successfully prevented delinquency. . . . We found little reason to believe that a major breakthrough in delinquency prevention is forthcoming."[16] Probably the premier preventive program was advanced in 1972 by the Youth Development and Delinquency Prevention Administration (YDPA) of the then Department of Health, Education, and Welfare.[17] The YDPA recommended a national strategy of establishing youth services systems to divert youth from juvenile justice handling.

The YDPA projected a 25 percent decrease in youth being brought to juvenile courts. If enough services were supplied, it was argued, the numbers going into the juvenile justice system would inevitably decline. The opposite happened. The number of youth service bureaus increased, yet more youngsters were brought into the juvenile justice system. In no case was there any effect on reform school and detention populations.

Diversion.   Diverting young offenders from the juvenile courts was another strategy. The idea was to refer them for counseling, mediation, or other measures short of the formal court process. The concept is interesting, since it implies that there is an inherently destructive aspect to the juvenile court. What researchers found, however, was that the children being "diverted" were youngsters who ordinarily would not have been brought to court anyway. The usual cases continued to parade through the courts. As Paul Nejelski concluded, "These projects may be useful in themselves because they aid juveniles, but they increase state intervention without reducing the workload of the courts. They are supplemental, but they are not diversionary."[18] While some local communities were successful in diverting middle-class youth who generally don't penetrate the system anyway, they were notably unsuccessful with youth in the urban ghettos.

Deinstitutionalization. Deinstitutionalization was another catchword. It referred to the practice of removing juvenile offenders from institutional settings (detention centers, training schools, and jails). Although it would be difficult to find another juvenile justice issue over which so much has been said, there is precious little evidence for any effective deinstitutionalization in juvenile justice.

Whenever the number of inmates in state reform schools has dropped, there has been an equivalent rise in youth populations in other institutions (child welfare and psychiatric). But curiously, though some were simply relabeled, a significant number were not the same kids. This speaks less to the pathology of the youth than to the other social and political mechanisms which sustain institutions. It suggests that institutions have a life of their own, unrelated to their stated task. Should the requisite number of youngsters from one group or class be unavailable, others will be found to fill the void.

When consensus-driven deinstitutionalization was allowed, it was aimed at groups like status offenders. *Status offender* refers to runaways, truants, or disobedient children. Were it not for their status as children, these offenders would not be brought to court. The removal of status offenders from reform schools and detention centers didn't lower the total numbers of juveniles in institutions. It simply culled the most tractable for the community-based ministrations of social workers, psychiatrists, psychologists, and educators.

In those few cases where removing status offenders actually lowered reform school populations, other youth were soon taken in to fill the void. Labels and diagnoses were escalated to justify filling the beds in training schools and detention centers which might have been vacated. For example, a juvenile judge might order a truant to go to school every day. If he missed a day, he violated a court order and became a bona fide delinquent fit for institutionalization. This common practice was upheld by the California Supreme Court.[19] In cases where it was too risky to relabel the juvenile, the institutions were renamed to justify their continued usage. For example, when it might draw too much attention to send nondelinquent youth to reform schools, the schools became treatment centers for PINS (persons in need of supervision).

A telling example of the politics underlying such euphemistic manipulation occurred in Ohio. Following a drop in population at the Fairfield School for Boys, the legislature inserted a budget amendment requiring the Ohio Youth Commission to keep a minimum number of boys (300) in that reform school whether or not they were appropriately assigned. The chairman of the Ohio Youth Commission stated he had to "practically kidnap" boys and incarcerate them long past their release dates in order to obey the law.[20]

The amendment was attached by a legislator in whose district the reform school was located. He denied it had anything to do with jobs for his constituents, insisting he wished to ensure quality vocational programs. To do so, Fairfield's population had to be kept at a given level. One seldom sees the issue so well defined. The school was eventually closed to juveniles when it was renamed an adult correctional facility. The number of juvenile inmates in reform schools statewide grew.

An example of a similar dynamic occurred under California's Probation Subsidy Program. Initially the program caused a dramatic drop in the numbers of youth committed to state institutions, as the state reimbursed counties for not sending youngsters to state institutions. The purpose was to stimulate local alternative programs. The counties soon realized, however, that they could use state probation subsidy dollars to staff county institutions if they were run by local probation departments. By the mid-1970s, California was harboring the largest per capita youth population of any state in the Union in its county-run detention facilities. Ironically, by 1988, the California Youth Authority also had the largest number of youngsters in its state reform schools in history.[21] Probation subsidy had created a county reform school system as an addition to the state reform school system.

Some say that we routinely institutionalize a given percentage of the population in our society. As we close one type of institution, we fill another.[22] Inmates of tuberculosis sanatoria were replaced by mental patients, by prisoners, and by youthful offenders. Other studies suggest that we fill prisons to occupy empty cells.[23] The states that build more prisons have more prisoners. Those that do not build have fewer prisoners. Numbers of prisoners in both cases are unrelated to crime rates. If this analysis is accurate, it is no more than logical that, following the massive dumping of mental patients, we incarcerated the largest number of prisoners in our history. The former patients did not just all transfer themselves to the prisons (though some did). The criteria for becoming a member of the new prison population included a person's vulnerability and political usability for institutionalization. Recent calls for the return of the large orphanage can be viewed in this context.

Reforming the Juvenile Court

Some reformers walk a tightrope between abolishing the juvenile court and totally supporting it. This was the tack taken by the Twentieth Century Fund's task force on sentencing policies toward young offenders. The report put it bluntly:

> The theory behind the juvenile court is not merely obsolete; it is a fairy tale that never came true. The court has helped some young offenders, but it has punished others. From the beginning, juvenile court judges have considered the interests of the state as well as those of the offender. It is pointless to pretend that social policy toward youth crime is based solely on the best interests of the young offender or that the best interests of the offender and those of the state are always the same. But the juvenile court need not rely on hypocritical rhetoric to justify its jurisdiction over youths charged with crime.[24]

The task force then went on to justify a discrete policy toward youth crime which included the principles of culpability, diminished responsibility resulting from immaturity, and proportionality. It recommended sentencing parameters dictated primarily by the level of the offense and supported custodial confinement and waiver to adult court of selected cases. The task force also recommended reforming the management of institutions and criticized the attitudes, actions, and professional inadequacies of certain judges, police and corrections officers, and magistrates.

The task force's conclusions just moved the chairs about on the deck. Issues were realigned on a continuum between the juvenile court system and the adult correctional system. In many ways it was a retreat from reform—a rearguard action against what was perceived as a law-

and-order backlash. The state of Washington eventually used this model, ostensibly as a way to bring reason and consistency into the juvenile justice system. State planners anticipated it would lead to fewer youngsters in reform schools. The reverse happened: undeserving delinquents were moved closer to the adult system, while the deserving were steered toward the juvenile system.

Why can't we break out of this vicious cycle? The reasons reside in the system itself. It makes even occasional "successes" questionable. Too often, as Edmund Leach put it, cure represents "the imposition of discipline by force—the maintenance of the existing order against threats which arise from its own internal contradictions."[25] To the degree that this is so, the success of revolutions in juvenile justice will continue to be limited.

Disillusionment with the child-saving movement and cynicism toward the juvenile justice system are well founded. The disillusionment, however, is more a function of bureaucratic traditions than of a failure of ideas. Practice has never approached its goals. Perhaps it never could. Perhaps youthful captives can never expect accountability from those who treat them. Perhaps reform will always be subject to the altruism of those who provide the service. Yet altruism is notoriously undependable, eventually wears away, and often deteriorates into violence. That has been the sad history of the juvenile justice system from its beginnings.

I dimly understood this when I set about the task of reforming a juvenile corrections system mired in scandal and abuse. So it was a slight surprise when the endeavor turned out not to be so quixotic as predicted. There were ways to make a difference. Whether those differences would be allowed to survive was the more crucial question, and it has yet to be answered.

2   *A Preview of Deinstitutionalization*

On a chilly March morning in 1972, a ragtag assortment of cars and vans drove onto the grounds of the Lyman School for Boys, a cluster of decrepit stone and brick buildings on a hill outside the town of Westboro, Massachusetts. Opened in 1846, Lyman was the first state reform school in the United States. It was founded following an 1836 law prohibiting incarceration of certain juveniles in state prison. If the offense did not call for life imprisonment and the young offender was deemed a proper subject, he or she was committed to the State Reform School for Boys or the State Industrial School for Girls.

Massachusetts pioneered reform schools. In 1842, Charles Dickens visited Boston's House of Reformation for Juvenile Offenders, noting the boys there "had not such pleasant faces . . . and in this establishment there were many boys of colour." But Dickens was nevertheless impressed.

> The design and object of this institution is to reclaim the youthful criminal by firm, but kind and judicious, treatment; to make his prison a place of purification and improvement, not of demoralization and corruption; to impress upon him that there is but one path, and that one sober industry, which can ever lead him to happiness; to teach him how it may be trodden, if his footsteps have never yet been led that way; and to lure him back to it, if they have strayed; in a word, to snatch him from destruction, and restore him to society a penitent and useful member.[1]

Such was the promise of the reform school. It became the model for hundreds of similar youth institutions which opened across the United States and Europe over the next century and a half—an unlikely collection of reform schools, industrial schools, reformatories, training schools, learning centers, youth development centers, and institutes for juvenile guidance. But the Lyman School for Boys was the granddaddy of them all.[2] Lyman had outlived a century's worth of visits, investigations, reforms, and name changes. It would not survive this March morning's events.

Lyman was the last of the seven Massachusetts state training schools we closed between 1970 and 1972, making Massachusetts the first state to do away with all of its reform schools. Having invented them, it seemed fitting that Massachusetts should be the first to abandon them. Though we'd quietly planned this day for months, the institution went out with few of the graces usually afforded a 130-year-old tradition. I had told the superintendent only a week before that all the boys in his facility would be moved out the following week. He told the staff three days before it happened. Why this belated notice, which flies in the face of the tenets of planned change? Because we had learned our lessons well. By now, we knew that any lengthy phasedown of a reform school invited problems. Within days of the announcement, we could expect a dramatic increase in kids sent there by the juvenile courts, the judges' way of showing opposition. That would be followed by an inordinate number of incidents—escapes, riots, assaults, and fires—often set off by less-than-subtle messages from staff to inmates well-conditioned to act on cue in proving the need for their own institutionalization.

When the Lyman staff were told the school would close in a few days, most dismissed the news as a fantasy. Their skepticism gave us the respite we needed. No weekend incidents occurred. The place was relatively calm. But now the truth was out. Today the inmates were leaving Lyman. An administrator's muttered, "They'll be back," told the story. The experiment would fail, the kids would soon get in serious trouble and be returned to the institution, the cottages would be filled again. That's the way it had always been. Why should this be any different? The staff simply had to wait it out. And wait they did. Lyman remained fully staffed but empty of inmates. As the waiting stretched from weeks into months, everyone finally recognized that the inmates weren't coming back.

We hadn't come easily to this day. I had originally hoped to reform the reform schools, make them more humane—maybe even utopian—islands of care in the otherwise coercive and destructive milieu of juvenile corrections. We began new programs: individual therapy, guided group interaction, positive peer culture, transactional analysis, special tutoring, and a variety of other models. We brought in the British pioneer in therapeutic communities, Maxwell Jones, the inventor of "positive peer culture,"[3] Harry Vorrath,[4] and Al Trieschman, with his marvelous psychoanalytic therapeutic model.[5] By these measures, we were successful. The institutions grew more in touch with the world outside. The kids felt better about themselves. The brutality slowed and the violence subsided.[6]

But whenever I thought we'd made progress, something happened—a beating, a kid in an isolation cell, an offhand remark by a superintendent or cottage supervisor that told me what I envisioned would never be allowed. Reformers come and reformers go. State institutions carry on. Nothing in their history suggests that they can sustain reform, no matter what money, staff, and programs are pumped into them. The same crises that have plagued them for 150 years intrude today. Though the casts may change, the players go on producing failure.

The decision to close the institutions grew from my frustration at not being able to keep them caring and decent. If I'd been able to stay away, I probably could have tolerated them. But as I came to know the young people in them, my responses to the system altered in ways I hadn't planned. It was, after all, *my* system. As long as I was in office, I was responsible for it. Now, years later, it's easier to admit my inability to sort out my own feelings for those who were caught in a system which made as little sense to me as it did to them. Had I known what I now do of government, politicians, and professional helpers, I probably would have abandoned the effort. By the time I'd come to that March day at Lyman, there wasn't much room for neophytes. I'd lost my political virginity.

Conflict dogged virtually all our attempts at reform. Whether we wanted to loosen up a tight and coercive institution or move the youngsters into the community, most of our reforms were greeted with cacophony, partly blather and partly threats, couched in dire warnings of chaos and crime in the streets. When it became obvious that I intended to close the state institutions, the upset among Massachusetts politicians was matched by the turmoil among my fellow correctional administrators.

National delinquency program administrators voted to censure me.[7] State employees' unions picketed on the capitol steps. Immediate staff fed information to hostile legislative committees. A department lawyer, sitting next to me at legislative investigations ostensibly to advise and defend me, was allegedly giving the committee staff selected internal departmental reports and documents aimed at nailing me to the wall. There were a host of colorful verbal variations on the theme of getting my ass, putting me in jail, or running me out of the state.

I turned to my professional peers: psychiatrists, psychologists, and social workers. A few offered support, for example, Eveoleen Rexford and Katie Van Amarungen, who were child analysts at Boston University's department of psychiatry; Hubert Jones, then with the Roxbury Multi-Service Center; Paul Quirk, who headed the state's association of child-care social workers; and Don Russell, a psychiatrist and expert in juvenile violence. But they were the exceptions. We were in uncharted territory. The helping professions were as intimately tied to the institutions as any old pol in the legislature. At best, they treated the whole affair with detached tolerance, leaving themselves room for a quick bailout should things collapse. At worst, they waited for business as usual to resume—doubtless with the hope of a few consulting contracts and increased professionalization of the reform schools. I was effectively isolated. To use a term of the American psychiatrist Harry Stack Sullivan, I had very little "consensual validation." From time to time the realization of my abandoned state threw me off stride and severely tested my emotional equilibrium.

Although we herd hundreds of thousands of inmates through our prisons, jails, detention centers, and reform schools, and show a notable lack of curiosity about them, much would be written about the tumultuous three and a half years leading up to that day at Lyman. The Harvard Center for Criminal Justice produced six books and a few dozen articles devoted solely to the Massachusetts Experiment,[8] and it also became a case study in a number of universities, including the Kennedy School of Government at Harvard, the University of Pennsylvania's Wharton School (under Thomas Gilmore), Duke University (under Robert Behn), and the London School of Economics. Most textbooks on delinquency and its treatment now routinely include a section on the Massachusetts deinstitutionalization—with about as many interpretations and versions as there are authors. Scholars like Ivan

Illich and Michel Foucault, whom I knew only from their writings, made inquiries.[9] We had visitors from Germany, France, Italy, Japan, Switzerland, Norway, Sweden, the Netherlands, Spain, Turkey, Israel, Australia, Denmark, and even South Africa. This was remarkable for a field so shy of examination.

It is a rare correctional institution that can yield very much detail about its inmates, their life histories, their strengths and weaknesses, or their eventual success or failure in keeping out of trouble. Aside from routine statistical data—age, sex, crime—personal details about a particular inmate are, for the most part, used to serve collective myths—the ax murderer, the serial killer, the sex offender. Such war stories fuel political speeches and "attack" journalism while rationalizing institutions. Paradoxically, personal tales usually ensure further depersonalization of the inmates. In this system, any authentic chronicling of the life histories of individual inmates is threatening and must be invalidated. The categories we allow, the theories we use, and the labels we apply limit information to the sorting and deterrent task at hand. Selective inattention, which Sullivan associated with paranoia, is endemic to penal institutions. Too close attention to individual lives, too much knowledge of later adjustment, too much personal involvement would quickly undo the rationale for the institution and make it unmanageable. One cannot individualize en masse. Except for rare lapses, institutions must remain Procrustean beds where limbs are stretched or amputated to meet institutional norms.

We deinstitutionalized a relatively small number of inmates. Depending on the time of year, the Massachusetts youth institutions held fewer than a thousand delinquent youngsters. Though as many as 8,000 to 10,000 went through our detention centers in the average year, and we had more than 2,000 under supervision on an average day, this figure was dwarfed by the deinstitutionalization going on at the same time in mental health and retardation facilities. While we were moving a few hundred delinquents back to the community, state departments of mental health across the United States were deinstitutionalizing thousands of mental patients. But the numbers alone didn't tell the story.

Asylums, prisons, and reform schools have hidden tasks to perform. They rest uncomfortably close to what holds a society together. It is a delicate balance, a societal cohesion that authentic deinstitutionalization threatens. To bring back into the community those who test the boundaries of its tolerance, beliefs, and safety is to invite a barrage of harsh questions and a resurgence of dark impulses. Institutions provide more than one kind of asylum. While they lock away those who offend our sensibilities or threaten our well-being, they also allow us to escape the deliberation we might otherwise expect from a compassionate society. They relieve us of responsibility. It's relatively unimportant whether an institution succeeds in its public purpose, whether curing the mentally ill or setting criminals straight. Its private task is to give absolution to society. Whatever treatment is allowed, whatever cure is sought, whatever control is imposed, the institution must first reassure us that we have no share in the malady. This is why authentic deinstitutionalization almost never happens and, when it does, seldom survives. The pull is always toward exile. Even on those rare occasions when resources follow the inmates to the community, what often happens is a perverse reconstituting of institutional regimens in the community. For finally, deinstitutionalization is not a technical problem. It is not a matter of means. It has to do with values.

The cars and vans winding their way toward Lyman's administration building that crisp New England morning were driven by university students and a few trusted youth workers from around the state. As the students and youth workers left their vehicles and fanned out over the grounds to help this or that boy get packed, their upbeat mood was tempered by an occasional sarcastic remark from a cottage parent who stood on the sidelines watching the circus, but missing the message of these prophetic clowns—a hundred or so boys, some shaking hands with administrators or staff members, others saying nothing, sauntering down to the waiting cars. Cardboard boxes half full of the boys' meager belongings were packed into trunks and on luggage racks—a pair of sneakers, a few socks and shorts, here and there a picture or a charm—simple possessions which lie about on chairs and bureau tops in most teenagers' bedrooms but are obsessively hidden and treasured by youngsters in reform schools. Lyman had always been awash in poor kids. But today, for a while, their delinquent identities seemed blessedly less secure. In the dress-down manner common to the early 1970s, young, mostly middle-class men and women wandered about the grounds and cottages with this or that youngster in tow, excitedly talking of hopes and plans for the next few weeks. Except for their age, one couldn't tell the keepers from the kept.

I felt relieved as I drove off the grounds. Most of the boys seemed pleased and left Lyman with few regrets. But a lone fifteen-year-old boy put it all in perspective. He came up to me on the arms of a cottage parent. He was crying and begging me to let him stay at the institution. The irony was palpable. This impersonal and occasionally violent place had become his home. It was probably less violent and more stable than his family home. Cottage staff added to the confusion by telling him that an uncertain, probably dreadful, fate awaited him on leaving Lyman. My reassurances didn't help. I finally told him he'd have to leave. He walked off with a student, albeit unwillingly.

This distraught adolescent epitomized the paradox of the Massachusetts Experiment. What I saw as humane reform and greater freedom for a generation of youngsters relegated to brutal and ineffective institutions this boy saw as a threat. He was successfully institutionalized. He believed he needed what the institution gave. His anguish defined the moment. Were we doing the right thing? Were we hurting the kids? Were we headed for disaster? As I left, I knew only that we were all out on our own.

3   Background

When I was just out of graduate school in 1957, I was assigned to Sheppard Air Force Base with the Air Training Command in that dusty tornado alley between the Oklahoma border and Dallas. All day, every day, lines of basic trainees would trudge into the psychiatric clinic, telling me about all the maladies common to a group of near-adolescents who had gone into the service for as many reasons as their complaints mirrored. For the next ten years, I worked as a psychiatric social work officer in military psychiatric facilities, stockades, schools, and family service agencies.

The military was apt preparation for what came later. One learns to keep one's own counsel in bureaucracies which take themselves too seriously. Psychiatric clinics in the service (at least those worth their salt) were always on the edge. They were needed, but only tolerated, as they turned over rocks and nosed about in things most unmilitary. Reluctant clients kept falling out of their assigned cubicles and personal closets. I saw a series of transvestite nuclear bomber pilots; a young officer not long out of the Air Academy caught masturbating with women's panties in the Base Exchange; a bombadier with moral scruples over the effects of his handiwork; a young sergeant caught caressing the body of a teenage girl he'd taken from a freshly dug grave. Getting "help" was as ambiguous and risky as giving it. A pilot who showed up in the clinic put his career in jeopardy. No records were confidential. I learned to write clinical notes in a personal code. More often, I didn't make notes at all—a habit which later served me well in state government.

After Sheppard, I was part of a small unwelcome psychiatric clinic in Curtis LeMay's Strategic Air Command (SAC). LeMay had no use for psychiatrists or social workers anywhere near his troops. But Karl Menninger, who had pioneered American military psychiatry during World War II, wanted a psychiatric clinic at Forbes Air Force Base in Topeka, Kansas, the home of the Menninger Clinic. Menninger, a general in the Army Reserve, prevailed on the Air Force surgeon general at the Pentagon to establish a clinic at Forbes. It was the first psychiatric clinic in SAC.

There were three officers on the staff—El Cook, a Menninger-trained psychiatrist, Dan Brown, a clinical psychologist, and myself. Given the official ambivalence, we kept a low profile. Menninger was our close consultant and adviser, usually spending Wednesdays with us. He brought with him whichever eminent visitor happened to be at the Menninger Clinic that week. Our small staff meetings became marvelous seminars. (Because I was the junior officer, I was assigned the less formal tasks, ending up as chauffeur and tour guide to Aldous Huxley, Margaret Mead, Konrad Lorenz, Nathan Ackerman, and other notables who visited the Menninger Clinic in those halcyon days.) It didn't take long, however, for us to understand the resistance of a single-minded military leader like LeMay to having any shrinks around the Strategic Air Command—the backbone of our nuclear-deterrent national policy.

One afternoon, a young sergeant ambled into the clinic complaining of vague anxiety and problems in sleeping. He talked of visiting his mother in Wichita and getting into a violent argument with her. As the threats and shouting mounted, he grabbed his mother's kitten, strangled it, and threw it at her. He ran from the room, leaving the stunned woman rocking and moaning over the dead pet on her lap. He then drove the hundred miles to the base. On the way, he came upon a bloody car accident. He stopped to rubberneck. Looking at the guts and gore, he got an erection.

The next day he wondered why the day's violent events had been such a turn on. His anxieties warranted concern, and he was scheduled for another appointment. But with an offhand comment the interview took an unexpected turn. When I asked what his job was, the sergeant replied, "Oh, I fuse weapons." "Weapons" in the Air Force meant only one thing, hydrogen bombs. We removed him from his assignment pending further evaluation and informed Air Force Headquarters in Omaha, strongly recommending that SAC begin psychiatric screening of persons assigned to sensitive positions, particularly those who worked closely with nuclear weapons. Headquarters immediately classified the report secret, sent it back, and instructed us not to mention the case again.

A couple of months later, another distraught young airman came into the clinic ranting about his wife's unfaithfulness. His sergeant was having similar problems. In their frustration, the two talked of creating "Lake Kansas." Both worked with nuclear weapons. Although we never knew for sure, we had been told by others in the unit that at that time two persons acting in concert could detonate a "weapon." We sent this case to Air Force Headquarters with a more urgent request for screening to be initiated in SAC. We took for granted that similar cases were appearing elsewhere. We had stumbled on ours only by accident. The Air Force gave the same response: the case was classified, and no further action was taken.

At about this time I was selected by the Air Force Institute of Technology to return to graduate school. The Air Force wanted me to apply to Catholic University's doctoral program in social work. I scheduled interviews, and my trip to Washington provided an opportunity to bring a potentially disastrous problem to the attention of the new Kennedy Administration. El Cook put together a bundle of the classified cases he'd been obsessed with for months. I concealed the files in my luggage and hopped aboard an Air Force refueling tanker, hitching a free ride to Andrews Air Force Base outside Washington.

My best friend's father, Jim McDevitt, called Eugene McCarthy (then a senator) and asked that he see me. I gave McCarthy the case records and briefly summarized them. Although McCarthy seemed annoyed and didn't give the impression that he took me very seriously, he offered to pass the information along. I never heard from him again, but a few months later the Air Force announced a "human reliability" screening program for those who worked with nuclear weapons. I hoped we'd had something to do with it.

I transferred to Washington and began school. El Cook, overwrought by his concern with the laxity in Air Force screening of personnel who handled "weapons," attempted suicide. For a while he was hospitalized at Andrews Air Force Base in Washington, and we had the chance to go together to see Stanley Kubrick's *Dr. Strangelove.* Neither of us laughed much. A couple of years later El succeeded in killing himself, leaving his wife and three preadolescent sons. When I met Senator McCarthy at a fundraiser fifteen years later and reminded him of our meeting, now invested for me with tragic recollections, he was gracious but clearly had no memory of the event.

After completing my doctorate, I was assigned to the tactical air forces in England. I worked in Air Force psychiatric clinics and hospitals for the next five years, living "on the economy" rather than on the base. Through my clinic work with British therapists and social workers, I got to know some of the experimental psychiatric and child-care programs which would never be allowed in the States, but which, paradoxically, the strait-laced British considered routine.

For example, there was the startling George Lyward, a 73-year-old former headmaster and lay psychoanalyst. During the Blitz he had wandered from London to Tenterden in Kent with a group of troubled adolescents. There, in an old monastery, he began Finchden Manor, a therapeutic community. Lyward's model stayed with me over the years—a place of openness, unconditional care, and emotional growth that followed the lead of the child therapist August Aichhorn.[1] I placed some difficult and disturbed adolescent sons of American servicemen there, at Finchden Manor, and visiting the place was a therapeutic experience for me. Finchden Manor became the standard I later applied to programs for troubled adolescents.[2] When I took over the Massachusetts reform schools ten years later, I hoped to recreate Lyward's model of care and acceptance on the grounds of a U.S. reform school. It was a naive expectation.

I found Lyward through A. S. Neill, whose more talked about (and less impressive) Summerhill was a short drive down the road from the village in which I lived.[3] Neill had put me in touch with Lyward after I'd asked him for help in finding a residential school for an Air Force pilot's son who insisted on wearing his mother's clothes. The boy's behavior sent his macho father up the wall, and the kid was desperate. Neill said, "There are only four schools in England that don't teach hate—Summerhill, St. Francis, Redfern, and Finchden Manor." I called them all. They were all full. But Lyward, true to a form I later came to know well, suggested I stop by with the youngster anyway. Perhaps something could be worked out.

Neill was a big bear of a man in his eighties. Following the American success of his book *Summerhill,* a treatise on child care fit for the fitful sixties, his school had been inundated with the rejected and troubled children of wealthy American families. They tested Neill's therapeutic model, so dependent upon the basic civility and traditions which characterized the English, to the limit. I vividly remember sitting next to him during a house meeting. The house meeting was the touchstone of Summerhill, the kids' self-government. As one particularly domineering and big-mouthed American youngster took over the meeting, Neill softly muttered, "Can't someone shut the little bastard up?" No one could. The success of Neill's model was so tied to his own decent persona that Summerhill declined with Neill's health.

I also got to see the worst of organically oriented British psychiatry and authoritarian behaviorist psychology. The horrifying visions of H. G. Wells and George Orwell took life. I sat in a staff conference at prestigious Fulbourne Mental Hospital near Cambridge as disciples of William Sargant, the polemicist for brain surgery, ordered a lobotomy for a sixty-year-old woman troubled with cycles of depression. The fact that her depressive episodes were triggered annually on the anniversary of her husband's death was of no interest or relevance to the assembled psychiatrists and psychologists.

Behaviorism held sway in England in the 1960s. For example, psychologists working at a British approved (reform) school for delinquent boys treated one boy's predilection for stealing cars with a bizarre mixture of aversive conditioning and a naive reconstruction of psychoanalytic theory. Placing the boy in a chair, they showed him color slides of cars. As each Rolls or Rover flashed on the screen, he was given a stiff electric shock in the groin. This pattern was varied by occasional slides of nude women (the car thefts putatively stemming from the boy's unresolved sexual feelings). At this point, the boy was given tea, toast, and marmalade. When he returned to the streets after the course of treatment, he promptly stole another car. This time, however, it was a Morris Mini. Formerly he had stolen Jaguars. This was taken as a sign of progress—the object of his desires was less phallic!

The closest I got to the British correctional system was Rampton Hospital, a facility for the so-called criminally insane. The psychologist, a disciple of H. J. Eysenck,[4] had been engaged in a decade-long search for the "criminal mind." The result was an office overflowing with the machinery of the behaviorist research psychologist. There were polygraphs, shock machines, skin galvanometers, and other imposing armamentaria. To his disappointment none of the procedures, measurements, or mechanical stimulants proved predictive of the criminal mind.

I felt almost sorry for this man, who was being inexorably crowded out of his office by the tools of his trade—and all for naught. But I could have spared my pity. With a quick smile he told me that he had, after all, found meaning in his decade-long efforts. He had discovered a reliable way to predict a new inmate's adjustment to Rampton. His prediction was based on how intimidated and agitated the inmate became when first confronted with the useless machinery, dials, wires, and buttons which crowded the psychologist's office. It was a fitting denouement, a variation on the Hawthorne effect.[5] The research technique had become its own justification.

By this time the United States was well into the Vietnam War. Things changed in the clinic. Fighter-bomber pilots from our base "reflexed" regularly to Vietnam. A new breed of Air Force psychiatrists came to be in charge, some of them back from duty in the Far East. The sheltered and relatively decent inpatient community, which we had worked so hard to establish, collapsed. The electroshock machine reappeared (and was quietly rendered unusable by myself and a staff nurse). The Air Force had finally become comfortable with its psychiatric clinics. We were no longer on the edge. We were all becoming, in H. G. Wells's term, "psychojusters" who were expected to label those who questioned what was happening as emotionally disturbed or otherwise flawed. Such pathology had to be controlled immediately or excised, lest we glimpse its sources.

Meanwhile, I'd made major, but accepting the promotion would have meant another four years in the Air Force. Leaving was not the moral decision I wish I could say it had been. The truth is, the Air Force had become wearing, and I wanted to do something new. It was time to leave. I'd met Charlene, my wife-to-be, in England. She was a psychiatric nurse at the base hospital, and she was being transferred back to the States. We decided to get married when I returned.

After having worked with prisoners in Air Force stockades and set up a clinic in England for troubled teenage dependents of American military and embassy personnel in Great Britain, my interest in the causes and treatment of crime and delinquency, always present, had become preeminent. I decided to look for that kind of civilian job as I hopped Air Force and U.S. Navy planes back to and around the States over a frenetic ten days. I received a number of offers and decided to take a position as Assistant Director for Research and Training with the newly formed Maryland Juvenile Services Administration. It was an important job in a new state agency and my first civilian job of any consequence. It was also my introduction to state government human services. I lasted six weeks.

I arrived in Baltimore and settled into the new job, meeting with staff and visiting youth institutions and camps. I was excited at being part of a reform administration. The Maryland legislature had passed one of the most progressive juvenile justice laws in the nation. We had an adequate budget and a group of skilled young professionals at the top. Everything was in place for effective and innovative programs. We could place youngsters in treatment, design the programs, and decide the length of time. But there was a drawback: the agency was run with a pollster in the anteroom.

It soon became clear that bureaucratic survival was the watchword. Nothing was proposed without first running it past a hodgepodge of union representatives, local judges, sundry advocacy groups, local politicians, and others. This seemed democratic enough. But in agencies with a captive clientele, compromises tend to be made at the expense of those who are excluded from the process.

One morning I attended a meeting in the superintendent's office at the state's largest boys' reform school. Most of the top administrators were there. We had a thoughtful discussion about plans for new treatment and educational programs at the school. Clearly this was a well-motivated, decent group of men (no women) with progressive ideas about reforming an ineffective system. After the meeting, I wandered upstairs, mulling over the possibilities. Strolling down the hallway directly above the superintendent's office, I glanced to the right. There were isolation cells containing this or that youngster, stripped down and learning whatever lesson the institution was teaching that day. At our staff meeting no one, including myself, had made any mention of this brutal practice within shout of our deliberations. We all knew about it. If a poll of those in the meeting had been taken the majority would have opposed this use of isolation. But it was unseemly to talk about it. In pursuit of larger goals we passed over the misery countenanced by existing policies.

I walked back downstairs. It was only too clear that if I were to make a career here, I'd have to avoid seeing too much, particularly in the individual faces of the adolescent inmates. It was a lesson I never learned. Years later I found a rationalization in the work of a conservative philosopher, Karl Popper, who warned of the brutal potential in planning which overlooks present evils in its pursuit of eventual nirvana.[6]

The next morning I called Dick Medhurst, dean of the School of Social Work at The Ohio State University, and asked if his earlier offer of an associate professorship still stood. It did. I left Maryland a few days later, apologizing to Dick Batterton, the director, leaving my concerns unspoken and giving difficulty in finding suitable housing as my reason for quitting.

Although I'd taught a few courses in the University of Maryland's overseas programs, Ohio State was my first teaching experience on a major university campus. I was assigned graduate and undergraduate courses in human behavior and delinquency. Things started on a sour note when, a few days after my arrival, a group of students protested my occupying my office, which they had been using as an informal meeting place. That I had come to Ohio State from the military didn't help. A petition was circulated demanding my ouster. Looking over my assigned space, I agreed it wasn't much of an office and signed the petition. I got a different office.

I enjoyed the students and the university atmosphere immensely, and it was a productive time for me. I caught up on the literature and had several articles accepted for publication in professional journals. I was an occasional consultant to the Ohio prison system and the Ohio Youth Commission. I also learned a bit more about academic bureaucracies. Along with some young administrators with an inner-city poverty program and a group of OSU graduate students, we used federal Comprehensive Employment Training Assistance (CETA) funds to get a couple of hundred inner-city youths and adults admitted to OSU. Using a general letter of support from the University's Vice Chancellor, John Corbally, we talked a number of department heads into admitting our clients (most of whom lacked high school degrees) into their programs, allowing each catch-up time at the beginning (one quarter's credit for two quarters' work). Most eventually got bachelor's degrees, and a few went on to graduate school. Many of those involved in setting up the program—Tom Jeffers, Paul DeMuro, Magnus Lewis, and Rudy Adams—later joined the reform effort in Massachusetts.

The following spring, the dean told me I'd be getting a full professorship and would be recommended for tenure in the fall term. I was elected to the faculty senate. To top things off, Charlene and I had lucked out with a pair of fifty-yard-line season tickets to OSU's annual football rituals. Things looked good at Ohio State.

4   *The Invitation*

In midsummer of my first year at OSU, the personnel information bulletin of the National Association of Social Workers came across my desk with the morning mail. Massachusetts was looking for someone to head its newly created Department of Youth Services (DYS) the state's youth corrections system. The new department had been created following a series of scandals regarding abuse of youthful inmates.[1] The idea of working there was one of those "What if?" fantasies for me. I'd been teaching a course in delinquency and social deviance at OSU, with particular emphasis on therapeutic communities, but my only foray into the field in Maryland still gnawed at me.

A faculty sociologist with a radical bent sarcastically suggested that since I was constantly berating the Ohio Youth Commission's training schools, I might want to put up or shut up. We laughed and went about preparations for the fall term. With little reflection and virtually no intention of anything serious happening, I threw a résumé into an envelope and sent it off to Massachusetts. A couple of weeks later the chairman of the search committee called and invited me to Boston for an interview. I was flattered, but I still didn't take it very seriously. I planned to be at OSU in the coming term, but the invitation was an opportunity to visit Boston and, perhaps, to influence the direction the committee might take in assessing candidates.

I flew out to Boston in mid-August, arriving about twenty minutes early for an 8:00 P.M. interview. The screening committee was meeting in the central office of the Massachusetts Youth Service Board (YSB), then housed on the seventh floor of a rundown office building near the capitol. As I waited in the hallway, a prospective candidate emerged from his interview along with a couple of the panel members. It was a friendly scene, with backslapping and handshakes all around. They were going to meet later for a few drinks. Though I'd been told there were about thirty candidates, clearly this one had an inside track. It reinforced my view that nothing much was likely to come of the interview. Search committees in state government routinely conduct national searches for executives. They then, just as routinely, nominate a member of the search committee. As a matter of fact, that's what almost happened in this case, but other matters intervened.[2]

I went into the interview feeling pretty much free of any need to tell the committee members what they might want to hear. I saw it as a forum for discussion and argument on the always controversial subject of delinquency. I was introduced to the members of the committee. True to form, I remembered no names. They asked about my experiences and my views on youth services and treatment models for offenders. One asked me what I might do if I were directing a state juvenile corrections agency. I said something about making the institutions more humane and setting up aftercare programs. I thoroughly enjoyed the hour-long interchange and left feeling that though it had been stimulating, it would lead nowhere. I'd had a free trip to Boston, a chance to wander down to the Union Oyster House for a lobster, to walk about the Common, and to poke around Harvard Square for a couple of hours—in the summer of 1969, a "trip" in itself. I flew back to Columbus expecting to hear no more.

A few days later Leila Deasy, a former professor of mine at Catholic University, called. She had been contacted by Lloyd Ohlin, professor of criminology at Harvard University's Center for Criminal Justice. He had asked a good deal about me, and she had the impression it was a serious inquiry. Then a faculty member from the Ohio State English department called and asked me if I was applying for a job in Massachusetts. I was surprised he knew. Though I'd not kept it a secret, I hadn't mentioned my trip to Boston around campus. A friend of his in city hall had asked, "Who's Jerry Miller?" Someone in Boston was making inquiries of the mayor's office and the police department, asking what they might know about me. It turned out that the inquiries came not from the search committee but from others who had caught wind of my name's being on the list and who were looking to head off the governor from nominating me.

I hadn't expected this. It sent me to the phone to try to find out more about the job. I had no contacts in Boston, but I'd recently had a paper accepted for publication in the *Family Law Quarterly* of the American Bar Association. The editor was Father Robert Drinan, then dean of Boston College School of Law. I called and asked his opinion. He was more politically informed than I'd expected a cleric professor to be. I'd forgotten he was a Jesuit. He sent a sheaf of news clippings on the Youth Service Board, commenting that the Massachusetts legislature had a tradition of creating new programs and then refusing to fund them. Though he wished me well, he wouldn't advise me to take the position.

The following week, Chris Armstrong, an aide to Massachusetts governor Frank Sargent, phoned. He asked me to come out to meet with members of the governor's staff. I made another trip to Boston and, eventually, met with Governor Sargent, an amiable and forthright man of old Yankee stock. He was unusually open about the problems and scandals in the Youth Service Board, weaving an intriguing yarn about the difficulties he had had getting John Coughlan, the former head of the board, to resign. He told me how he'd invited Coughlan to his office one morning and kept him there well into the evening, until he agreed to submit his resignation. Years later a former aide to the governor told me that the act had bordered on kidnapping. The governor got his way, and Coughlan signed the resignation letter drawn up for him. Later he tried to withdraw his resignation, but the governor refused.

Governor Sargent bluntly told me I wasn't his first choice. He preferred Frank A. Maloney, the acting head of the department. At the governor's request, Frank had taken the job as an interim assignment. Following Maloney's swearing-in at the governor's office, he was accompanied by state troopers for the short trek down School Street from the capitol to the offices of the YSB. He fully anticipated that Coughlan, having announced he would not vacate his office, would have to be carried out in his chair.

Maloney, an affable, nonabrasive social work administrator, quickly settled things down in the department. He enjoyed his job and had expressed interest in the new commissioner's position. The search committee, however, had recommended me. Despite his preference for

Maloney, Governor Sargent felt obliged to honor the committee's wishes. He told me I could have the position if I wished to accept it. I'd never met a governor before and was frankly flattered by such high-level attention. The ambivalence that had dogged me from the day I sent in my résumé took flight. I said I would be honored to accept the position.

As I left his office, the governor remarked somewhat cryptically, "I hope you'll get along with Frank Maloney." I was slow to pick up on his meaning. Chris Armstrong clarified it outside. I was expected to appoint Frank deputy commissioner. The governor wanted to cover his bets, so that if I fell on my face, he'd have someone to pick up the pieces. But there were other conditions attached to this prearrangement. I had to make another flight to Boston for a two-hour airport meeting with Frank to see whether we were compatible. We were. I'm not sure what would have happened if we hadn't been.

Massachusetts politics being what they are, things weren't going to be smooth. I was an outsider—at best an unknown, at worst a threat. My nomination had to be confirmed by the Executive Council, a hold-over from pre–Revolutionary War days. This group was originally created as a check on the absolute power of the British governor of the Massachusetts Colony, but over the years its role had degenerated. Known on Beacon Hill as the "swap shop," it was a place to trade favors and bank influence. My nomination was in limbo while this group went about its work. Some council members objected to the way Coughlan had been treated. Councilman Walter Kelly was particularly perturbed. His brother, a former fireman, was assistant superintendent at one of the reform schools. Before confirming anyone, Councilman Kelly wanted to guarantee his brother's job. Other councilmen wanted less definable favors. I was not privy to the kinds of negotiations the governor engaged in, but I took it for granted that trades had to be made to soften the blow. After a month of haggling, I was confirmed.

During those long days of waiting, I strolled over to the YSB offices (a block and a half away from the statehouse) and walked unannounced into the same seedy office building in which I'd met the search committee a couple of months earlier. I took the rickety elevator up to the seventh-floor administrative offices and wandered down the poorly lit hallways, introducing myself to whatever staff I found here or there at a desk. People were friendly but guarded. The new Department of Youth Services was peopled with the same staff and administrators who ran the now defunct Youth Service Board. It had just been renamed. I later concluded that the old YSB could have done virtually everything the new DYS would accomplish. The legislation provided a respite rather than a new mandate. Reform is always more a matter of will than of legislation, and most youth and adult corrections agencies have the capacity to reform themselves within existing legislation and budgets. They seldom use the means at hand and, as the least accountable of state bureaucracies, they maintain an entirely reactive stance, waiting for mandates which seem never to arrive.

Since I was in the building, Frank Maloney offered to arrange an informal get-acquainted session with administrators. I tried to put everyone at ease with light talk about my excitement at coming to Massachusetts. For most of my professional life I'd been a therapist in one or another psychiatric setting, and I used whatever therapeutic skills I could muster. The staff seemed a beaten-down group, understandably concerned with where they'd land in the newly reorganized department. They had little reason to worry. The state legislature had been unduly responsive to intense lobbying by DYS staff. Though more than nine hundred of the approximately one thousand YSB employees were political appointees, the legislature gave them all civil service tenure. Whatever uneasiness I sensed at that first meeting didn't have to do with whether they'd keep their jobs. In fact, many of those sitting in the room had been applicants for the job I got.

After the meeting I flew back to Columbus, and the next morning I got a call from Chris Armstrong. A summary of the meeting had appeared in the *Boston Herald* in a political column written by Thomas Gallagher. I was portrayed as an arrogant outsider who insisted on being called "Commissioner" while proposing a series of radical changes in the department—all this before my appointment had been confirmed by the Executive Council.[3] The meeting reported was not the one I remembered. I had no plans for the department. The reference to wanting to be called commissioner gave my students at Ohio State a few laughs. But I learned to take the Gallagher columns seriously, not for their accuracy but because they gave a clue as to what the opposition was up to. Gallagher's opposition ran deep: "Nationwide searches to fill state positions are, of course, ridiculous, in light of the depth of the talent in every field of endeavor which abounds in Massachusetts." He added that, on those few occasions when Massachusetts governors or mayors had plucked department heads from other states, "the results have ranged from unsatisfactory to disastrous."[4] Gallagher's favorite candidates for the commissioner's job were a former Suffolk County sheriff, John Sears, who had recently lost his reelection bid, and George McGrath, a well-known political figure in Massachusetts who was then commissioner of corrections in New York City and a member of the search committee that had selected me.

Over the years Gallagher attacked almost everything I did and became the favored press outlet for disenchanted staff, who fed him a regular diet of gossip, rumors, scandals, and fantasies. That the happenings in DYS were written about primarily by political columnists fitted the traditions of that department well.

My first days on the job were a haze. It's not that my recollections have grown misty. Rather, the experience was a confusing blur of meetings—kind faces, hostile glances, pols on the make, imperious judges, troubled staff, child advocates with mixed motivations, meetings with no purpose, speeches, press briefings, cocktail parties, and private dinners. The activities weren't motivated by any sudden demand by public and private figures to make my acquaintance. But I headed a small state agency which was tied to strong special interests—ideological as well as political. Virtually everyone had an agenda—to lobby for favorite programs, jockey for position, seek contracts, bless union agreements, become consultants, tell of new scandals, cajole, manipulate, support, and occasionally threaten.

I later learned to put some of this in perspective, or at least to keep my own counsel until I knew what I wanted to do. Every new head of a cabinet-level or other large state agency goes through this stage, but Massachusetts was my first experience with it. I simply didn't know what I was getting into. I'd been a clinician for most of my professional life and had no more than a passing interest in the mechanics of government. The most difficult problems came from those who presented themselves as, and who should have been, my natural friends and allies.

My political education was a case of sink or swim. I almost undid the hope of reform while learning to survive. I wandered through the halls of the historic Massachusetts State House not unlike the professor who, I'm told, wandered about Chicago's West Side during the riots following Martin Luther King's assassination. Aside from police, he was the only white man in sight but was left untouched by the gangs of rioters. His naïveté apparently saved him. Anyone so bereft of common sense must be held to a less demanding standard.

I was in a game in which I knew neither the rules nor the players. Only later did I find out how vulnerable I'd been. It's not that I didn't try to inform myself. I wanted to understand state government and know who held the levers of power. This might seem relatively easy—the most powerful people, one would expect, can be identified by their office. But that's not the way it works. The vice chairman of a committee might have more power than the chairman because of a personal interest or a stake in a particular department or issue. Nearly invisible advisers and aides at various levels often called the shots, screened the information, and made the final judgments. I'd been told that the reform legislation had broad support in the legislature, but not that the support was also shallow. My own position wasn't funded for a year after my appointment, nor was that of the deputy commissioner or the four assistant commissioners called for in the legislation. I paid myself and Frank Maloney by leaving other positions unfilled.

The assault on the old YSB had come from a small coalition of liberal legislators led by Brookline senator Beryl Cohen and a young new legislator, Michael Dukakis. The rest of the legislature eventually joined in with a wider range of motives. I later concluded that the reform legislation was passed not because the legislature wanted more effective handling of delinquent youngsters. Instead, it grew out of such cause as feeling slighted over not sharing in the well-known patronage pot, getting even with YSB administrators, and the herd instinct which routinely seduces legislators when there is the smell of blood—anyone's (in this case, Coughlan's). In that kind of atmosphere even old loyalties collapse pretty quickly.

Despite Massachusetts' liberal reputation, liberal is not an apt description for its brawling state politics. On local issues, the legislature was conservative and provincial. The problem was compounded by its large size—240 members. (The number of legislators was later cut back under pressure from a coalition of citizens' groups led by the League of Women Voters.) This conservative legislature was totally dominated by Democrats. I worked for a liberal Republican governor. Theoretically, the Democrats should have had no problem passing any legislation they wished. But the Massachusetts legislature resembled the Congress of forty years ago, with some legislative committees being controlled by conservative Democrats who would have been equally at home in Mississippi. Boston city councilwoman Louise Day Hicks personified that aspect of Massachusetts politics best as she resoundingly won her seat with a less-than-subtle appeal to racial fears—while the state voted for George McGovern for president.

There were exceptions to the self-serving in the legislature. Jack McGlynn, a legislator from Malden, was one example. Though liberals were not his natural constituency, Jack carried the ball for the Massachusetts Committee on Children and Youth in getting the reform legislation through the House. Without him there would have been no reform. He was one of those rare birds in politics who are able to hold onto that part of one's character where one does what seems right despite the political repercussions, all the while playing the public game with the best (or worst) of the old pols. Jack chaired the House Committee on State Administration, and in this role he protected and shepherded the reform legislation through a legislature usually hostile to this kind of reform. He later guided me through some difficult investigations and attacks from the legislature.

My original guide around the statehouse was Mark Burke, the public relations person in the department. Mark, a rotund, red-faced Irishman, offered to acquaint me with the state's political powers. He also had his own agenda firmly in mind as we proceeded up and down the halls, meeting the senate president, the speaker, the chairman and vice chairman of Ways and Means Committees, and a wide assortment of legislators. Mark led me from office to office, introducing me as the new commissioner and telling the various dignitaries he was trying to ease my way into the workings of government. I was a prop in Mark's show, but I dutifully went along, speaking when spoken to, answering the kinds of empty questions such occasions elicit, and trying to get a fix on the cast of characters I came to know well.

My first meeting with Dave Bartley, the Democratic speaker of the house, was particularly memorable, not for its content, but for the fact that I didn't realize it was important. I was sitting with him and the majority whip, Tom McGee. The speaker sat in his JFK rocker, an affable man who had more than a passing interest in what I wanted to do in the department. He jokingly asked what I was doing in Mark's company, and we all laughed. I enjoyed the meeting, and Mark told me it had gone well. As we walked down the marble hall from the speaker's wood-paneled office, I remarked that he seemed a nice person and appeared to be in an influential position. Mark replied sarcastically, "Yes, Jerry, he's an 'influential' person." The speaker had afterthoughts as well, but of a different kind. He quietly got word back to me through the lobbyist for the Massachusetts Committee on Children and Youth, Ceil DiCicco, that I was being introduced around the legislature by the wrong person. Mark was seen as tied to the old guard. Bartley went out of his way to be protective of me, and his low-key support meant the difference between success and failure over the next four years.

Mark was well known on Beacon Hill. His uncle was Michael Paul Feeney, a legislator from Boston. I got a firmer impression of Mark's political involvements later when he casually remarked that he'd be taking a leave to run for the Massachusetts legislature—"But don't worry, Jerry. I won't be elected." It seemed curious that he would spend so much effort on a lost race, but in Boston it made sense. Mark's uncle was opposed in his reelection by a fellow named Michael Burke. Mark ran as "M. Burke," to draw off a portion of Michael Burke's supporters. Mark was back in his office the day after the election. Michael Feeney was back in the legislature.

The speaker's advice made it seem wise for me to be reintroduced to the legislators. This time my guide was George O'Shea, an administrator in the department who had formerly been in the legislature. George had had a good reputation as a legislator, though he too was a patronage appointment in the department. He knew both the liberal and the conservative blocs in the legislature, but he went out of his way to ensure that I was introduced to Mike Dukakis, Beryl Cohen, Jack Backman, Marty Linsky, and others who had supported the reform legislation. George also took me back to Speaker Bartley and to the senate president, Maurice Donahue, as well as to Joe Early, chairman of the house Ways and Means Committee, and a somewhat menacing "Blackie" Burke, chairman of the senate Ways and Means Committee. Burke and I carried on no discussion of issues. I was warned simply not to antagonize him. His only interest was funding for the Maritime School, which was in his district and apparently had some program money from my department.

Mark initiated me rather quickly into the local political traditions: going to a nearby bar for a couple of beers after work, chatting with the hangers-on and assorted pols who routinely conducted much of their business there, sharing stories and gossip. It was usually in some bar or other that I first met members of the Boston City Council, legislators, and local political appointees. "Dapper" O'Neill, for instance, then head of the Liquor Control Board, was a Boston pol to fit an outsider's worst stereotype—given to sitting briefly at the table, speechifying loudly about crime and permissiveness, telling a dirty joke, waving the flag, working the crowd, scoping me out, and occasionally offering "a bit of friendly advice." But not so friendly that, if the opportunity arose, he wouldn't do me in with a crowfooted wink of a usually red eye. Despite his backslapping and his loudly shouted "Commissioner," to Dapper I was in the enemy camp.

In an attempt to be helpful Joe McCormick, a respected local political figure formerly associated with the YSB, invited me to address a Holy Name Society Communion breakfast in his large West Roxbury parish. I brought along a copy of one of the logbooks from the Lyman school. I thought it might be instructive to this group of two to three hundred (mostly Irish) Catholic men to hear about the ethnic history of the reform schools. I began by reading a log entry from the late 1800s. "Kevin O'Reilly," went the intake summary, "typical Irishman, coarse and stupid." It was a lame attempt at making the point that those sent to our institutions were on the lower rungs of the socioeconomic ladder—that though the Irish had been replaced by blacks and Hispanics, today, the mechanics remained the same: inmates were never taken from among the sons and daughters of those who made the laws. My point fell flat. I got polite applause and thanked Joe for the invitation and the Jerusalem Bible given me by the Holy Name members.

My tenure as commissioner was uncertain, but I hoped to survive long enough to keep the lid on a set of reform schools I couldn't avoid changing. Tommy Sheehan, the department's child legal counsel and head of the Democratic City Committee for Boston, told me the betting on Beacon Hill was that I wouldn't last more than six months. I'd been in office a couple of months and had provided plenty of raw meat for politicians. I'd made some pretty outlandish public statements which, though true, were not the kinds of things anyone bent on staying long in state government should say. But I had a poor appreciation of this at the time and went about my business unaware. Now, twenty years later and looking back over the news clippings, I realize how insensitive I was. I'd like to think it wasn't so much arrogance as ignorance, but I'm not sure. My insensitivity certainly didn't make things easier. I was preoccupied with this or that inmate in a detention center or training school and tended to make my judgments relative to that individual case. At times, an unannounced off-hour visit to this or that facility would leave me in a state of panic. What I'd see was so at odds with what I'd envisioned that I would get sick to my stomach. The images stayed with me for days after. I fell prey to an obsessiveness which allowed little room for compromise and was a recipe for failure in the politics of state government. I had to learn to let up without selling out—a tightrope act which, even when I was successful at it, ground away at my innards.

Maurice Donahue, a former schoolteacher serving out his last year as senate president, was strongly interested in the department and stressed the need for better educational programs in the institutions. He suggested I might want to consider running for office. My name had been in the papers so often, though usually associated with problems, riots, and escapes from the institutions, that I could win. Donahue told me it didn't matter much whether the press was good or bad; it had provided name recognition.

In politics a new incumbent is usually given a "honeymoon" by the press and political adversaries. But for me, no honeymoon was on anyone's agenda. I was fair game before, during, and after assuming office. Some of my friends in human service might say, "But you are a professional. Your position wasn't really political." Unfortunately, that's not how it is. I was immersed in politics from the day my name surfaced as a candidate for commissioner. That it took me a while to understand simply delayed getting on with the business at hand.

5   *Punishment vs. Restoration*

Massachusetts reform schools had more than a century to become a tradition, even setting the course of institutionalization for the nation. Though they grew and prospered, periodically a dark side emerged. Comparing Dickens's characterization of Boston's House of Reformation for Juvenile Offenders as a place "to reclaim the youthful criminal by firm, but kind and judicious, treatment"[1] with a report to the Massachusetts legislature in 1969, one might conclude that the reform schools had greatly deteriorated over the years. But some nineteenth-century reformers like abolitionist Samuel Howe had questioned the concept from the beginning, proposing alternatives for institutionalized youth.

There had been changes over a century and a half. The Lyman School no longer maintained the policy of giving boys over to clipper ships—often never to be seen again. The early schools were strict. A visitor to the House of Reformation for Juvenile Offenders in 1832 described how "the boys worked their tasks without talking, using sign language and gestures as the sole means of communication" and how "they took their meals at prescribed periods at long tables and were forbidden to eat at other times." This regime of the reformer superintendent, the Reverend E. W. P. Wells, was apparently not strict enough, however. The institution was closed four years after its opening with charges that discipline was too lax for a penal institution.[2]

Strict regimens and liberal use of corporal punishment were the rule in nineteenth-century reform schools. Flogging a youngster in the mid-1800s was less unusual than it became later. But the forced haircuts, the demeaning silence and marching, the occasional beatings, the planned, ritualized violence of discipline cottages, and the restraint to beds in the 1970s were mightily out of keeping with the larger society of that period. Still, if one visited the reform schools in 1920 (in an unguided tour) or in 1900, the institutional regimens would probably have made the average contemporary visitor uneasy. But unguided visits were as "uncivil" in Victorian times as they are "inappropriate" today.

But state institutions with captive inmates and a deterrent role have always had convoluted aims. Twelve years before Lyman School opened its doors, British law had found such a gruesome use for its public institutions. Before the nineteenth century, hanged criminals provided the only legal source of bodies for medical dissection. When hospitals made surgery respectable, there were no longer enough available bodies. Medical schools began purchasing them from grave robbers and murderers. This scandalous situation was mitigated by the Anatomy Act of 1832, making it legal to dissect the bodies of those who died in public institutions. Two years later, this was tied to the Poor Law Amendment Act, which attempted to deter applications for public assistance by requiring recipients to be placed in institutions where, should they die, they would be subject to dissection. It was a particularly effective deterrent to application for aid among the religious poor, who saw the mutilation of the body as threatening the afterlife.[3]

The Lyman School was established in 1846 from funds contributed jointly by the state and by Theodore Lyman, a former mayor of Boston. It seems initially to have been seen as a caring, relatively homelike setting, though the length of the sentences belie any expressed good intentions. The old logbooks from the period tell the familiar stories of nineteenth-century child welfare:

> Oril J. Barden, age 9, committed in 1856 for larceny. Both parents died when he was a year old. Lived with aunt and uncle. Both respectable people. He was in the habit of stealing fruit. Stole 28 cents at one time and cried when he told his aunt.

> John O'Daniel, age 11, a 10-year sentence. Father sometimes gets drunk. He played on Sundays with idle boys, stole apples, stole money from his mother. Got whipped pretty hard, but seems like a sweet boy.

Simon Leary, 14. Mother and father would fight and strike each other. Got turned off from work places because breakfast was late served. Has been punished for talking in school.[4]

Over the next 140 years, there would be periodic investigations, charges, updates, and reforms—new buildings, probation, parole, diversion programs, and professionalization of the staff. But the reform schools only grew larger and more numerous. The reforms never broke their institutional tether.

The logbooks, huge leather-bound ledgers written in longhand in fastidious Victorian prose, sketched the history of every boy sent to Lyman from 1846 to 1910. One could trace the waves of ethnic immigrants into Massachusetts as their children were sent to the reform school . . . along with a small but overrepresented sampling of "coloureds."

In the late 1800s Lyman was inundated with Irish, Portuguese, and Italian youngsters from the streets of Boston. An annex was created—a ship in Boston harbor. Boys were held there until such time as a passing clipper or other cargo vessel sailed by. The ship's master stood on the bow calling out, "One boy!" "Two boys!" If a ship's captain had need of a cabin boy or other young laborer, the youngster was sent off. "Kevin O'Reilly [for example] was last seen off the South China coast."[5]

But even with this seagoing alternative, the model of choice remained the reform school. Each school had its own methods and population characteristics (age, sex, offense). A loose statewide system developed around each facility's traditions. Some took older boys, some younger. Others took boys who were difficult to manage, likely to run away, or in need of discipline. One school took girls. Some intakes were based on the ability of the institution to break the recalcitrant.

Four years after the Lyman School for Boys was founded, the Lancaster Girls' Industrial School was established, first as a foster home for wayward girls. After a few years, more homes were opened on the same grounds and were placed under a central administration. Over the protests of Samuel Howe and others, Lancaster devolved into a girls' reform school not unlike Lyman.[6] Those who ran the Massachusetts reform schools soon cultivated their own political power bases within the legislature. Superintendents of mental hospitals, wardens of prisons, and sheriffs of jails tend to gauge their effectiveness by the buildings and staff they can acquire. By these measures, Massachusetts reform school superintendents were very effective indeed.

Reform schools sprouted across the state. Though there was never much evidence that any of these nineteenth-century institutions was effective at its stated goals—curing the mentally ill, humanely caring for the retarded, reforming the delinquent, or calming the recalcitrant—all were highly successful at exiling the unmanageable, the unproductive, and the threatening. Their purpose was custodial, despite the gloss succeeding eras placed upon them. Humane reformers tried less to make institutions succeed in rehabilitating or otherwise fixing the inmates than to mitigate the harm the institutions did. Boards of visitors were established to ensure minimum standards and inhibit the tendency to slip into frankly brutal practices. They provided a way to keep a cap on things when institutional abuse strayed too far beyond the boundaries of civility. But the Victorian sense of proper order, of taming the wild, of celebrating "the imposition of human structure on the threatening chaos of nature" provided the backdrop. Harriet Ritvo's analysis of the metaphorical purposes of the Victorian obsession with zoos is equally apt to the role inmates still play in many state-run mental hospitals, and in most prisons and reform schools. These institutions corroborate the claims of the Caucasian male to superior status; they embody his anxieties about the maintenance of social discipline; and through the maintenance, staffing, and funding of the institutional system, they justify enterprise.[7]

But the governing principle of virtually all state institutions, whether for the retarded, the mentally ill, the delinquent, children, or adult offenders, was soon established. Reform schools were bound to the political power of local legislators. In those states in which I have been responsible for such state institutions—Massachusetts, Illinois, and Pennsylvania—they were immersed in patronage. Local officials sponsored a large percentage, if not a majority, of state employees on the institutional grounds. Though civil service requirements were meant to alter these arrangements, they failed.

The word *reform* always has a different meaning when a state institution is at stake. As the number of institutions grew, so did their influence in state legislatures, a fact that people routinely ignore. Any proposed change in services to or supervision of those who would otherwise be inmates had first to pass the political test. Innovation had to be accomplished without threatening the institution's stability. In politics, this means the institution must survive. Reform strategies must therefore absorb existing staff, add new institutional staff, and bolster the institutional plant.

Their foundations firmly set in a century's worth of rough-and-tumble Massachusetts politics, the reform schools were joined under one administration in 1948—the Massachusetts Division of Youth Services. It consisted of a three-person board with a chairman and came to be known as the Youth Service Board. The goals of the new reform were spelled out by the special commission devising the legislation, a commission distinguished by its emphasis on diagnosis and application of "modern knowledge of human behavior to the treatment and rehabilitation of young offenders."

The first step is diagnosis—physical, mental, emotional and social—to determine, if possible, why a child is delinquent and the type of treatment most likely to restore him to acceptable behavior. The Board is required to make this thorough study of each child, on commitment. This may be done in the existing training schools or in a separate reception and diagnostic center. The job requires a team consisting of a pediatrician, psychiatrist, psychologist and social investigator, plus properly trained teacher and other supervising personnel.

The second step is treatment to fit the diagnosis. Accordingly, the Board may place the child under supervision in his own home or in a foster home, or in one of the training schools, or in any public or private institution that can best meet the particular child's need for treatment and retraining. The Board is given control of the three training schools in order to control commitment to them not merely by age, but according to the needs of the youngsters, and thus to transform them eventually into treatment centers for specialized groups capable of effectively re-educating children. Any other training schools that may be established by the Commonwealth in the future will also come under the Board so that it may provide a wider variety of units to fit the needs of different categories of personality disorders.

The third step is the goal of the whole process, namely, successful replacement in the community. The Board is necessarily the paroling agency and responsible for supervision of parolees. The intent of the act is to return a child to the community as soon as this can be done with some hope of success, so the Board has power to grant parole as well as to discharge at any time.[8]

As rational as all this appeared, political realities dictated that the institutions be left untouched. The independent superintendents were politically unassailable. The 1948 reform legislation fixed their jobs and the institutions more deeply in the state bureaucracy. In addition, the legislation mandated *new* institutions: reception and detention centers with diagnostic services. It also established a state system for parole (aftercare) and preventive services, a treasure trove of patronage jobs.

John D. Coughlan was appointed director of the Youth Service Board in 1953. His academic background was in education and his doctorate from the Staley School of Speech in Boston. As I learned later, he could give a stem-winder of a speech, particularly when threatened, as he was wont to say, "by vipers at my breast." Coughlan directed Massachusetts youth corrections for seventeen years through a succession of Democratic and Republican administrations—a remarkable feat for an appointee without civil service protection. He was unusually adept at courting state legislators, the governor's executive council, and county government officials.

Coughlan made liberal use of a tradition which reached its zenith in the administration of Boston mayor James Curley—the political patronage system. After I left Massachusetts, I held cabinet-level positions in other states, some much devoted to patronage—but Massachusetts took the prize, hands down. In 1969, the *Boston Globe* estimated that over 90 percent of YSB employees were non–civil service appointees.[9] With the advent of the 1969 legislation, all the politically appointed administrators and staff were given civil service protection by the Massachusetts legislature under a grandfathering clause.

Patronage was neither hidden nor embarrassing to either party. I can recall an aide to Governor Sargent asking me to run a new hiring past the "patronage office"—a particular cubbyhole in the statehouse where new applicants to state agencies were screened for political purity or "trading" potential. I went over expecting to see "Patronage Office" etched in the frosted glass of the door. I soon learned to disregard these requests, which were usually made by a second-level operative in the administration. The governor was not going to insist that I follow traditional hiring protocol.

The degree to which patronage drove the department was brought home to me a few days after I took over. I was rummaging through the old gray metal desk in my office, and there, in a thick maroon folder, were notes listing employees in the department. Alongside each name was penciled in a sponsor—the legislator, county commissioner, or party official who had referred the employee for hiring. I later learned that most of those who came in the front door of the YSB looking for a job were told first to step across the street to the Golden Dome and find a legislator willing to request the hiring as a favor. Every favor carried an obligation, and the system was designed to ensure administrative longevity. The department had only three blacks among its thousand employees, but it couldn't hold out indefinitely. The cast of characters changed as some legislators lost elections, original sponsors went on to other things, and opponents won elections and wanted their own people in the jobs. Although there were attempts to keep new legislators happy with jobs for constituents, there were never enough openings to keep pace with the demand.

In the mid-sixties tales of brutal abuse of youngsters leaked out: stories of beatings, widespread use of solitary confinement, isolation in unheated rooms, rapes, staff discontent, violence, and dilapidated buildings. Scandals are usually poor harbingers of reform. The sensation they cause is settled with cosmetic change. But the times were unusually ripe. The question was whether, this time, things would be different—whether the state could finally break loose from the reform roundabout which usually follows exposé.

Massachusetts had been through the ritual many times before, and each crisis had ended in new buildings and more staff. Massachusetts reformers were never much into the third tenet of traditional reform—professionalization. The YSB had never brought in many psychologists, psychiatrists, social workers, or educators. This was probably because of the extensive patronage. When I took over the department we had only one full-time psychologist with a Ph.D. and one social worker with an M.S.W., along with three part-time consultant psychiatrists.

Ironically, the fact that the YSB was relatively unprofessional made it more vulnerable to substantive change. If it had had more social workers, psychiatrists, and psychologists it would have been far more immune to any significant moves to create alternatives. I doubt, however, that it would have been any less brutal. A study of reform schools done by Robert Vinter at the University of Michigan found an inverse relationship between deinstitutionalization and professionalization.[10] From this point of view, corrections reform is probably more easily accomplished in a state like Alabama or Arkansas than in California, routinely among the worst in the nation.[11] California's brutal Youth Authority is overrun by M.B.A.'s, M.S.W.'s, and Ph.D.'s. They do the same things which cried out for reform in Massachusetts, but with more technical finesse and professional arrogance.

The Massachusetts Experiment came to be discounted not because it didn't work, but because it happened in Massachusetts. It must have been, people seem to think, a criminological as well as a political anomaly. Certainly the 1988 presidential campaign added fuel to that fire. The state's delinquents must have been "different." There was one surprising difference. The Massachusetts system held a large number of youngsters who in other states would have been in adult prisons. In 1988, for example, a total of twelve juveniles were waived to adult courts in Massachusetts. In that same year, Maryland waived 900, Florida 4,000, and Virginia 800. But Massachusetts is no more liberal when it comes to law and order than other states. It continues to have some of the most brutal prisons in the nation.

Who were the inmates in Massachusetts reform schools? They varied little from those in institutions in other states. They were no more nor less criminal than youngsters in the Texas Youth Council's infamous Mountain View reform school in the early seventies, Los Angeles' Juvenile Hall in 1988, New York's maximum-security facility for delinquent teenagers at Goshen, Illinois' St. Charles Reformatory, the District of Columbia's Oak Hill, Tennessee's Taft, Oregon's MacLaren, or Florida's Dozier. I mention these particular institutions because I was subsequently involved in lawsuits against them making court-ordered visits, studying statistical and case records, and interviewing youngsters, staff, and administrators. The average age of inmates in the Massachusetts reform schools was fifteen and a half. Most were sent to the facilities for breaking and entering or other property crimes. Though blacks formed less than 5 percent of the state population, they made up more than 30 percent of the reform school population, and at times almost half of those in pretrial detention. Hispanics accounted for an additional 15 percent of the reform school population. As is still true, most were involved with alcohol or drugs (acid, speed, heroin, and the beginnings of the cocaine epidemic). As is the case in almost all jurisdictions, most of the youths were the offspring of teenage unions, and almost half had themselves fathered or borne children. Of the approximately two thousand youth under DYS supervision, usually no more than fifteen or twenty had been committed for murder or manslaughter (about five or six youths per year). These fifteen or twenty constituted virtually all juveniles convicted of murder in the state. Approximately 25 percent were formally charged with crimes of violence or crimes against persons. When distilled case by case, however, those who demonstrated a capacity for personal violence were less than 5 percent of the youth committed to DYS. This is because charges don't necessarily reflect the particular violence or dangerousness of the individual young-ster. The difference between aggravated assault and simple assault, both crimes against persons, may be the difference between impulsive-ly pushing a policeman away and beating an aged stranger senseless. Despite the common mythology, most juvenile courts tend not to lower the level of charges, but rather to overcharge. Massachusetts was no exception. To suggest that juvenile courts routinely mollycoddle delin-quents by disregarding serious crimes is nonsense. When juvenile courts latch on to a kid caught in a violent act, they hang on with a tenacity far beyond that of most adult courts.

Another interesting fact about the delinquent youngsters in Mas-sachusetts is how little they differed over the years. Though one fre-quently hears that juveniles have grown more violent than the rest of the population, the statistics do not bear that out. There was a growth in crime nationally—adult and juvenile—in the twenty-year period be-tween 1960 and 1980, and again in the early 1990s, but it has been much overdramatized with reference to juvenile crime. Juvenile crime rates rise or fall pretty much in line with adult crime rates.

Even with the spread into the suburbs of drug abuse—along with more burglary, petty crime, and the occasional armed robbery—the percentage of middle-class youngsters inhabiting state reform schools or detention centers didn't rise. The offenders incarcerated in state juvenile institutions are predominantly black, Hispanic, or econom-ically disadvantaged whites.[12] The youngsters in Massachusetts deten-tion centers and reform schools supported the thesis that reform schools and detention centers are not for our own—for the sons and daughters of legislators, academics, judges, journalists, politicians, or any other of a host of middle-class parents. They are for others, though local stan-dards may call for variations on who those others might be.

One other thing characterized the many young people in the Mas-sachusetts reform schools and detention centers: they were often prod-ucts of the very programs set up to treat them—particularly the child welfare system. Early on in my administration, I brought in Joe Leavey as assistant commissioner for community-based programs. Joe had been an administrator with the Division of Child Guardianship, the state child welfare agency. As we walked through the institutions, Joe kept wandering off to this or that room. He was constantly getting hailed by the inmates. Joe knew too many by their first names. It was like old home week as he went up and down the hallways. Here were the alumni of child welfare. Our children were theirs. Theirs were ours.[13] These kids were not the failures of a caring child welfare system, but the perverse successes of a neglectful child welfare system—its by-products.

II

A Brief Tour

6 *Waiting Rooms*

Roslindale

The Judge Connelly Reception and Diagnostic Center was in the Roslindale section of Boston. Built in the early 1960s as a centerpiece of reform, it stood hidden down a side road between a cemetery and a dump. In it were juveniles awaiting trial or transfer to a reform school. The kids had aptly dubbed the place "Rozzie"—a place of random punishment and occasional deliverance through identification with the aggressor—it produced sufficient dread among its inmates to guarantee the obligatory macho overreaction, particularly in the strongest of the frightened.

I drove out to Roslindale with Frank Maloney. We were met by Len Avery, the superintendent Frank had recently appointed. Len had worked for the Youth Service Board as an assistant superintendent following his retirement from the FBI. He was a big, soft-spoken man who kept his natural sensitivity to troubled youngsters subdued through a lifelong immersion in law enforcement ideology. He was naturally kind, but like so many graduates of the American Catholicism of the 1940s and 1950s—people assiduously recruited by the FBI and the CIA— he was a true believer in the ideology of discipline which was the backbone of Roslindale. Nevertheless, Len was someone to depend on. He tried his best to carry out whatever reforms were proposed, and put up with me in spite of his fear that I was an insufferable bleeding heart. He would never attempt to undermine me.

Roslindale, originally designed with eighty-four small cells and four small dormitories, was rated to hold one hundred. It was filled to overflowing with boys eleven to seventeen years old. Len outlined the new intake procedures, educational programs, and gym repairs. Because of allegations of staff brutality, he was trying to make shift supervisors more accountable. I sat through the presentation by Len and his assistants and congratulated them on the progress they were making. The scene reminded me of military briefings with its charts, projections, pointers, and so on. I tried to be polite and ask appropriate questions. Len then took me on a tour of the institution.

As I walked the buffed floors, I soon saw that, despite the administration's efforts, the place was not much more than a giant, walled waiting room. The boredom was overwhelming. Rollo May was absolutely right when he said that the opposite of love is not hate, but apathy. Going into a locked living unit, I was confronted with a hundred or so mostly sullen boys dressed in institutional dungarees and T-shirts. The boys were watched and ordered about by a coterie of generally young, bulky "masters"—virtually all of them political appointees, and most hardly above their charges socioeconomically. The halls got darker, dirtier, and smellier the farther we wandered from the front office. Individual cells didn't meet minimal standards. There was a small gym with a cement-backed tile floor (the source of many injuries) and a large empty swimming pool, now closed as a health hazard. All the horrors were there—the open, doorless, seatless toilets, the occasional crying youngster, the pervasive stench of urine, the herding by size and age—all the accoutrements and routines of rabble management, which occasionally produce the personal violence that revalidates the system.

Some youngsters were locked in rooms in their shorts for punishment or control. Their shoes stood outside with their pants and T-shirts, which were wrapped in neat bundles. If this was not enough control, the more recalcitrant could be mechanically restrained in isolation cells downstairs. At bedtime, usually 7:30 P.M. (for the sake of the staff), the boys were made to stand at attention outside their cell doors and were ordered to strip. Each was then inspected by a master, after which he could enter his locked cell for the night. The whole procedure was a cross between boot camp and a castration ritual.

There were no toilets or sinks in the rooms. "Head call" was held before the boys were locked in. They stood silently in lines along the walls outside the congregate johns, waiting their turn to sit on an open seatless toilet to relieve themselves in full view of the waiting line. Each boy wiped himself with the number of toilet tissues dispensed by an observing staff member. Because many of the boys had serious emotional problems, mattresses and floors were regularly soiled and soaked in urine and occasionally in feces. During the night, the more resourceful youngsters, rather than trying to rouse the slumbering staff member locked in the control unit at the end of the long hall, would urinate out the barred window. On hot summer days the sides of the brick building reeked.

The day I visited was barber's day, and I walked by the silent line of boys waiting to be shorn. This was in the heyday of the youth culture of the late sixties, when hair was of more than usual importance to kids. Each boy had most of his hair shaved off. Although the reason given was to prevent hair lice, the ritual served to brand the teenager as a Youth Service Board boy. Youngsters regularly cried during the ordeal, a response that seemed oddly satisfying to staff. My own thoughts went to the classic 1930s study by the University of Chicago sociologist Clifford Shaw in his marvelous *Natural History of a Delinquent Career*. A young man described the haircut he was given at the St. Charles Reformatory in Illinois. After it was done, he said, "I knew I was a criminal."[1]

Here and there was a youngster with a scarred face or a black eye—an accident or the result of some street altercation. Battle scars were routine at Roslindale, and not all were street wounds. Youths were herded into a classroom or gym for occasional activities, which served as a means for better institutional control. The ostensible purpose of schooling—education—was beside the point, but if a boy learned something along the way, all the better.

I was told that the most dangerous youngsters in the state passed through Roslindale's portals. That statement was hard enough to believe on those first visits. When I left the state four years later, with more experience and knowing most of this group personally, it was even less believable. "Can you get out of here?" "Would you call my mother?" "What's Lyman like?" "I didn't do what they said I did." Such were the questions and hustles of these predictable settings. It was no chore to be taken in by a story. What neither the staff nor most of these youngsters understood—and what I probably couldn't explain—was that being conned was never much of an issue with me. I think I knew when it was happening. If an adolescent in this strange place manipulated or dissembled, it was only normal behavior in an incredibly abnormal setting. Although the staff constantly worried about being taken in, to me it hardly seemed crucial to call a youngster's bluff just to bolster my own ego. There's usually more risk to the integrity of the therapist than benefit in that technique. Awareness of that risk made me come to mistrust many of the so-called therapeutic community programs based on confrontation and group peer pressure. Too often they seem aimed at reassuring the therapists.

Though about 8,000 young people went through Roslindale each year, Roslindale, like virtually every other youth detention center in the United States, didn't hold many violent youth, nor were many particularly threatening. Though these deep-end delinquents provide the rationale for a massive national system of locking up juveniles, they seldom make up more than 3 percent of the institutionalized population. This means that of the 80,000 to 100,000 youngsters in the nation who are locked in detention facilities and reform schools on any given day, only about 2,500 need to be in "secure" settings. In Massachusetts, the state with eighth-largest detention population in the Union, we lowered the daily population of our largest locked detention facility from 250 to twenty-five at no increased risk to the community. We could have lowered it to five or ten.

Huntington Avenue

The Detention Center at Huntington Avenue in Boston was our only facility exclusively for girls awaiting trial or placement, though there were girls in two other smaller detention facilities in western Massachusetts (Westfield) and in central Massachusetts (Worcester). The center bordered a busy thoroughfare on Huntington Avenue and looked like a deteriorating warehouse. It was a self-contained brick building with a large adjoining parking lot. Only by going around the building could one see the barbed-wire-topped security fence surrounding a tarmac yard, which clearly distinguished it as something more than a storage facility.

Most girls at Huntington Avenue were awaiting transfer to the Lancaster Girls' Industrial School or an opening at Madonna Hall or the

House of the Good Shepherd. The old YSB had had ways to contract with private, nonprofit agencies. I learned fairly early on that I was expected to keep Madonna Hall, a Catholic girls' home, supplied with a given number of girls. The state house speaker's office would call my office if the population began to fall at Madonna Hall. We were expected to supply enough girls to keep the place solvent. At first I couldn't object, since their care and services, though rigid, seemed a cut above the services of the only alternative we had—the Lancaster reform school.

Despite its rundown, grubby appearance, Huntington Avenue was kept in rigid order under a superintendent who tolerated no relaxation of control. Any mildly sassy girl found herself in isolation. Most girls came to Huntington Avenue for status offenses like truancy, incorrigibility, and running away—crimes which wouldn't have been crimes if they had been committed by an adult. This was a common pattern in the department. A large number of the boys were also charged with status offenses. After Congress passed the Juvenile Justice and Delinquency Prevention Act in 1972, a national effort was launched to remove status offenders from the juvenile justice system. It failed.[2] The same kids were just relabeled as bona fide offenders and committed to detention centers and reform schools.

A common ploy used by the juvenile courts was to order a truant to go to school, or a disobedient child to be home by 9:00 P.M. At the first day of school missed or the first 10:00 P.M. return home, the status offender became a delinquent in violation of a court order liable to juvenile corrections like any other. This procedure has recently been upheld and endorsed by a conservative California Supreme Court.[3] Huntington Avenue was a good example of overkill—control gone awry. Though we heard the routine myths about increasingly violent delinquent girls, we didn't see many then, and I haven't seen many since. Most were status offenders or other lightweight delinquents in need of individual care and supervision. From informal interviews, it was my impression that at least a third were victims of incest.[4] As we began to relax things a bit, one of my new staff found a girl ordered to us as incorrigible on the complaint of her father, who brought his daughter to court when she stopped honoring his nightly request for a bed partner.

As we walked along the narrow hallway of the admissions unit, girls peered out from isolation rooms—their faces pressed hard against the small scratched windows of the heavy security doors. Here and there a door was ajar. Many wore hospital-type gowns and cloth slippers. It was hard to get a fix on why so many girls were in isolation. I'd seen it justified for escape risks or for young people who were violent management problems, but here girls were in isolation who, as best I could tell, were simply waiting for classification or placement. The phrase *medical isolation* kept popping up as a kind of official rationale meant to put the procedure beyond question, at least to a "layperson" like myself. Finally the nurse told me that each girl coming into the Huntington Avenue detention facility was locked in solitary for up to two weeks following the policy dictated by the physician in charge. In his view medical isolation was necessary to avoid the spread of venereal disease even in those cases where there were no allegations of sexual promiscuity. As part of this rite of entry, each girl was given a vaginal examination. I'd heard staff at the central office occasionally joke about "Dr. Goldfinger" at the Huntington facility. Now I knew what they meant. A virgin's hymen would frequently be broken during the exam—a practice which a study committee of the Harvard School of Public Health would later call barbaric.

Despite their surroundings, the girls seemed giddily upbeat and verbal (though softly so), and they reached out for help and support. Those not locked in isolation were dressed in housedresses or smocks. They sat in small circles on the floor, whispering and playing jacks, a game I hadn't seen since the 1940s. The aura made me uncomfortable: infantilization with a tacky erotic quality. The girls called the female staff "Auntie"—adding their first names or initials—"Auntie B.," Auntie Alice," and so forth. Against the unvarying backdrop of neglect, isolation, and occasional strong-arm handling was this fawning, clinging quality. Girls held onto and wound their arms around the necks of staff members who were as likely as not, in another instant, to lock them in.

7   *Warehouses*

The Boys' Industrial School at Shirley

A few days after my swearing-in, I began a series of trips around the state to visit the reform schools. Herb Willman, a staff member in the central office who was an ex-Army sergeant, offered to help me get to know the system. I felt an immediate affinity for him. He made me feel as if I were back in the Air Force again. Herb had been in the Youth Service Board for most of his working life, with time out for a stint in the service. He knew where most of the skeletons were buried, and I had the impression he'd also been on most sides of the issues affecting youth care in the YSB.

It was natural that I gravitated toward Herb. He had the street smarts of a lot of NCOs I'd known in the military: they were masters at manipulating young officers who were fresh to command but afraid someone might betray their incompetence. Experienced NCOs perpetually walked the thin edge between insulting a dumb new CO and carrying him along. I'd been properly handled by a few such NCOs during my time in the military. But I'd learned a few lessons as well. The best technique was to allow someone to think he was using me while I learned as much as possible from him—and never openly to acknowledge the process. Both parties, of course, know what's happening, but it becomes a comfortable, even relaxing, game. My relationship with Herb had something of that quality. During the hours of driving, he spun out anecdotes intended to advance his own agenda. I neither trusted the information nor neglected it. Instead, I listened and filed things away. Herb was a great gossiper, and his evenings sometimes seemed to be taken up with phone calls to superintendents, cottage supervisors, and others, listening, advising, passing on stories and rumors. His offhand comments and jokes were a good barometer as to how things were going, what problems were coming up, and what I'd best look out for.

My first trip to Shirley Industrial School, more than any other, set me on the path that eventually led to my closing the reform schools. Shirley was about an hour's drive from Boston, near Leominster, Massachusetts. Many of the buildings dated from the late 1800s when Shirley had been a Shaker community. But as the celibate Shakers declined in numbers, they had no further need for such a large facility. The state acquired the property and added new buildings. There was a logic to all this: the industrial school was as utopian a concept as the eccentric religious settlement. Shirley Industrial School was to be a place for retraining and teaching discipline and proper ways. Though it never worked very well for the inmates, it was if anything even less rehabilitative for the staff. Shirley traditionally held 150 to 200 of the oldest boys in the department. In earlier years, its Cottage Nine was also the end-of-the-line institution for obstreperous youngsters who were management problems in the other institutions. The YSB developed a special discipline program for these boys at Shirley. Later, it opened the Institute for Juvenile Guidance at Bridgewater to handle this hard-core population.[1]

We drove slowly up the narrow road which circled a long central mall between lines of cottages facing each other. At the top stood the administration building. Behind it were the school and shops. It could easily have been a prep school or college campus. Lawns were neatly cut, flower gardens in place. It was really quite impressive. But I didn't see any boys. I asked, "Where are all the kids?" There had to be a couple hundred somewhere on the grounds. Herb's facetious reply was that they were stashed in tunnels under the quadrangle. "Where are the kids?" became a sick joke as we toured institutions. The more presentable the reform school, the less visible were its inmates—an inverse ratio between neatness and care. Like those who can't chew and walk at the same time, many state institutions find it difficult to maintain tidy institutions while giving personal care to the inmates.

This isn't universally true—most youth correctional institutions are both dirty and uncaring.

On this first visit, I simply wanted to meet the superintendent and get the amenities over with. Instead Herb and I were ushered into a large room adjoining the superintendent's office. The superintendent, assistant superintendent, director of education, and chaplain sat around an impressive conference table. The flags, comfortable chairs, carpets, and paneled walls testified to a well-ensconced administration. I was given a presentation describing the types of boys in the institution, its programs, and building plans for the future. This was followed by a guided tour of the chapel, the school, the kitchen, and an empty cottage.

I saw the auto repair shop (where the staff's cars were repaired), the upholstery shop (where the staff's furniture was reupholstered), the bookbindery (where the staff's books were rebound), the machine shop, and the dining hall—all the appendages of reform schools for the past century. I looked in on a vocational program and an empty cottage dorm. Then there was the arts and crafts room, where one is shown things "made by the boys themselves" as though this were an epoch-making accomplishment, given their supposed deviance. (It's characteristic of many institutions with captive inmates that the usually pathetic products of their arts and crafts programs serve only to reinforce the outsider's perception of deviance in the inmate population. Walpole prison sold chokers made by the Boston Strangler. Chillicothe prison in Ohio sells miniature electric chairs "made by the inmates themselves.")

The boys I encountered were polite when spoken to. Otherwise they were mostly silent. The administrators were loudly off-the-cuff as we passed this or that inmate in a shop or classroom: a shouted "How we doing, Jimmy?" to a somewhat startled inmate sweeping a floor. "Did you get a chance to see your parole officer this week, Harry?" "How's the food, Billy?" The hail-fellow-well-met ambience was decidedly one-directional, and I grew more uneasy, though I said nothing. After an hour or so, I thanked my guides for their time and apologized for having to leave so early, citing the need to visit the girls' reform school at Lancaster a few miles down the road.

As we drove away from the administration building Herb pointed out Cottage Nine standing halfway down the mall. Since no one had mentioned it, I suggested we stop briefly. Herb hesitated. He didn't think the superintendent would want us to visit this particular cottage unannounced, adding somewhat cryptically, "You're the boss, though." That piqued my interest, and Herb knew it. He said he wasn't sure the staff on duty would let us in.

We negotiated the steps of the old stone building, and Herb pressed the doorbell. After a long wait, a beefy, unsmiling master cracked open the heavy door and eyed us up and down. Herb was ill at ease, though he seemed to get something of a kick out of the whole scene, as if we were a couple of students breaking rules. He assumed an officious tone and announced that the new commissioner wanted to tour the cottage. We were ushered into a sparsely furnished room. The whole place was deathly silent. The master picked up a phone and called the administration building. After a few mumbled words, he hung up and escorted us inside.

There they were—about a dozen fifteen and sixteen-year-old boys with clipped heads and institutional garb sitting across from one another, four at a table. Nothing was happening. There was no talk, no reading, no movement, nothing. They just sat with their hands folded on bare tabletops. Another burly master sat up front, blankly staring out on the sullen assemblage from behind a scarred desk. I said hello and got a grunt in response. A more talkative staff member came in from an adjoining hallway and struck up a conversation, explaining that this was rest period. The boys had just finished chores and would later be involved in programs. He said a group therapy program was conducted every Wednesday or Thursday. A Boston psychiatrist, Irving Kaufman, met with individual boys as needed. The name resonated uncomfortably. I had used Kaufman's material while working at various clinics in the Air Force. He was a nationally respected expert on character disorders, a psychoanalytically oriented psychiatrist whose approach seemed unusually humane in a field not particularly distinguished by humaneness.[2] I thought it odd that he would be a consultant here.

I walked uneasily across the room to the boys sitting silently at their tables and asked a routine question: "What's your name?" I got a slight smile and a couple of whispered words—"James, from Lowell." That was it. This was no place for banter. I was caught up in some sort of local drama. Everyone in the room seemed to hang onto whatever slight utterances might be exchanged. Talking seemed like a deviant act, and the silence overwhelmed my puny stabs at civility. I withdrew with the comment that I'd be back, and hoped to get to know them better.

The more talkative staff member showed us the rest of the cottage.

There was a small kitchen, though food was apparently bused in from a central dining hall. Upstairs, I was shown the large dorm where the boys slept, complete with the fenced-in booth for the staff member who watched them. At the far end stood an open seatless toilet. As we headed back toward the stairs, I noticed a closed door across the hallway. I asked if we might see that area as well. There was a noticeable hesitation before the staff member ushered us into the "tombs"—a series of cement cubicles not quite reaching the vaulted ceiling of the old building. The coffinlike rooms were aptly named. I asked to look inside one. The master unlocked the steel mesh door, and there, on the floor, nude in the darkness of his own tomb, sat a sixteen-year-old. He was being punished for having caused a scene in the cottage a few days earlier. I asked our guide how long the boy would be kept in the tomb and was told it was usually a matter of days but could go on longer. I asked the boy his name. He approached the doorway, blinking at the light from outside, and told me his name and what he'd done to get himself confined. The hovering staff, and the prospect that any conversation would get back to the silent room below, served to make me limit my remarks to the impersonal rituals and bureaucratic inanities which traditionally attend this kind of insanity. I wished the boy good luck and walked away as the master secured the door.

We went downstairs again, past the roomful of cropped heads. I thanked the staff for showing me the facility and left without comment. I had to get out. I feared that the superintendent would arrive shortly, and I didn't want to meet him then. I didn't know what to say. As we drove away, I tried to sound detached, commenting that it was an interesting place. Herb said he didn't think I'd made a good impression by visiting Cottage Nine unannounced. I was less concerned with the impression I'd made than with an obsession that was beginning to take me over. Our tour had touched something that would make the reform schools my personal ghosts.

The Girls' Industrial School at Lancaster

We left Shirley and drove the few miles down the road to Lancaster's Girls' Industrial School, which dated from 1848. The plain red brick buildings scattered about tree-lined grounds held about 150 girls. Buildings had been added over the years as the institution grew, but the place had a certain sense of architectural integrity, giving the impression that, except for a few conveniences like phones, the buildings, offices, dormitories, and dayrooms were probably much as they had been in the mid-1800s.

This was to be the most formal of visits. A staff person ushered us into a waiting room outside the superintendent's office. After a twenty-minute wait (which seemed somehow appropriate to the occasion), Mrs. Van Waters, the superintendent, made her appearance. She was a proper, distinguished-looking woman who appeared to be in her late sixties. Though she was gracious, it was a studied, supremely controlled graciousness.

Mrs. Van Waters was a survivor. As the daughter-in-law of a famous Massachusetts prison reformer of the early 1900s, she had developed a close relationship with local community groups who supported her way of running the school. She suffered the occasional intrusions of the YSB central office into her programs without ceding any control to Boston. She'd kept the place pretty much incident-free. There were few escapes. The town of Lancaster considered the girls' institution as integral to it and was well pleased with Mrs. Van Waters' tenure.

Mrs. Van Waters outlined the programs, describing some of the rather wild girls and their need to be resocialized to be proper ladies. After her presentation, we adjourned to the dining room and sat down at a long Victorian dining table, with Mrs. Van Waters at the head. Her foot touched a button on the floor under the table. A bell rang faintly in the next room, and presently a teenage girl appeared. She was dressed in a long pinafore smock and wore a cloth granny cap secured with elastic to cover her hair and ears. I felt as if I were caught in a time warp as the blushing girl served us. Mrs. Van Waters introduced her and asked her another of those pro forma questions meant not so much to be answered as to exhibit the youngster.

After lunch, we were shown one of the cottages. Girls in frumpy housedresses and granny caps sat at tables knitting, sewing, and reading. A couple wore something resembling a nightshirt. Apparently those girls were security risks. The place was mostly silent, though occasionally a girl would raise her hand and, following a nod from a matron, would run across the room to whisper in the ear of an "auntie." A few years later when I toured girls' reform schools in Tennessee and Texas, I learned, alas, that the girls there didn't call the matrons "Auntie" but "Mommy," and in the case of male supervisors, "Daddy."

Like Shirley, Lancaster wasn't a place for spontaneous conversation. From reading the Children's Bureau report, I knew Lancaster had its own isolation unit hidden in the basement of one of the cottages. Unruly girls were placed in whitewashed brick basement rooms. As we left, I asked Herb if it was equivalent to Cottage Nine. He said he didn't think anyone would be in it, if for no other reason than that the administration knew I was coming. He suggested we defer visiting Lancaster's version of the tombs to another time. A few days later, I returned unannounced and had a maintenance man unlock the doors of the isolation unit. It was empty.

The Lancaster Girls' Industrial School was a brick-and-mortar embodiment of a pattern noted by the social historian David Rothman. Institutions sprang up in the United States in the Jacksonian period—prisons, jails, mental hospitals, and reform schools—and were, in a sense, designed to re-create for the people of the mid-1800s the more disciplined world which had ostensibly spawned the American Revolution.[3] But memories falter and such re-creations can survive only inside institutional walls. Institutions are different. Inmates can be coerced into the most extreme caricatures our selective memories conjure up, giving us blessed, though false, reassurance.

John Augustus Hall

In a quaint twist of logic the department's institution for seventy-five to one hundred seven to twelve-years-olds was named for John Augustus, a nineteenth-century Boston shoemaker who invented probation and devoted his life to keeping offenders out of institutions.[4] The idea of sending a twelve-year-old, much less a seven-year-old, to a reform school seemed peculiar to me. It was a "liberal" Massachusetts reform school for toddlers.

John Augustus Hall was the newest institution in the department. The modern building looked much like an elementary or junior high school. However, as soon as we set foot inside, it was clear this was no ordinary school. It was run by a kind of troika that showed the kinds of alliances Coughlan had forged with the legislature. The superintendent, Paddy Creedon, was a benign gentleman in his fifties or sixties, a bachelor who lived in a room at the institution. He was often seen wandering up and down the hallways in slippers and nightshirt, checking to see that the boys were tucked into their beds. His political connections came from the Worcester area. The Children's Bureau consultant had been impressed by Paddy: "While . . . John Augustus Hall fails to meet many of the minimum staffing, program, and physical plant standards, it would be a gross disservice to the present superintendent and staff to fail to state for the record that the institution is being operated in a compassionate and humane fashion."[5]

The assistant superintendent, Joe Kelly, seemed an equally friendly sort, but I had no way of knowing the friendly from the hostile during those first weeks. I had not yet learned to recognize the blarney which masks less-than-salutary motives. Joe's brother Walter, it turned out, was a member of the governor's executive council and had led the battle against my confirmation, so Joe had no reason to love me. The third member of the troika was the institutional psychologist, a woman in her fifties who spoke gushily about the "poor little boys" who peopled John Augustus. Though she did some psychological testing and, apparently, some counseling, I didn't believe she was a clinician.

Our guides took us on a quick tour of the institution. It was an architecturally updated version of Roslindale. The inmates occupied individual cell-like rooms with solid doors and steel bed frames. Unlike Roslindale, however, these rooms had toilets in them, though they were solid steel jail toilets without seats and with attached sinks. There were even isolation cells if a seven or twelve-year-old should get defiant. I had the impression, however, that they were rarely used.

What had these kids done? Joe told a couple of war stories—the kind that would make a kiddy reform school seem reasonable—of a twelve-year-old burglar who led older teenagers to follow him and an eleven-year-old car thief who kept getting picked up because his head barely showed above the dash when he drove. That was about as bad as they got at John Augustus. But it was clear that the people who ran the place really didn't know why most of the children were there. They knew the offense, and occasionally they read probation reports or met a visiting family member. The personal and family tragedies which attended most youngsters who had landed in John Augustus were purely tangential to running a clean, incident-free institution for little tykes. At best they were material for a good story. Less entertaining problems had a way of undoing the myth that John Augustus Hall was a happy place for youngsters wrested from ill-disciplined families. As I passed a pile of sheets lying on the hallway floor, a familiar stench greeted me. Most of these kids wetted or soiled their beds.

Joe invited us to have lunch in the staff dining room, a glass-enclosed room off the main dining hall. Joe told us that this would allow us an opportunity to see the inmates. Shortly, seventy or so small boys with burr haircuts and striped T-shirts filed in and sat at tables. They were mostly silent, though a few words were exchanged. As we sat observing these children eating, we were served by the kitchen chef. Lunch was chow mein—a glutinous plateful which appeared the same as what the kids were eating. After the first forkful my mouth was on fire. I looked across the table at Herb, whose face was turning shades of purple. The boys seemed to be having no trouble at all downing their chow mein, and I figured someone was trying to make some sort of point. We ate our chow mein, drank a lot of water, and said nothing.

The Lyman School for Boys

Lyman was the first reform school in the nation. It began with great hopes. As Massachusetts governor George Briggs said at its opening:

> Of the many and valuable institutions sustained in whole, or in part, from the public treasury, we may safely say, that none is of more importance, or holds a more intimate connection with the future prosperity and moral integrity of the community, than one which promises to take neglected, wayward, wandering, idle and vicious boys, with perverse minds and corrupted hearts, and cleanse and purify and reform them, and thus send them forth in the erectness of manhood and in the beauty of virtue, educated and prepared to be industrious, useful and virtuous citizens.[6]

But Lyman strayed from these ideals. Jon Connearney and Robert Dellelo were in Lyman School as teenagers in the early 1950s. In 1970 Connearney, at age thirty, was in Walpole State Prison for murder. He described his memories of Lyman to a reporter from the *Boston Globe:* "My first day there I talked in the dining room. I got 50 dollars. That's 50 blows with a stick on your open palm. Makes it swell up good." Robert Dellelo, also in Walpole for murder, had vivid memories of being "drop-kicked" like a football and learning to hate authority.[7] Lyman was a testament to institutional longevity—an odd agglomeration of decrepit stone, brick, and wooden buildings scattered about low rolling hills. It had accumulated a century and a half's worth of annexes, tacked on to reflect whatever changing ideologies the politics of the times dictated—from punishment to education to military training to vocational training to rehabilitation and back again. It routinely held between 250 and 300 thirteen to fifteen-year-old boys.

I was given the grand tour of the grounds, the school, the shops, various cottages, and the farm. As the afternoon progressed, the superintendent, Frank Ordway, kept referring to this or that beast, building, barn, or gym as his own—"my cattle," "my farm," "my pond." He'd succumbed to the besetting temptation for wardens and superintendents, which afflicts competent and incompetent alike, whose chief symptom is a tendency to turn a state institution into a personal fiefdom. It infects those most perniciously who invest themselves in trying to develop effective institutional programs, a process which inevitably undoes itself. I think it has something to do with the overwhelming sense of futility one feels at seeing the failed products of the institution return again and again. One retreats to a benign acceptance of the inmates as flawed beyond hope, and focuses instead on having a spiffy facility.

Lyman's administration was more humane than most. Frank and his assistant, Bob Brown, devoted themselves to trying to make the school responsive to its inmates. When I visited, I would almost always find them in the superintendent's office trading stories and discussing ideas for programs. But their innovations were no more than rearrangements. This was Lyman's Achilles' heel: they couldn't get much beyond their institution. Even their community-based ideas were institutionally bound, and the tie to the institution undid their efforts. In the midst of all their well-intentioned activity stood Lyman's discipline cottage, the stigma of failure.

The U.S. Children's Bureau consultant had noted that, when he visited Lyman, more than 25 percent of the institution's population was in the discipline cottage. "This was regrettable inasmuch as the experience in the security program did not seem at all constructive to the consultant." Noting that discipline seemed to place considerable stress on boys' polishing floors to keep busy, the consultant described a cell in the basement of the discipline cottage. "The only furnishings are a floor mat for each boy. Boys are placed in this area who need maximum control. When the consultant first came into the cottage there were at least six boys sitting next to each other on their mats. At the time of another visit to the cottage all boys had been removed from the cell so a boy suspected of having syphilis could be placed there for isolation purposes."[8]

Frank Ordway was unhappy about the discipline cottage and peri-odically shut it down. But after an incident, or because of staff pres-sure, he'd reorganize and reopen it. I was forever being told that he planned to close the discipline cottage finally, but it remained open well into my tenure. It had some illustrious alumni, among them Albert Di Salvo, the Boston Strangler.[9]

But despite this, Frank ran Lyman more creatively than the other reform schools were run. He tried to normalize Lyman. He and Bob thought it could be a home. But no home, at least no nonabusive home, would have a discipline unit where youngsters were forced to sit in silence for weeks or to scrub floors with toothbrushes a number of hours a day. No caring home would treat every youngster's defiance, sassiness, or running away in the same manner as every other. That is part of the dilemma of the institution. It *must* handle all inmates alike. To do otherwise undermines order. But now and then a child grabs normalcy even from the institution's repressive environment.

Billy, a grinning, hyperactive fourteen-year-old, had spent long periods in discipline. He had no family and no prospect of one, but was forever looking for a home. He was a mascot at Lyman. With Frank's permission, Billy painted the walls of one of the unfurnished rooms in a crumbling old cottage. Late one afternoon, as I walked alone past that cottage, Billy came up quietly behind me. He pulled me by the arm and led me into the room. In colorful crude letters from ceiling to floor, he had written his favorite song. I read some of it aloud:

Here comes the sun
. . . and I say it's alright.
. . . It seems like years since it's been here
It's alright—it's alright.[10]

"Do you like it, Mr. Miller?"
"Yeah."
He smiled and folded his arms.

The Institute for Juvenile Guidance

Bridgewater's Institute for Juvenile Guidance (IJG) was what finally brought the Youth Service Board down. The abuse of inmates and the public confrontations between the superintendent and the assistant superintendent were too much. But the IJG had begun as a major reform. It was the single locked institution set up by Coughlan to house violent and obstreperous youngsters away from all the other institutionalized teenagers in YSB.

What about violent youth in correctional institutions? Inmates who end up confined to discipline units, holes, and segregation are not necessarily those who've committed the most serious crimes. Most cause management problems for the institution. They rebel, have problems of attitude, try to run away, goad cottage staff, or threaten to embarrass the administration. The paradox is that these harsh units are often filled with the institution's lesser offenders, the youngsters who most resist their own institutionalization. Chronic serious offenders usually succumb willingly to the demands of institutionalization. They are more likely to be alumni and to recognize the routines and the proper role of the inmate. They follow the axiom of the good con—"Keep your mouth closed, your nose clean, and do your time"—biding their time until they are poured back onto the street. An inmate's institutional "adjustment" is one of the worst predictors of later behavior.

In its earlier years, Cottage Nine at Shirley sufficed for the perceived need for isolation, at least for the older boys. Though the brutality of the place was well known within the administration, no one said much. As time passed, however, even Cottage Nine wasn't a sufficient "hammer." It held Shirley Industrial School together, but it wasn't enough to contain inmates from all the reform schools. A larger facility was needed. Though Bridgewater was meant to provide treatment beyond having youngsters scrub floors with toothbrushes or sit rigidly mute at tables, the new facility wasn't to be mollycoddling or permissive. It was a place to separate offenders, as Coughlan put it, "through restraint heretofore impossible."[11]

State institutions were a cottage industry outside the town of Bridgewater. It was already home to Bridgewater State Hospital—made infamous by Fred Wiseman's controversial documentary, *Titicut Follies*. The IJG opened in 1955, two years after Coughlan took over the agency. Between 100 and 150 boys were to be housed in a large nineteenth-century building with a yard surrounded by a stone and stucco wall. The building's history gives some insight into the survivability of these kinds of facilities. It had been a county farm, a men's prison, a place for defective delinquent women, and finally a warehouse for recalcitrant teenagers. Shortly before I arrived, a seventeen-year-old parolee from the IJG was found hanging from a tree in the front yard of his home, his hands handcuffed behind his back. His death was ruled suicide. Staff commented that the boy had been kept in the same isolation cell his mother had occupied twenty-five years earlier as a defective delinquent.

The scandals at the IJG were brought to Governor Volpe's attention in 1966 following the publication of a highly critical U.S. Children's Bureau report. It became a cause célèbre of reformers, and when Lieutenant Governor Frank Sargent became Massachusetts' chief executive in 1969, he made cleaning up the IJG a priority. Feelings about the institution ran high. An influential citizens' reform group, the Committee for Youth in Trouble (CYT), formed around the scandals at the IJG, was unhappy with the attempts of the new superintendent, Bill Mac-Donald, to salvage the place. The CYT touted professionalization—more psychiatrists, psychologists, and social workers. MacDonald preferred to rely on trusted staff from within the department to ensure better management. He instituted new regulations and rules to ensure greater consistency, placing limits on using isolation and mechanical restraints. They did, however, continue to be used periodically. He began new programs and brought in tutors and a part-time psychiatrist to meet individually with some of the more disturbed boys. Things quieted down, and the IJG was off the front pages.

Frank Maloney took me on my first visit to Bridgewater. I remember my shock at coming upon this rundown, gray-walled institution along a narrow country road outside the town of Bridgewater. It was an ominous-looking place, and I wondered what thoughts went through a youngster's head as he sat shackled in the back of the state van delivering him to this broken-down, God-forsaken slab of concrete and stucco. A master came down to the front gate in the wall, opened it, and escorted us up to the central building. The IJG was decaying—it had cracked walls, ceilings, and floors—as well as the familiar institutional stench, in this case smelling not so much of antiseptic or urine as of the cloying scent of Pine-Sol meant to cover the smell of bodily excretions.

Maloney had appointed MacDonald superintendent, and he was anxious that I recognize MacDonald's progress. We sat in the superintendent's office while he went over various charts outlining programs—tutoring, upholstery, bookbinding, and so forth. Then we had a quick tour, with emphasis on the newly painted walls in hallways and rooms. We met a few youngsters along the way—here and there in a classroom with a teacher, or else mopping the floors. Though there was an occasional smile, the smile looked like what one sees in a state mental hospital.

MacDonald showed us the isolation unit, where youngsters had been kept stripped in unheated rooms. They had slept on the cement floors or been shackled to steel bed frames welded to the floor. He stressed that he was not using isolation anymore. The IJG was trying to be decent and effective. I wasn't immune to the self-deception. It would come to me later masked as reassurance that at last, after wearying battles and bloody skirmishes, I had accomplished something. Such self-deception gives one respite, but it is the bane of true reform.

The premise according to which the IJG operated was epitomized in the person of sixteen-year-old Jimmy, whom I first met in four-point bed restraint (hands and feet strapped spread-eagled to the bed frame corners). He had been tied down because of his verbosity and bad attitude. I got to know Jimmy well in the next four years. He became a symbol to me of what we were about, what we had done to our charges, and how difficult it would be to reclaim them. Eighteen years later I received a letter from Jimmy, who is now in the adult institution for the criminally insane at Bridgewater, still one of the most despicable institutions in the nation and not half a mile from the room where I first met him. A couple of weeks after the letter came, I got a call from a local radio station, followed by an inquiry from the White House Secret Service. Jimmy had escaped and given out as his intention the assassination of Vice President Bush. He was caught on his way to Washington and sent back to Bridgewater.

Topsfield

I had been in the state only a few days when the subject of Topsfield first came up. Chris Armstrong mentioned it almost as an aside following my first meeting with the governor—"We've made arrangements to buy a convent on the North Shore to replace Bridgewater." Topsfield had been a Catholic convent and had stood empty for a few years as vocations declined. It was a well-maintained building that with some adjustments could probably be converted into an acceptable institution for up to a hundred youngsters. The problem was how to make it secure for the—ostensibly—most dangerous youngsters in the department.

Staff had reconnoitered the facility to see what would be required to bring it up to security standards. In those days relatively few such standards existed. The hardware-and-shackles crowd which now dominates the American Correctional Association (ACA) had little interest in juvenile corrections. If we had had to meet current ACA standards, we would have produced a juvenile version of the "new generation" prison touted in recent years by the U.S. Justice Department—concrete and steel behemoths combining the best of twentieth-century technology with the worst of nineteenth-century ideology.

We hoped to make Topsfield reasonably escape-proof through perimeter double fences. The fact that the individual rooms didn't lend themselves to the kinds of security which characterized more traditional correctional architecture seemed to me an advantage. We would have to try something new. In the back of my mind was the hope of creating caring, therapeutic communities in the state's reform schools. Topsfield's inadequacies could be turned to advantage by making staff rely on program, one-to-one interchange, and personal involvement rather than electric doors and isolation. Eyeball and program security would be our watchwords.

The idea was not that farfetched. Years later, I started other programs in Massachusetts and Pennsylvania for hard-core and violent youngsters in which the hardware security was minimal, relying on staff-to-inmate ratios for program security. These programs demonstrated the feasibility of unwinding from the overkill most juvenile corrections practices. The citizens of Topsfield, however, wanted no part of any correctional facility, traditional or otherwise. They just wanted to keep us out. A local opposition group formed headed by Jordan Patkin, a Cadillac dealer from Boston.

After my first week in office, Frank Maloney introduced me to the Topsfield town selectmen. The meeting was chaired by a state senator, Bill Saltonstall, son of former U.S. senator Leverett Saltonstall. The selectmen took pains to conceal the meeting from the Topsfield citizenry. We met in an almost deserted private club near Manchester. Despite this initial display of paranoia, the meeting was cordial. The selectmen were concerned that a scheduled town meeting, at which I was to defend the placement of dangerous delinquents in Topsfield, not get out of hand. There'd been threats, particularly from some residents who'd recently moved to the quiet, rural North Shore community. Senator Saltonstall asked me to reconsider the plans to acquire Topsfield. I told him that not everything had been decided and that we were open to compromise, though I wasn't sure what shape it might take.

New England is firmly wedded to its town meetings, and this was one to remember. About five hundred people showed up. The meeting was broadcast on the local radio station and presided over by the chairman of the board of selectmen. I gave a forty-five-minute apologia for our plans, pointing to the unacceptable conditions at the Bridgewater institution and the need to replace it. I tried to describe the inmates in some case-by-case detail, expressing my hope that the people of Topsfield might get to know them, start volunteer groups and tutorial programs, regularly visit the institution, and help us work with these difficult young offenders.

Though a few supported my position, most people were loudly hostile. After my presentation came the question period. The first query, which set the tone for the evening, was in the form of a statement. It went something like this: "Someone ought to shoot you with a rifle." The elderly man who said this was roundly applauded amid a din of muffled boos and self-conscious laughter. The selectmen, true to their promise, kept order, reminding the audience that I was a guest and had not come to be tarred and feathered. Things settled down, and I thought I might even be making some progress—if in nothing else, at least in engendering a smidgen of guilt in some of the more liberal members of the audience. Questions and comments began to be prefaced with "I know you mean well, but" or "It's not that we have anything against these boys, but," and usually ended in an offer to help me look elsewhere in the state to place the institution.

The town meeting confirmed the conventional wisdom holding that local communities don't want prisons and jails in their own neighborhoods. That is true as far as community-based facilities like halfway houses and day treatment centers go, but it doesn't always obtain when it comes to prisons, jails, reform schools, and detention centers. Communities just as commonly vie for new correctional institutions.[12] Most local leaders recognize the potentials of a large prison or reform school—jobs, contracts with vendors of services, building and architectural services, and so on. But Topsfield was different. It was an old and secure community. Unemployment was not a problem. Even if it had been, I had the impression that the community would rather have had those who needed employment consider moving elsewhere. The incentives which usually work toward acceptance of a reform school were absent in Topsfield.

But something else happened at that town meeting. As I stood there loudly defending our projected move from Bridgewater to Topsfield, I realized that I didn't see the new facility in the same light as those in the department and in the governor's office. Up to then it hadn't occurred to me that we might scrap the very concept of an institute for juvenile guidance or that we could close Bridgewater without replacing it. I saw Topsfield as offering a modest chance for some new approaches to the troubled young people I'd seen at Bridgewater. But in the argument that night, I found myself concluding that, if we got the Topsfield facility, it would have to be something quite different from the simple maximum-security institution it would replace. I began privately to question whether that kind of facility was needed at all for most of the Bridgewater youngsters. As I drove home, I mulled over the possibility that the old convent might serve a different purpose. Perhaps it should be a small, fifteen- or twenty-bed open therapeutic community. Perhaps it should even be a model program not unlike Lyward's Finchden Manor.

As the weeks went by, the opposition from Patkin's pressure group got nastier. I was asked to come to meetings to discuss plans for the Topsfield institution. The group was less open to compromise than even the hostile speakers at the town meeting. Allegations were made that I, as a former Maryknoll seminarian, had arranged some quiet deal with the Maryknoll order, which owned Topsfield; that money had changed hands; that I intended to move the youngsters in during the middle of the night. Our last meeting was on my birthday. As Frank and I rode up the dark, winding road to the Patkin country estate, it seemed as if we were involved with some kind of pseudomilitary intelligence network. We were met by men in trench coats walking about in the rain and fog, taking license plate numbers, and asking for identification. The birthday cake Patkin's group had prepared only compounded the unreality of the situation, and I was more stubborn than my embryonic plans justified. Things moved wholly into the realm of the fantastic a few weeks later, when I was walking around Boston Common during lunch hour and chanced to look up. There, written against the blue sky, was the name "PATKIN." I was dumbfounded and decided to keep this obvious hallucination to myself. I stole another quick glance. This time it read: "PATKIN CADILLAC." It was just an advertisement. So goes paranoia.

But Patkin unwittingly did me a favor. His group doggedly opposed us every step of the way, finally attaching itself to an issue which delayed our occupying the convent for several months. Though in years past fifty nuns had lived in the buildings with nary a murmur from the town, the sewage system was now judged inadequate for the same number of delinquent youngsters. I made a few unseemly remarks regarding discrimination in evaluating feces, but the environmental problem delayed our coming to Topsfield. New tests and ground taps had to be made, new contracts signed, new approvals gotten. By the time all this was done, I had closed Bridgewater without sending any of the inmates to Topsfield. (Months later, I recommended Topsfield's use as a staff training center connected to a ten- to fifteen-bed treatment program for youngsters with drug problems. We contracted with a group to begin the program. It never got off the ground. Though a dozen or so youngsters lived there for a few months, Topsfield mostly stood vacant during my tenure.)

As it turned out, Patkin's group wasn't totally off base in its allegations of financial hanky-panky in the purchase of the convent. A few weeks after my last meeting with Patkin, Frank Maloney and I were called before a closed session of the governor's executive council. To our surprise, we were berated by members of the council for having tried to "rook" the nuns. We had paid them a quarter million less than their asking price. We explained to the council members that we'd done our best to bargain and that the nuns had agreed to the lower offer. We thought we should be commended for getting the institution at a savings to the state. But that wasn't the way it worked. A couple of years later, a *Boston Globe* investigative team alleged that kickbacks (not involving the nuns) had been arranged in connection with purchase of Topsfield.[13] I had wandered through this political minefield like a blind man.

Brewster

The Forestry Camp at Brewster was a bright spot in the state system. Its Outward Bound model—though much longer than the classic program—in which kids spent a few months cleaning up the forest, seemed unusually humane next to the rest of our institutions. We eventually adjusted the program by shortening it and adding an after-care component. My first response to the idea of a forestry camp was mildly negative. What could a kid learn in the woods that had any relationship to his living at home or in the inner city? I'd missed the point. It was not a matter of learning marketable skills so much as it was an opportunity to succeed at something. Though the program was demanding, no one failed who tried. The peer support and the intense staff involvement all made for a satisfying experience. The Outward Bound philosophy—an unlikely mix of machoism and sensitivity—was made to order for many of the youngsters sent to us. Though there was little formal therapy, and problems weren't likely to be talked about in much depth, the atmosphere was caring. An evening campfire's sharing of the day's rock climbing, hiking, or rappeling was probably as therapeutic as anything we could have given at that time, as later research demonstrated.

The Outward Bound program inhibited recidivism, at least for a while. But after a youngster had been back in the community a few months, the positive results tended to get washed away. To sustain the good effects of the program there had to be solid aftercare and follow-up supervision, a lesson that apparently is not easily learned. Fifteen years later, a book on another Massachusetts Outward Bound–like "boot camp" program on Penikese Island near Cape Cod bemoaned the poor success rates of its graduates, attributing failure to the depth of the youngsters' pathology and maybe even to their bad genes. The author had views of therapy as wrong as his sense of what the reforms in Massachusetts were all about.[14]

The cantonment-type wooden buildings, the camping atmosphere, and the openness brought out the best in those who ran the forestry program, as well as in the boys sent there. There wasn't enough staff or hardware to allow the kinds of things which undermine good intentions in institutions. The young people had to be controlled and motivated through means other than intimidation or coercion. An overabundance of correctional armamentaria inevitably leads to deterioration in relationships. If the average suburban tract house were outfitted with an isolation cell, or if goon squads sat waiting in the parlor to handle unruly teenagers, a fair number of otherwise sane parents would, from time to time, make use of the available technology. Convenient coercion is too tempting. Forestry's strength lay in its lack of facilities.

Al Colette, the superintendent at Brewster, didn't agree. Through his contacts in the legislature Al got funds to erect permanent buildings, a large brick gym, and a dining hall at the forestry camp. I opposed the appropriations. I felt it would move forestry back to being another institution. The neat, rambling old wooden buildings were part of the reason the place worked. The staff *had* to learn other ways to deal with a withdrawn or temporarily out-of-control youngster. After I left the state, Al got his appropriations. I hope he's proven me wrong, but I doubt it.

III

Reforming Reform Schools

8   *Finding a Direction*

Competently administering a corrections system is of course a difficult task. Success is measured by a very peculiar set of criteria. Robert
Hitt, the writer and researcher on state-run human service agencies,
has put the qualifications succinctly. You are a successful state administrator if you (1) keep staff happy; (2) stay within your allocated budget; and (3) avoid untoward incidents (escapes, suicides, riots, blatant
incidents of abuse) which might come to public attention.[1] None of
these has much to do with the purposes of the agency—rehabilitating
offenders, deterring crime, making the streets safer, or whatever. But in
corrections, the goals of the agency are mostly irrelevant.

Correctional reform in this country of lawyers and management
experts has taken the form of setting minimum standards and ensuring
that rules and regulations are well written and properly promulgated
and enforced. Ignoring the possibilities of more basic reform, these
actions try to mitigate abuse. Through a variety of suits on conditions
in institutions, most states are under court order about or supervision
over conditions in prisons and jails. Looking at the results, one wonders
whether the effort was worth it. Court decisions have no doubt moder-
ated harsh prison conditions and softened some of the grosser bru-
talities. The court's involvement, however, has simultaneously served
to reinforce reliance on the failed institutional model as our primary
correctional response to crime.

Any halfway intelligent corrections administrator can use a lawsuit to cajole reluctant legislators into voting higher budgets for more staff and buildings. And that's precisely what has happened in the United States over the past twenty-five years. Court-ordered reforms are eventually swallowed by traditional correctional ideology. Reforms directed at meeting minimum standards through regulatory procedures end up driving the same vicious cycle that brought about the original problems. New institutions are built to meet court-ordered standards. They soon become overcrowded. More lawsuits follow, then more prisons, more guards, and more hardware. In a warped and minimal way, it works well for all concerned. The inmates (most of whom wouldn't be in prisons or reform schools if the same funding had been made available for alternatives), get minimal standards for a while. Lawyers and federal masters get a virtually unending source of funding for their efforts. Prison administrators and sheriffs get more buildings and staff. And politicians get to scream about being tough on crime while more criminals are created in the correctional system and crime rates rise, refueling the whole cycle. This is reform based on minimum standards and efficient administration. Had these standards been our goal in Massachusetts, the reform schools would be more numerous, bigger, and more firmly ensconced in the political structure than ever . . . and by now undoubtedly overflowing with children.

At first I had no specific agenda, only hazy ideas. I wanted to stop the brutality and lessen the harm we were doing, and I hoped to challenge some traditional correctional approaches to young offenders. That seemed like enough. But these modest goals turned out to be much harder to achieve than the more radical step of closing the institutions. My experience corroborates Margaret Mead's comment that, in the late twentieth century, massive change would be easier than incremental change.

Reform legislation had laid out a structure, a series of administrative positions and bureaus. It didn't mandate deinstitutionalization, and I didn't intend to start it. At most the legislation called for professionalization of the department. The U.S. Children's Bureau report which provided the impetus for the reform called for civil service tests for employees and more professional caseworkers, clinical psychologists, and psychiatrists. It recommended restrictions on overuse of isolation and less severe discipline practices—and more structured institutional programming. Perhaps the best example was its approach to John Augustus

Hall, the reform school for seven to twelve-year-olds. Not pausing to question the concept behind this bizarre facility, the Children's Bureau report merely asked for its professionalization: "The long range goal for an institution of 80 boys would be a half-time psychiatrist, a half-time psychologist, three full-time caseworkers, and a social group worker."[2]

Similarly, when confronted with the Shirley Industrial School which, according to the report, "exudes an atmosphere of defeat and negativism," the suggestion was to appoint a "qualified" person to bring in specialized services. This after making note of Cottage Nine's tombs, the silence, and the fact that the outdoor play area had not been used "since a boy escaped by going over a fence more than a year ago."[3] The reform schools would stay, but would be properly run and accredited. Community-based programs were seen as additional resources rather than as replacements for the institutions.

As I traveled from meeting to meeting it became clear that most wanted to hear the same things—qualified staff, new facilities, better salaries, better classification, better isolation hardware, perhaps uniforms, stainless steel toilets with sinks attached, staff training in techniques for subduing aggressive teenagers, and more emphasis on teaching discipline to the recalcitrant. These are the pronouncements one routinely hears, for example, from the leadership of the American Correctional Association—the old boys club of present and former guards (now risen to administrative positions), right-wing academics, and construction developers which speaks for professional corrections in this country. It's as if standards for the practice of medicine were being dictated by a cabal of semiskilled nineteenth-century barbers.

Though my policies changed with events, a direction eventually emerged for me. To borrow a phrase from Robert Theobald, I had not so much a map as a compass.[4] We were mapping uncharted territory as we made our way. It couldn't be otherwise, for no one had been there. But the reasons for change were often embarrassingly personal. Again and again I altered plans in response to the presence of some boy or girl. They were always catching me up in the hurtful conundrums created by the agency I headed, even as I was trying to keep a lid on the upset caused by meddling in reform school affairs on behalf of some youngster. But I was getting an education of sorts. As I beat this or that tactical retreat, I found myself reconnoitering the institutions and their administrations, looking for points of vulnerability, and finding a few allies among the generally hostile or apathetic staff.

My visits convinced me that I couldn't claim the institutions as my territory. Over the months I grew more alienated. My frustration was compounded by legislators, investigative committees, professional groups, and an edgy governor's staff communicating an imperfectly muffled faintheartedness which occasionally rose to thundering threats: "Don't move too fast." "Be sure to touch all the bases." Sometimes the message was a less benign: "You'll be lucky to last ninety days." "We'll have you in jail before this is over." Or even this: "I'll flush you down the toilet."

What we did was characterized by some as radical correctional reform. Indeed, the *Boston Phoenix* called me the only anarchist to run a state agency. I didn't consider myself either radical or an anarchist. I had been an Air Force officer, I had been educated in Catholic schools, I was not given much to worrying about class struggle. I had no grand scheme or ideology for reforming youth corrections, and I was as wary of doctrinaire explanations for crime and delinquency as I was of recipes for treatment, whether concocted from the narrow nosologies of the psychiatric professions or derived from the grand social and economic theories in vogue among left-wing criminologists. My views were conditioned mostly by clinical experience. This cast me as a liberal incrementalist, a person frightened of confrontation, willing to spell out lofty goals but unwilling to move toward them without majority support before the fact. Radical sociologists pretty much dismissed what we were doing. Only after we had finally closed the institutions did they pay much attention, and then it was to discount as basically irrelevant whatever we might have accomplished, calling it a classic liberal reform that ignored the economic roots sustaining the institutional tradition.

After a few months in office, I was invited to speak to a citizens' group made up mostly of angry Harvard students and leftist hangers-on who, as was their wont in the early seventies, were briefly hobnobbing with the oppressed working class from the rowhouses of Somerville and outer Cambridge. The group wanted to know what I intended to do about the state's reform schools. When I said I wanted to do better by individual youngsters, the audience was in near riot. At my suggestion that by going kid by kid I hoped we might actually reduce the populations of some reform schools, I was all but hooted off the stage.

Most of these politically involved students could not have cared less about knowing an individual youngster unless he or she was a good follower. When, in frustration with staff, I hired some radical university students to work in one of our institutions, I soon found them knocking youngsters off the wall with alacrity, matching blow for blow the presumed fascists who traditionally worked the floors. There were exceptions: Toby Yarmolinsky, for example, who at times seemed to be wherever I needed help, and Jim Kunen, who had recently written *The Strawberry Statement* and who came as a conscientious objector to teach the girls at Lancaster. Both were totally committed and unthreatened by the difficult youngsters with whom they worked.

Setting Wide Goals

I hoped that certain small actions of mine might carry wider implications for social change. My workaday approach was more at home with the ideas of social reform laid out by the British conservative philosopher Karl Popper, who distinguished between "utopian engineering" and "piecemeal engineering." Attributing utopian planning to Platonist thinking with all its authoritarian implications, Popper explained it this way:

> The Utopian approach may be described as follows. Any rational action must have a certain aim. It is rational in the same degree as it pursues its aim consciously and consistently, and as it determines its means according to this end. . . . Only when this ultimate aim is determined, in rough outlines at least, only when we are in the possession of something like a blueprint of the society at which we aim, only then can we begin to consider the best ways and means of its realization, and to draw up a plan for practical action.[5]

Popper contrasted utopian engineering with what, in an unfortunate phrase, he calls piecemeal engineering.

> It is an approach which I think to be methodologically sound. [The planner] may or may not have a blueprint of society before his mind, he may or may not hope that mankind will one day realize an ideal state, and achieve happiness and perfection on earth. But he will be aware that perfection, if at all attainable, is far distant, and that every generation of men, and therefore also the living, have a claim; perhaps not so much a claim to be made happy, for there are no institutional means of making a man happy, but a claim not to be made unhappy, where it can be avoided. They have a claim to be given all possible help, if they suffer. The piecemeal engineer will, accordingly, adopt the method of searching for,

and fighting against, the greatest and most urgent evils of society, rather than searching for, and fighting for, its greatest ultimate good. . . . It is the difference between a reasonable method of improving the lot of man, and a method which, if really tried, may easily lead to an intolerable increase in human suffering. It is the difference between a method which can be applied at any moment, and a method whose advocacy may easily become a means of continually postponing action until a later date, when conditions are more favorable.[6]

Popper, of course, spoke mostly of geopolitical issues, of doctrinaire Marxism and Fascism. But the model is just as apt for the discrete elements of political entities, including the structuring of youth corrections. Whereas utopian experiments must be on a large scale and

must involve the whole of society if they are to be carried out under realistic conditions . . . piecemeal social experiments can be carried out under realistic conditions, in the midst of society, in spite of being on a "small scale," that is to say, without revolutionizing the whole of society. In fact, we are making such experiments all the time. The introduction of a new kind of life insurance, of a new kind of taxation, of a new penal reform, are all social experiments which have their repercussions through the whole of society without remodeling society as a whole.[7]

This was precisely what I hoped to accomplish: the amelioration of individual suffering and the bringing about of small changes which would carry wider repercussions without demanding the whole society to change first. It was a minimalist approach, the small, unadorned specific containing larger implications—the "unadorned specific" in this case being a young offender for whom I was, for a time, responsible. I felt closest to the conception of William James, "The trail of the human serpent is thus over everything."

Making Small Actions Count

The work of the American sociologist Neil Smelser had provided the framework for my doctoral thesis a decade earlier. Building on theories of Herbert Blumer and Talcott Parsons, Smelser developed a model within which to consider any social action. It had four components: values, norms, roles, and situational facilities. Smelser described them as follows:

(1) the generalized ends, or *values*, which provide the broadest guides to purposive social behavior; (2) the regulatory rules governing the pursuit of these goals, rules which are to be found in *norms;* (3) the mobilization of individual energy to achieve the defined ends within the normative framework. If we consider the individual person as actor, we ask how he is motivated; if we move to the social-system level, we ask how motivated individuals are organized into *roles* and organizations; (4) the available *situational facilities* which the actor utilizes as means; these include knowledge of the environment, predictability of consequences of action, and tools and skills.[8]

Smelser posed four questions: What values legitimize action? Which norms ensure that action is coordinated and kept relatively free from conflict? How is the action structured into roles? What kinds of situational facilities are available? He arranged these four components into a hierarchy and explained his scheme as follows:

> As we move from top to bottom, we approach components which are progressively less central to the integration of the social order. A change in values will demand changes in norms, roles, and situational facilities. But the same logic does not apply by reading up the hierarchy from bottom to top. . . . Changes in the basic values entail changes in the definition of norms, organization and facilities. Changes in norms entail changes in the definition of organization and facilities, but not values. Changes in organization entail changes in the definition of facilities, but not norms or values. Changes in facilities, finally, do not necessarily impose any changes on the other components.[9]

It was put more simply by Blumer, who described the successful agitator not as the person who comes into town and challenges the system, proposing radical action or change, but as the one who asks the questions that lead others to reflect on the situation and change its definition.

Traditional reforms in corrections are directed to the more specific levels of Smelser's hierarchy—situational facilities and occasionally roles. Such actions are concerned with matters like improving staff skills, building new buildings, and creating new programs which won't threaten institutional routines. Such reforms assiduously avoid anything that might affect values and norms. Even the most brutal institutional systems can absorb reform if it is confined to such things as management procedures. Smooth management is as crucial to inhumane systems as it is to humane systems. Perhaps the best example of this kind of reform was the introduction of the so-called control model into the Texas prison system in the 1960s. An efficiently run system of minute rules, unbending regulations, and obsessive accountability, it was violent to its core. The values which countenanced depersonalization and chronic abuse of inmates were left untouched. Things were simply managed better.[10] This seems to be the goal of contemporary corrections.

Here, for example, is how the ACA viewed standards for the use of isolation in juvenile training schools. First, the rule book—setting the line across which you dare not cross—which contains all chargeable offenses, breaches of institutional rules, ranges of penalties, and disciplinary procedures is posted in conspicuous and accessible areas. Then, for major violations, a youth may be placed in isolation for twenty-four hours. "Confinement for periods over 24 hours is reviewed every 24 hours by the administrator or designee who was not involved in the incident." If this doesn't work, one can escalate to "security room confinement," commonly known as "the hole." The ACA recommends the keeping of a log with name, date, and reasons for confinement. If the breach of the rule can be interpreted as a crime, the ACA recommends reporting it to the local prosecutor for charging and trial.[11] This is not so much wrong as it is irrelevant. It's the rational approach for the large institution, but it has no place in the rehabilitation of already alienated youngsters.

There are simpler ways to regulate the use of isolation. I eventually made it a rule that whoever ordered a youngster into isolation should sit in the isolation cell with him until his release. This seemed appropriate, given the purportive rationale for isolation—to allow the youth to calm down. The rule effectively stopped use of isolation.

Of Symbols and Gestures

Because of their symbolic meanings, certain very small acts can shake a system from top to bottom. I sought less to avoid conflict than to take small actions which made others rethink the values that were at the source of the conflict. Our small actions challenged the values which justified the reform schools and detention centers. The values were ambiguous, even contradictory (Should we punish or rehabilitate? Can we do both?). Even questioning them created hyperambivalence, weakened norms, and blurred roles. It was no recipe for smooth management, but management wasn't my purpose. I wanted to assure that the day-to-day decisions I made would challenge others to question the premises sustaining the reform schools and detention centers. Training staff in new methods of supervision or therapy techniques, reorganizing the department, and reclassifying the youngsters wasn't likely to have much lasting effect without a reordering of the goals and values behind the actions. I therefore began scrutinizing actions for their symbolic power and for their potential for reverberating across the spectrum of action outlined by Smelser.

I looked for issues which touched the reason behind the institutions' existence but which could be contained in an individual youngster. The rationale underlying corrections is the violent, irredeemable offender or intractable delinquent. The whole system rests on those difficult and dangerous youngsters at the deep end. If they weren't there, there would be no need for the system. Violent and dangerous youth became my symbol. If I could do something decent and humane with these most threatening delinquents, then the whole system would be shaken. If we didn't isolate and abuse the intractable we weren't likely to institutionalize a simple burglar. If we didn't institutionalize a burglar, we couldn't very well institutionalize a truant or a runaway.

This decision to focus on the deep end led inexorably to the Institute for Juvenile Guidance and Cottage Nine. They contained the "worst," most difficult, least likely to succeed, and most militantly rejected juveniles in our system. I would change the way we dealt with these "dangerous" inmates first. I would demonstrate that we could listen to, understand, assist, treat, and care for those least deserving delinquents. Doing things differently with these youngsters would demand that we address the values justifying our system. The strategy was to undermine the whole institutional system. Our reforms would be accomplished in precisely the opposite way from most reform in corrections. We would go first to the deep end.

Undoing the Silence Rule

The superintendent of the Shirley Industrial School was an avuncular man who'd been in the department for more than thirty years. He had nurtured close relationships with the community and commanded unusual loyalty from the staff. But beneath the administrative tidiness and high staff morale, the place occasionally slipped into near barbarism in handling recalcitrant youngsters. It didn't take more than a few weeks to see that the administration wouldn't support even my most minimal suggestions for change. Though the superintendent voiced his support, I sat in frustration as my puniest recommendations were undone. I concluded that, so long as he occupied his office, not much was going to happen. I couldn't attack him head on. He was a decent man at least twenty years my elder. It would have been an unseemly display, and I would have lost. But as conditions at the school deteriorated and incidents multiplied, I hit on an option. Browsing through the red book of personnel rules and regulations, I discovered that though I had no power to remove administrators, I could send them on leave for health reasons. I suggested he take some time off at full salary. He had heart problems and in the past had wintered briefly in Florida. He took my offer, and with his departure the staff lost their champion.

The assistant superintendent was another problem. He'd been at Shirley for more than a decade. Though he presented himself as an agreeable person, he was the hammer who enforced rules and regimens quickly and harshly. This sort of role splitting is common in penal institutions. To get a fix on a prison, a jail, or a reform school, it's often more useful to look past the top dog to the second in command—an assistant warden or a deputy for operations. Somewhere on that level one usually finds the enforcer who holds the place together by delivering on the implicit threats, never far below the surface in institutions. It's not unlike the administrative structure of some public high schools.

The assistant superintendent was a charming enough man. His major complaint was that the boys weren't institutionalized long enough for the discipline to have its effect. This is a common lament among institutional administrators, notwithstanding the fact that the longer an inmate stays, the less likely he or she is to make it on the streets. The assistant superintendent wasn't shy about his philosophy of treatment. As he told me in an unguarded moment, "You have to totally break a delinquent boy—break him down." I mentioned this later to Irving Kaufman, the consulting psychiatrist to Cottage Nine at Shirley. He shook his head—"What kind of people are these?" The surprise of this eminent clinician regarding what went on in a building he had visited weekly really disconcerted me. The well-known child psychiatrist and writer Robert Coles had likewise been a consultant to the Lancaster Girls' Industrial School. Coles later wrote of Lancaster, "The place wasn't as bad as some of its critics would allege." These professionals seemed to lose their bearings when they were absorbed into the regimens of total institutions.

Our problems seemed to be no one's fault. There were no convenient scapegoats. The keepers were as much victims as the kept. Staff were so wedded to institutions that I took it for granted that those who eventually supported me probably compromised their own integrity in the process. Most lay back and waited. But I was obsessed with other things. Late one evening, I stopped by Cottage Nine again. It was the same scene I'd witnessed on my first visit—sullen boys, hands folded in front of them, facing each other over scuffed square tables. Nothing else was happening—no talk, no reading, no television, no movement, no programs. A burly master sat up front. A torn magazine something like the *Police Gazette* lay on his desk. The atmosphere was heavy with violence and made eerie by the numbing silence.

I pulled up a scarred chair. "What's your name? Why were you sent to us?"—The words resonated across the silent room. A long pause, then a few words slipped through the clenched teeth of a thin, dark-haired youngster who was smiling ever so slightly. "I'm Joe Kerry. I stole some tires out of this guy's garage." Having broken the ice, I pursued things a bit more. "Why are you in Cottage Nine?" Smirks broke out around the silent table, and there were quick glances to the front of the room, where the master sat looking at us with a fixed stare. I was beginning to feel as much a ward as a commissioner. The fifteen-year-old muttered, "I tried to run away from here." I thought to myself, I'd probably try to run away from here, too. I tried conversing briefly with each of the twenty or so boys over the next couple of hours. Each boy was about as forthcoming as a paranoid personality being publicly interviewed in the auditorium of the CIA—and not surprisingly, given the surroundings.

I took another quick trip upstairs. There were a couple more youngsters in the tombs. I asked the guard to open the doors so I could chat briefly with those inside. One boy was there for having yelled in Cottage Nine, another because he'd tried to escape. They would now spend a set number of days in the tombs, followed by more weeks in Cottage Nine. I later learned that this could go on for months and even, in some cases, for a year or more.

As I drove home, I mulled over what to do next. Why not simply close Cottage Nine down? But it was the threat which kept youngsters in line on the larger campus, and its symbolism resonated throughout the department. Closing it would probably destabilize Shirley. I decided to wait. It was a mistake. I should have followed my first impulse.

In the following weeks, as I made unannounced visits to Bridgewater, Shirley, and Roslindale, other unsettling facts emerged. There was an even darker side to these places. I was told that a local state trooper to whom the task of returning runaways to Shirley had fallen dreaded bringing the boys back. As he walked away from Cottage Nine after dropping off a handcuffed or shackled teenager, he could hear the shouts and moans, part of the intake at the tombs.

As certain staff grew more relaxed at seeing me so often, they were less guarded in their comments about the need to "hit the little bastards for distance." Programs consisted of such things as kneeling in a line in silence, scrubbing the floors with toothbrushes, or being made to stand or sit in odd, peculiarly painful positions. Having spent some time in the service and having counseled a few hundred young men from the Army, the Air Force, and the Marines, I was aware of some of the odder aspects of basic training. But the regimen in Massachusetts reform schools was not basic training. It was a demeaning ritual: an exercise in symbolic castration with no resolution. In their perverse way, these bizarre practices defined the whole system.

Then there was the silence. It's not that I don't respect quiet. I have fond memories of my silent year in the Maryknoll novitiate, which I spent on a farm along the river near Bedford, Massachusetts. Except for Compline, Sext, Matins, and Lauds, we spoke hardly at all. Occasionally, conversations were allowed, but they were relatively rare. That had been a time for thoughtful reflection. Reform school silence was quite something else.

When I asked an administrator why the boys didn't talk, he replied with a straight face, "They don't want to talk." When I sat at a particular table the inmates at the other tables would whisper softly to one another, producing a whirring sound, an odd white noise that prevented our words from being understood by the staff. "Why doesn't anyone talk around here?" I'd say. "Because they'll beat your ass." Other things began to happen, too. If a cottage supervisor saw me talking to a particular youngster, that boy was singled out for grilling after I left. This lengthened my visits considerably, because I had to talk with every boy every time I visited. That way no one could know who said what. One by one we'd go into the small lobby of the building and close the door into the cottage to get some semblance of privacy.

If Cottage Nine was the linchpin of the Shirley Industrial School (and in some ways of all our reform schools), the silence rule was what held Cottage Nine together. If these "worst" delinquents could be allowed to talk, it would resound throughout the institutions. But first, I had to establish that there was a silence rule in Cottage Nine. To anyone unaccustomed to correctional bureaucracies, this might seem simple enough. It wasn't. No staff or administrator would admit that there was enforced silence. "Well, if that's the case, there should be no problem with the boys speaking in Cottage Nine." "No, none whatsoever," was the reply of the superintendent, seconded by the assistant superintendent and the director of education. After a meeting like this, I'd traipse down to Cottage Nine and inform inmates and staff that there was no silence rule. It was all a misunderstanding. They could talk. There'd be a slight hubbub, and I'd leave. When I happened back in a day or two . . . dead silence.

We actually had prolonged meetings in the impressive conference room adjoining the superintendent's office to establish whether a silence rule did or did not exist in Cottage Nine. The administration denied its existence. I replied that the youths in the cottage said that there was indeed a rigid rule and that if they broke it, they were beaten or put into the tombs. "Nonsense," was the reply. "Well then, it might be helpful to post a memo in the cottage, noting this fact." "But that's not necessary. There isn't any silence rule." Round and round we went.

A few weeks later, after a particularly grueling exchange, the director of education got carried away. Even the inmates acknowledged how helpful Cottage Nine was. He plopped a questionnaire down on the conference table—a poll of the Cottage Nine boys—as proof. It was an "I like Cottage Nine because" study. I picked up the two-page questionnaire and absentmindedly scanned it while the discussion continued. There it finally was, on page two: "I think the silence rule is "helpful," "mildly helpful," or "not helpful." At last, acknowledgment that there was a silence rule. Reform then became a possibility.

Cottage Nine had characterized Shirley for a long time in other ways. I'd heard from the inmates about sadistic discipline: having to drink from toilets or kneel for hours on the stone floor with a pencil under one's knees. One morning my secretary dropped a dog-eared letter-size manila file on my desk. A note on the file read, "You might find this interesting." The file contained case summaries for boys in Cottage Nine. These were internal investigations which were kept "inside."

"Donald, 16, beaten on the soles of his bare feet with straps." "Walter, 16, handcuffed for 22 days and nights when returned from escape. He was forced to sleep and eat with the handcuffs on." "Charles, 17, padlocked to water pipe, given a cold shower for six minutes." There were descriptions of the *bastado*. A boy's feet were strapped to a bed frame and beaten on the bare soles with wooden paddles or the wooden backs of floor brushes. I also learned why the escape rate at Shirley had at one time been so low—one year there'd been only one or two runs from the institution. After being returned to Cottage Nine, the escapee's ring finger was bent back across the top of his left hand until the finger broke.

Staff Sabotage

Suspending or firing a staff person who didn't show up for work regularly, or who abused juveniles, seemed to be impossible. The parole agents, who would be integral to our community-based system, had other jobs as insurance salesmen, real estate agents, or liquor salesmen. Though they claimed to devote full time to their parole activities, this was questionable. I tried to make an issue over one particular parole agent who was listed as a job development specialist. When I asked him what he did, he said he found jobs for boys returning home from the reform schools. That seemed important enough. Our youngsters needed jobs. But his role was less complicated than that. He'd buy the Sunday paper and, after church, would clip the help wanted ads, put them in envelopes, and send them to the administrators of the reform schools. The whole thing couldn't have taken more than an hour a week. He collected a full salary.

Even more blatant personnel problems seemed beyond remedy. One cottage supervisor staggered drunk into a locked reform school dorm in the middle of the night, dragged a youngster out, and broke his jaw. After months of hearings, we lost the case. We couldn't fire him, and we had problems simply keeping him away from the inmates. The issue was resolved after we vacated the institution. He was assigned to a privately contracted community-based program. He eventually punched another kid in the face in full view of passers-by on a busy street. With that corroboration, he was forced to resign.

Though most staff belonged to the state employees' union, they weren't part of the militant American Federation of State, County, and Municipal Employees. Ties to the union weren't as strong as they might have been because of the extent of political patronage. Since most staff got their jobs through political connections, union membership wasn't seen as crucial. The union representative, Joe Correia, was an unusually moral and decent man. He'd been a union organizer for many years, and though protective of his members, he recognized the need for drastic changes in the ways they dealt with delinquents in the department.

Because reform schools are total institutions (to use Erving Goffman's term),[12] the staff held considerable power to undermine change. An important characteristic of total institutions is their capacity to shape information. Staff have unusual ability to control or to put a spin on information. Power relationships between keeper and captives distort the process beyond all reason. Minor changes in house rules or scheduling take on Olympian import.

I didn't have to do much to put an institution in turmoil. A simple chat with an inmate often sufficed. Admittedly, I wasn't the most adept of administrators. Many of our problems were the result of my poor management, of not informing the staff or bringing them along. But given the staff perceptions of the precariousness of my own position, it was unlikely that I would have brought many along anyway. When I shared my plans, the staff took it as an opportunity to head me off or make my actions politically untenable. Some couldn't resist the allure of sabotage. Plans which in most bureaucracies might have been seen, at least fleetingly, as positive or helpful were seen as threatening in our institutions. The upset was exacerbated when I retreated to doing what I could with one kid at a time.

Administrators felt undermined, and their frustration was felt through all the institutions. As incidents multiplied, I pulled back and devoted myself to administrative tasks in the central office—attempting to get new programs into the institutions, bringing in consultants, and planning staff training seminars. But events kept dragging me into more potentially upsetting situations. One day, as I was walking down the hallway outside an administrator's office at one of the schools, I heard a shout and a loud, repeated thump. A fifteen-year-old emerged flushed and red-eyed. An administrator had been banging the youngster's head against the wall. That incident provoked one of the rare written memos of my tenure. In it I stated that use of physical force with inmates would be restricted to restraining a youngster who was momentarily out of control and defending oneself against assault.

The memo wasn't particularly revolutionary. Three years earlier my predecessor had laid out a similar policy. But the context had changed. I followed this memo with another—inmates could wear their hair whatever length they wished. The institutions nearly went into disarray over that. Senior staff responded by publicly inviting staff and inmates to act out. At a staff meeting, one administrator commented that I was, in effect, telling staff they no longer controlled the institutions. "This means that if a kid spits in your face, you can't do anything about it." These less-than-subtle translations provoked more incidents, designed to prove that the new, "permissive" policies had given control of the institutions to the inmates.

Why should staff members show the need for an institution by causing incidents in it? It wasn't as paradoxical as it seemed. Incidents in institutions seldom call attention to the concept of the institution. They simply prove the need for better management. Staff-stimulated incidents are not meant to demonstrate the uncommon incorrigibility, violence, or character of the staff but of the inmates—inmates clearly in need of stricter regimens. The institution remains serenely unaccountable for its products. And what better incident than the escape? Escape has it all—threat, conflict, fear, hysteria, danger, suspense, and final resolution. It is the drama par excellence for proving that the institutions are needed.

Escapes

By late 1970, Shirley School was beset with more runaways than ever in its history. As I walked through the lobby of the administration building, I happened to glance to my left. There, pinned to the bulletin board outside the superintendent's office, was a crude map a young inmate had drawn for use in his escape. It had been confiscated and displayed for all to see. An administrator had penned large letters across the top: ESCAPE MAP. FREE COPIES GIVEN HERE. I took it down and tucked it in my coat pocket. When I later confronted the assistant superintendent with it, he said it was a joke and no more. I believe he thought it was, and I accepted his explanation that the map was too rough to be of much use anyway. (I later came to know well the youngster who had drawn it, Mike Radon. He eventually became director of a group home for youthful offenders. As far as he was concerned, his map was taken very seriously indeed. For possessing it he was thrown into the tombs).

The message was clear. The Shirley administration was encouraging runs from the institution for its own purposes. Later the flag on the administration building was flown upside down as a signal of distress over central office meddling. This was followed by open invitations to run. Keys were handed out to inmates by disgruntled staff. A Boston priest whose ministry was with runaway kids called me one afternoon to tell me the youngsters he was seeing were escapees from one or another of our state reform schools. They told him they'd been given an easy run by staff.

Escapes are an obsession in juvenile corrections. The concern seems reasonable enough. Reform schools and detention centers are supposed to keep violent and dangerous juveniles off the street and out of our neighborhoods. Law and public safety demand that we aggressively pursue and catch the fleeing inmate. Virtually all adolescent escapees are picked up at home or in their neighborhoods within a few days. A surprising number come back voluntarily at the urging of a mother, a sister, or a girlfriend. They usually run impulsively for what seems at the moment a valid reason—a slight, a worry about home. The run has less to do with any plan to get back into crime than with an impulse to hit the road. The sad reality is that most of these youngsters have no place to go. They run home and test the waters. Things haven't improved. The more seriously delinquent youngsters seemed often to be relieved at being returned to the institution. It confirmed their view of the world as essentially impersonal, rejecting, and ultimately violent. There is odd comfort in returning to a place where the abuse is regulated and predictable. But woe to him who upsets this hurtful regularity. To do so threatens a fragile identity—even one built on the worst impulses a society can give.

I remember Doug, a stocky sixteen-year-old addicted to heroin. Late one evening, returning from a meeting near Shirley, I decided to take a quick side trip by Cottage Nine. I asked the master on duty whether anyone was in the tombs. No. I guess he thought I wouldn't go upstairs and look. There, in the far corner of one of the dim cells, was Doug, lying stripped on the bare floor. I stood in the doorway, trying to talk through the mesh security screen which separated us. "How long have you been here?" The muffled reply: "A few days." "Why are you here?" His voice grew more agitated: "I tried to make it over the fence out back." I told him I wanted him to come out and go back downstairs. "We aren't using the tombs anymore." Doug let go a torrent of obscenities—"You naive asshole! You dumb motherfucker! Don't you know kids like me need to be in here?" Doug had become the well-socialized product of our reform school—a Cottage Nine "success" who believed what it taught. The way to handle unacceptable impulses is to be grabbed, beaten, handcuffed, dragged screaming up cement stairs, stripped, and thrown into a tomb.

Few juveniles in reform schools, if they get loose, immediately threaten public safety. Those who do weren't particularly violent or dangerous youths before their institutionalization. Few reform school inmates are committed for crimes of random violence, and nearly all will be returned to the community while they are still adolescents. Why then would they represent such danger in the few hours they're on the run? Usually, it's precisely because they are on the run. The ante has been upped, the stakes are higher. Though most want to go directly home with the least possible hassle, getting there is a problem. At this point the danger associated with escape resides less in the youngster than in the hysteria attending the incident.

A black youngster from Boston, with us for burglary, finds himself far from home in an almost all-white, rural part of the state. He is highly visible as he tries to make his way to Boston. He can't hitchhike. He can't walk openly during the day. His options are few—to run at night, to break into buildings, to hide until dark, to steal a car. If he is aggressively pursued, his situation is made more desperate and potentially dangerous. The need immediately to catch a runaway who would be released anyway in a few weeks or months heightens the likelihood of violence, a likelihood further enhanced by blaring sirens and the use of other inmates to chase escapees. It was an unwritten rule at Shirley that the chasers would beat the runner when caught. In return they were given favors which ranged from extra cigarettes to early consideration for parole.

Institutional tranquility demanded that we hound and catch escapees, but it seemed to me a dangerous policy, and I passed the word that I didn't want escapees aggressively pursued unless they were with us for crimes of violence. I wanted runaways to have the benefit of taking their time in getting home. We could pick them up later. We needed to de-escalate the whole sorry mess. In a sense, I was caught in a trap of my own making, for I hadn't yet been able to make the institutions caring enough to reduce youngsters' need to escape. But it would have been political suicide to allow escapes to increase, so I tried to straddle the dilemma—with mixed results. Although tightening security slowed our rehabilitative efforts, I wouldn't have been given the time needed if the escape rate had not gone down.

Once escapes became a political issue, it was self-defeating to tell some institutional administrators that a particular youngster needed close custody. If they knew, the kid was out a back door in record time. I had to keep a youngster's dangerousness to myself if I didn't want him disappearing into the streets, as the case of Eddie Mullaney illustrates.

Eddie was well known to the department. He lived in the Charlestown projects and had a long history with us. He'd been arrested a dozen or so times in the past for burglaries and robberies, had been committed to the department, and had duly spent time at Lyman and Shirley. Not unexpectedly, his delinquencies got more serious and more violent each time he was out.

Late on a Friday afternoon, I got a call from a Charlestown judge. He knew our problems with escapes from Roslindale and wanted to make sure that Eddy would remain locked up pending his hearing. Eddy had been arrested earlier that day on a charge of aggravated assault and attempted murder. He had rolled a sailor returning to the Boston Navy Yard after a night on the town, but in doing so had attacked his victim with more rage than simple robbery demanded, fracturing the young seaman's skull and leaving him for dead.

The judge set Eddy's bond at $30,000, a high bond unusual in juvenile cases. Clearly the judge intended to waive Eddy into adult court. I thanked the judge for his call and assured him we would take extraordinary measures to keep Eddy in Roslindale for Monday's court appearance. I called the superintendent and told him how important it was to hang on to Eddy. He was out by 5:00 that afternoon. I got a call stating that somehow he'd managed to run through an open door along with some visitors. The judge had gone home for the weekend before I called with the bad news. I took it for granted that Eddy had been let loose.

Saturday morning I went back into the office and pulled Eddy's address. I drove over the bridge to Charlestown and wandered up and down the project streets and alleys looking for the tenement apartment where Eddy lived. My knock got no reply. I strolled around outside, asking anybody I met whether he or she knew Eddy. A few youngsters did; Eddy was something of a local celebrity. I spread the word that I needed to talk with him, that he was on the verge of getting in more serious trouble and I wanted to help. I handed out a few personal cards, scribbling my home phone number on the back. "If any of you happens to see Eddy, give him a card and tell him to call me. It doesn't matter what time." Then I drove home.

Around 11:00 Sunday morning, the phone rang. It was Eddy.

"Why do you want to talk with me?"

I asked him how he was and why he'd run from Roslindale. I told him he'd put himself and a lot of others in jeopardy. Then I gave what seemed to me my strongest argument.

"I've been trying my best to change things around here, but when you ran from Roslindale, you screwed it up. I realize you're in a heap of trouble, and I can't say I wouldn't have run if given the chance but you've got to come back. It'd make matters a lot simpler for all of us."

There was a long pause. "What will happen if I come back?"

I promised Eddy that he'd be safe and that I'd come pick him up and take him back to the detention center.

He said, "I'll call you later," and hung up.

Eddy called again at about 4:00 P.M. He asked if I would come over. I was in front of his apartment forty minutes later. It was dusk, and as the door opened I couldn't see much in the room. The blinds were pulled, and a faint light reflected from a back bedroom. The musty smell took me back fifteen years to the South Side of Chicago, when it was still safe for a white welfare worker to trudge through the tenements visiting families on his caseload. Eddy asked me to wait. I heard a slight mumbling in the bedroom, then he came out and said he was ready. We drove off to Roslindale.

Eddy didn't say much during the ride. He certainly wasn't happy to be going back. I tried to encourage his resolve and told him how much I respected him for doing this. We talked about the accusations regarding the mugging and about his family. Then I found out why no one had answered the door to his apartment the first time I went by. His father was in the semilit bedroom, paralyzed from the neck down. His mother had died the year before. We drove up to the back entrance of Roslindale. I told the master on duty that Eddy had come back on his own and that I would be checking in later to see how he was doing. Eddie was escorted inside. I left feeling relieved. I'd been able to piece a potential disaster back together for myself, although I couldn't say the same for Eddy. I didn't have enough hold on my own department to ensure that this troubled, occasionally dangerous teenager would be dealt with sensitively.

Getting youngsters to hit the highways wasn't the only way staff showed their displeasure. There were other equally unsettling incidents—fires set by unsupervised youth, a few near riots. Often staff phoned the local press before the event. Once, at about 1 A.M., a local fire chief called me from the grounds of Shirley. A fire had been set in a cottage, but he wouldn't allow his men to go in and put it out until I came out to see "what your permissive policies have done." I asked him to put out the fire, promising I'd be there within an hour. By the time I arrived, the fire had been extinguished (it was a couple of mattresses), but the place was a shambles, with water everywhere. It reminded me of a story my father, a musician, used to tell—that a trained fireman, when entering a burning building with his fire ax, looks first to demolish the grand piano. Clearly there'd been a bit of overkill in the effort to demonstrate the terrible effects of permissiveness. But there was another more intriguing political angle to that night's firefighting which I learned about a few weeks later in the governor's office.

Occasionally I felt as if I'd been drafted for a role in an Ionesco playlet. Take the day I was sitting in my Boston office and got a call from an administrator at Shirley (fifty miles away) telling me a riot was about to begin in Cottage Nine. I asked him how he knew. He said a staff member had phoned him from the cottage (which was only fifty yards from his office). I suggested he walk down and check it out. He didn't think that was appropriate. He simply wanted me to know what was happening and, not too obliquely, what my policies were causing. I called around the grounds looking for a line staff member I trusted. I finally found one and asked him to go over to Cottage Nine and let me know what was happening. The "riot" had to do with the boys talking in normal voices. This noise, in a previously silent discipline cottage, was interpreted as a harbinger of riot. Inmates, attuned to the staff's uneasiness, tossed around words like "motherfucker," "riot," and "escape" for their shock value, saying them just loud enough to be caught.

But our problems at Shirley inevitably came to the attention of the governor. The state senate minority whip was from the Shirley area, and the governor couldn't duck his political responsibilities in connection with the turmoil. Chris Armstrong called and said the governor wanted me to attend a meeting in his office later that week with legislators, town selectmen, and other local representatives. That meeting came at a particularly bad time. The Shirley staff had circulated a petition through almost every bar and hamlet in the local area and obtained about a thousand signatures calling for the governor to oust me. A few weeks before, DYS staff had rallied on the steps of the statehouse carrying banners and signs with a number of messages—"Miller Lets Delinquents Run Free," "Training Schools in Chaos." I was particularly fascinated with the sign carried by a psychologist from Roslindale: "Miller Condones Free Sex." This was an allusion to my attempts to create coed programs.

On the morning of the meeting the governor called me over beforehand. "Jerry, these people are very upset with things out at Shirley. I hope you can get matters under control." I assured him that we were past the worst, that our run rate seemed to be falling, and that we were proceeding with our plans to lower the population. I'd kept Mrs. Sargent well informed of the bizarre incidents of staff sabotage, the encouragement of escapes, and the turmoil induced in our department. I trusted he knew of it through her. Over the preceding two years, I'd come to know the governor as a decent man who, when personal convictions clashed with political self-interest, usually took the high road. I hadn't felt under great pressure from him. The thought that he might sack me wasn't what was uppermost in my mind, so I was more outspoken than either the facts or my situation justified. I told him the petition had been circulated by Shirley staff and mentioned the phone call from the fire chief, who had later informed me that he wouldn't put out any more fires at the school. Although the governor said he understood my predicament, he was clearly perturbed. I was so obsessed with my battles that I had little real sense of the problems I was causing him. I later learned that his closest advisers were pressuring him to get rid of me. I was slow to get the message, but later, in the midst of a particularly vicious legislative investigation of me, it came through loud and clear. Earlier I confided to Chris Armstrong that I was considering the possibility of resigning, and to my surprise, he gave no response. Only after many years in government did I come to appreciate how much political courage the governor had shown in not firing me.

The governor outlined his plan for the meeting with the angry contingent. He would listen to their complaints (of which he had already been informed by the minority whip) and would then ask me for my side of the story. Following this, he would criticize me for not having a better hold on the department and reassure the group that he intended to solve the problems at Shirley. He wanted me to understand that despite the negative things he might have to say, he supported the direction I was trying to take with the department. Then he added, almost offhandedly, "Besides, all they want is a fire truck." The comment threw me. "A what?" "A fire truck. That's what they want. You'll probably have to put one in your next budget." Before I could ask what he was talking about, the delegation of citizens was being ushered into the office.

The meeting proceeded precisely as the governor had said it would. The complaints were presented in strong but civil terms. I outlined our plans for lowering the school's population. Things got slightly out of hand when a town selectman demanded I put the inmates back in state clothes and crop their hair. I responded sarcastically by suggesting that we might brand them on their foreheads. The governor interjected, "I'm sure the commissioner didn't mean that," and the meeting continued as planned. The governor gave me a mild dressing-down and ended by saying that he was sure I'd do a better job in the future. He gave his assurance that if I didn't, he'd deal with that as well. I waited behind as he escorted the now subdued delegation to the door. He returned saying that he thought the meeting had gone well and that he wanted me to put a fire truck in the next budget for the Shirley school. I did, and a few months later the town had a new fire truck. Apparently there had been an even earlier meeting with others at which this salient matter had been settled. We heard nary a peep from the local leaders after that.

Despite the successful meeting, things would get much worse. It was a lonely time, mostly of my own making. Though many staff were supportive, I was never quite able to trust any of them. I'd been burnt too often. Staff dubbed me "the phantom," a visage appearing at this or that cottage at some ungodly hour and then disappearing. The term wasn't one of endearment. I came to rely more on information from inmates than from staff. Though it sounds extremely unlikely, these supposedly most dangerous and deceitful delinquents generally gave more honest assessments of their situation and of the conditions in our institutions than did their keepers.

I needed to have some staff I could trust. I couldn't go it alone. I couldn't be everywhere at once, though I sometimes fancied I could. I couldn't go out and hire properly qualified people because there were no positions available—even if some itinerant psychologist or social worker had been interested in coming aboard what looked to many like a sinking ship. My own position hadn't been funded for almost a year, and neither had those of the assistant commissioners who were to be the first of my own appointees.

My desires to consolidate personnel, have a trustworthy staff, and be able myself to be as nearly ubiquitous as possible spawned one of the wackier ideas of my tenure—a proposal to purchase the former Cardinal O'Connell Seminary in Boston and turn it into one huge youth corrections institution holding almost all the children and teenagers in the department. My plan was to close most of the institutions and transfer the youngsters to this facility in Boston, where we would also move our central office. That way I could simply stroll out of my office and down a hallway to get a sense of what was happening. No more trips halfway across the state. I could run the whole thing myself. I got the support of the governor, the Harvard Center for Criminal Justice, and the *Boston Globe* for the plan to purchase the seminary, but was unable to get it through a legislative committee chaired by a perceptive state senator, Beryl Cohen, who vetoed the idea. If we had managed to get the appropriation, it would ultimately have stifled our reforms.

Meanwhile, I ran around putting out the brushfires that were too often the consequence of some action I'd taken to try to keep my wits about me. Frank Maloney attempted to keep a lid on things in the central office by taking on the thankless task of meeting with perpetually frantic superintendents and hostile line staff. He was outstandingly loyal during a period that must have been one of great personal frustration to him and in which I wasn't in control of the bureaucracy I headed—and which he had hoped to head. I finally realized I would have to rely on the staff I'd inherited. Most were going to be around much longer than I. Though only a few of them had ever seen a civil service exam, all were now covered by civil service protections. Our turnover rate was low, and I wouldn't be hiring many new people.

We began staff retraining programs. Though people seemed to accept some of the new concepts, the majority didn't share my views on the department or the youngsters in it. Most neither supported nor worked against the new policies. They just waited for things to collapse. An active minority with strong ties to local legislators and the governor's executive council worked hard to get me out.

At this time I was dividing my efforts between Bridgewater, Shirley, and the two Boston detention centers. Using a tactic similar to the one I had used at Shirley, I sent the superintendent of the girls' detention center on vacation with pay and replaced her with an unlikely team— Dan Bucci, a recent graduate with a master's degree in counseling from Tufts University, and seventeen-year-old Toby Yarmolinsky, the son of the Harvard Law School professor and former deputy undersecretary of defense in the Kennedy Administration, Adam Yarmolinsky. Toby had just graduated from high school. Dan had never worked in an institution before. Toby had never seen one. Dan was among the few degree-qualified persons who came by the office looking for a job. I hired him on the spot and sent him out to the Huntington Avenue center along with Toby to come up with some ideas as to what we might do to change the oppressive atmosphere. They came back with a whole series of plans and proposals. For the next ten months they worked fifteen-hour days to humanize the girl's facility. They brought in volunteers, tutors, new medical staff, visitors; they stopped medical isolation and began coed dances, busing in boys from the IJG. They got Polaroid to donate twenty-eight cameras for the girls to use in a photography class. (The cameras arrived one morning, and by evening, the staff had stolen all but two.)

Staff training seemed to be getting results. We opened therapeutic cottages on the grounds of Shirley and Lyman and began closing out admissions at John Augustus Hall. We opened a day-care center at Lancaster and set up a summer forestry camp annex out of the budget of the Shirley school—something which later greatly upset a legislative postaudit committee. Escapes from Shirley and Lyman decreased as more programs were introduced.

9 *Reverberations*

I probably survived my first two years because Governor Frank Sargent wasn't a rigorous administrator. If he had known what was going on in the department he would have demanded my resignation. Years later, writing in the *Boston Globe*, the governor likened his situation to hunkering down in a foxhole while I, on the one side, and the legislature and DYS staff, on the other, lobbed shells at one another. The description outlined precisely the role of a reform administrator. If the governor had been openly and loudly supportive, it would have politicized matters even more. I accepted my potential expendability as a political casualty, but I hoped the governor wouldn't fire me before I could accomplish something. I couldn't ask him to take the initiative. That was my job. Humane corrections is always a loser politically.

I had no choice but to forge ahead, but the more I pursued my concerns, the more things unraveled. Every abuse revealed another. Most people think an inmate who is being abused pines to tell others about it. Not so. Juvenile inmates hide their abuse and protect their abusers. It's not unlike what we've come to know about family secrets of sexual abuse and incest. Even those juveniles whom clinicians (too easily) label sociopathic or antisocial, from whom we might expect manipulation, habitually ignore their own victimization. They don't run to outsiders to spout tales of mistreatment. Some mention other inmates—

"He doesn't belong here." "They're beating on him." "They take advantage of him."—but that's about as far as it goes.

In recent years, I've prepared background studies on a number of young persons being tried on capital charges for particularly heinous murders. Even where the death penalty threatens, it's a rare offender who mentions his or her own physical or sexual abuse. They hide the memories from themselves as well as from others, and the history of their being abused has to be dug out with the tenacity of a private investigator. When such traumas are finally uncovered, the accused often asks for them to be kept secret for fear of embarrassing or hurting family members or friends. The idea of the delinquent wallowing in tales of his or her own abuse as an excuse for crime is another of the myths which nurture our misunderstanding of people who offend.

By the summer of 1970 we'd made progress. The beginnings of half-way houses on the grounds of some institutions, the introduction of group therapy models, the relaxation of the rigid silence rules, doing away with marching, state clothes, and so forth, all contributed to a calmer, less violent atmosphere on the institutional grounds. The new mood brought unanticipated side effects.

One morning, a young counselor we'd recently hired was conducting a fairly intense group therapy session. In the emotion of the moment, fifteen-year-old Craig blurted out that his parole agent had forced sex on him. When the group leader pursued the boy's comment, he quickly backed away—"I was just pissed. I made it up." A week or so later, as an aside in another conversation, the counselor casually mentioned the boy's accusation to me. "I don't think there's anything to this, but. . . ."

Craig lived in western Massachusetts and was well known to the department. He'd been in the Westfield Detention Center numerous times on burglary charges and had been committed to the Lyman School in his early teens, graduating to Shirley Industrial School when he reached fifteen. I telephoned the superintendent at Westfield. He was a psychologist and knew both the parole agent and Craig. He advised me not to trust much of anything Craig said, terming him a pathological liar, and I decided to drop the matter.

A month or so later, Bobby Bolster happened by the office. A former boxer who had grown up in the South Boston projects, Bobby made his way through college and graduate school and ended up as a vocational counselor with the YSB. He was a friend of Billy Bulger, the powerful senator from South Boston. I took for granted that Bobby's job came through the senator's office. Unlike many of those who came to the YSB via politics, however, Bobby was a highly motivated "kid-worker" and an advocate for the youngsters with whom he dealt. (Bobby occasionally went beyond the call of duty. Late one night I happened into the central office and noticed a light in the photocopying room. Bobby was creatively altering the school transcripts of a delinquent youngster to ensure his acceptance in a local vocational program.) I told Bobby about Craig's allegations, and he offered to see what he could find out. A couple of weeks later, Bobby came back. Craig had told him that what he had blurted out in the group had indeed happened. He said that other boys on the parole agent's caseload were also involved.

I telephoned the parole agent and asked him to come to my office. He apparently thought it had something to do with concessions I might be willing to make about job demands. In previous meetings with the parole agents, this man had been among the more outspoken against proposed changes. I wanted parole agents to become advocates and "brokers" for the youngsters on their caseloads, assisting them to find jobs, therapy, and services, instead of acting like cops. My view of their role was closer to that envisioned by the nineteenth-century shoemaker John Augustus, who created probation and parole in the United States. Many of the parole agents agreed, but the idea was particularly galling to a loud clique who yearly filed legislation which would allow them to carry revolvers as they went on their appointed rounds. Each year I opposed their legislation, and each year it was killed. I'm sure it's still being submitted and probably, some sad day, will pass. Fear and force have great staying power. My opposition had been very public, and there had been some heated meetings with the parole agents. I didn't want my concerns about Craig to be taken as part of a personal vendetta against an outspoken critic.

We chatted for a few minutes before I brought up the allegations. I said I didn't necessarily believe the boy, but because his allegations were serious, they would have to be investigated. If the allegations weren't true, the agent had nothing to fear. If there was proof that the agent had been sexually involved with boys on his caseload, criminal actions would follow. If, however, he chose to resign, I wouldn't pursue the matter, and he could seek help for his problem. I didn't want him working with youngsters who were subject to his authority, though I didn't come out and say so. He smiled and came back at me without losing a beat. "Why would you take the rantings of an antisocial delinquent seriously?" Nothing had occurred, and he had no reason to resign. It was part of my vendetta. After he left, I called Bob Quinn, the attorney general, and asked him to send over an investigator. A crusty detective stopped by a few days later, took some notes, and said he'd be in touch in a couple of weeks.

Three months later, the investigator came back with a thick file. The boy's allegations appeared to be true and went far beyond simple sexual abuse of this one boy. For over a decade, the parole agent had coerced sexual favors from a large number of parolees in return for easy supervision. But, and this was even more troubling, he had regularly returned individual teenagers to the reform schools as parole violators when they rejected his propositions. They had sat in brutal reform schools, some for two years or more—and not one had mentioned why he was there.

The parole agent ended up in Walpole State Prison. Predictably, when he was released a few years later, he demanded his old job back. (He'd saved up enough administrative and sick leave to cover most of his time in prison.) Joe Leavey, who succeeded me as commissioner, avoided having to rehire him only through some fancy administrative footwork.

What this incident shows is that, in investigating institutional abuse, truth is often better served by listening carefully to those inmates normally seen as being the least reliable. In the nearly two decades since Massachusetts, I have investigated abuse in reform schools in a number of states, and that premise has been confirmed. The best informants fall into three unlikely classes: (1) "emotionally disturbed" inmates; (2) developmentally disabled or mentally retarded inmates; and (3) the occasional middle-class inmate.

These three groups have one thing in common. They don't know, don't understand, or don't care about the codes which govern institutional life. Emotionally disturbed or retarded teenagers often misperceive or misjudge their situation and don't weigh the consequences well, whereas the middle-class teenager doesn't see himself as "appropriate" to the institution. He is an alien there and doesn't expect to return. Most inmates, however, know the realities of their situation only too well and are likely to return. They therefore do their best not to make matters worse for themselves by unnecessarily stirring things up. Investigators come and go. The abiding reality behind the bravado and the macho posturing of most reform school inmates is that they believe they deserve whatever abuse they may get—a belief which is fixed long before they enter the juvenile justice system.

As word got out about the changes in the reform schools, we began getting calls at the central office from adolescents in our care. That seemed natural enough. After all, we were supposed to be acting in loco parentis. But it was anathema to the institutional administrators, and much of the old guard in the central office, who saw it as blatant manipulation. Youngsters would call from pay phones on the institutional grounds or make collect calls from this or that office whenever they managed to get their hands on a phone without the knowledge or consent of staff. Usually they wanted me to know about their situation, what was happening to them at the reform school, problems with families or girlfriends. I'd put the word out quietly that no youngster on the run would be grabbed if he or she would call us or even come into the central office to discuss the situation. Everything was negotiable. Since we had the authority to set time, the conditions of confinement, and release dates, it was also all quite legal, albeit unusual. Before long we started hearing from former reform school inmates across the state and the nation.

Bill

Things had not gone smoothly for Bill. He called from Canada. He'd escaped from the Worcester detention center the year before and made his way north. He'd been involved in some burglaries and was awaiting placement in a program. He'd heard things were changing in the department and wondered if he could return without being sent to Lyman or Shirley. I told him to come back and we would discuss it. He showed up in the office a few days later, having hitched his way.

He was a slight fifteen-year-old more fit for the child welfare system than for youth corrections. He'd managed to survive on the streets in Toronto by catching part-time jobs and living with other street kids. As best we could determine, he hadn't been in any trouble with the law for the past year. I got his records of commitment to us. They confirmed our impressions—a nonexistent family, a throwaway kid, occasional drug use, minor delinquency. We were looking for an office boy, photocopier, and messenger the week Bill arrived, so we hired him in the central office. We gave him an advance so he could rent his own room in a Cambridge rooming house, and he set to work. He turned out to be a dependable employee, getting to work on time and fulfilling his duties assiduously. He liked to wear an antique stovepipe hat he'd been given in Canada. It looked a bit unusual in the state offices, but it added a note of whimsy. Bill was with us for about six months before problems developed.

Late one morning, Harry, a parolee and psychotic teenager we'd never been able to get the mental health department to keep, came into the office out of breath shouting, "A bunch of cops are headed up here to arrest you." I was used to Harry's exaggerations. He'd stop by once or twice a week to talk with and occasionally harass staff. We'd repeatedly referred him to psychiatric clinics, to no avail. He wouldn't keep appointments, and they wouldn't stretch professional protocol enough to reach out to him. His diagnosis was probably paranoid schizophrenic, and he was somewhat predisposed to pick up on rumors and possible threats. He said that he'd passed a group of police who were discussing a plan to come to my office, arrest Bill, and charge me with "harboring." I didn't know whether to believe Harry or not, but I called Bill into my office. While Harry talked on agitatedly about what he'd just heard, a secretary called from the front office to say that a group of four policemen was coming down the corridor. I told Harry to leave, and put Bill in my office while I went out to greet them.

There stood the head of the capitol police (those assigned to the statehouse), along with the Worcester chief of police and an assistant. The chief said he had information that Bill had been seen in my office. They were there to arrest him as a fugitive. The chief didn't say anything about charging me, but I expected that something to that effect would follow. It seemed curious that the police chief of a major Massachusetts city would travel fifty miles to my office to arrest a fifteen-year-old minor offender. But the potential headline was a corker: "Youth Service Chief Harbors Fugitive."

The capitol chief seemed embarrassed as he presented me with the warrant for Bill's arrest. I said I would have to inquire if Bill was around. I asked the police to wait, I returned to my office, and closed the door. I told Bill to crawl into the well under my desk for the time being. After a frantic twenty minutes or so, I was able to reach the juvenile judge in Worcester, an appointee of Governor Sargent's who had originally sentenced Bill and later issued the warrant when he ran.

I told the judge that I was unaware that there was still an outstanding warrant, that Bill had returned to our jurisdiction six months ago, and that he had been under our supervision working in the central office. The judge said that, since Bill was back in our custody, he saw no need to execute the warrant. I asked if he would speak to the police chief. I brought him into the office and put him on the phone, with Bill still under the desk. The chief scowled as he listened to the judge. When he finished, I thanked him for his vigilance, and the police left.

Todd

Sixteen-year-old Todd called collect one day from New York City to say that he'd escaped from the Lyman School a year before. He wondered if he could come back and, if he did, whether he'd be put in the discipline cottage. He'd talked with a girlfriend in Boston before calling, and she'd told him things were changing at the reform schools. Todd was from one of the blue-collar suburbs that lie just outside the Route 128 beltway, which circles greater Boston. He'd run from Lyman after a stint in the discipline cottage. Late one night he slipped away from a dorm and ran out onto Route 9, the highway that passed the school. He hitched a ride with a trucker and was into the Berkshires before he was missed. A few hours later he was out of Massachusetts. Most escapees went home, but the few who didn't usually headed for New York City, Florida, California, or Canada, depending upon the time of year. Todd landed in New York City.

Despite his history of burglaries, marijuana use, and general incorrigibility, Todd wasn't a sophisticated delinquent. He was like most kids in reform schools—bumbling, hostile, not terribly shrewd, and with a more than adequate share of impulsiveness. An hour or two on the Manhattan streets and he was already in a new bind. Though he'd heard of hustling (prostitution) in the reform school, he hadn't thought of doing it himself until a middle-aged man approached him near Times Square and offered twenty-five bucks for a blow job. Within a few days he was deeply into a scene he couldn't escape as easily as the Lyman School.

Todd was introduced to hard drugs by other young hustlers in Times Square and was always high after a couple of weeks. The hustling got more compulsive and more dangerous, culminating in his being tied up as part of a sexual game. He was handcuffed to a bed, shot up with heroin, and kept there against his will while a pimp brought in men who enjoyed sex with a shackled boy. Todd existed like this for a number of weeks. His diet consisted of Big Macs and Cokes brought in by the pimp, and he was released from the bed only for supervised trips to the toilet. Finally, a client felt sorry for Todd and called the police anonymously. Todd's pimp freed him as the police entered the building. They both ran out. Todd was too embarrassed to report what had happened. It was a day or two after this that he called. I told him to come back, and he showed up in my office a couple of days later.

I didn't send Todd back to Lyman, and therein lay a serious problem. It didn't seem right to return this damaged youngster to the institution to sit for a month in the discipline cottage, after which he would have to work himself out of the institution by jumping through all the hoops demanded of escapees. Instead, he needed individual programs, a therapist, a job, some sense of self-esteem, and a semi-independent living situation. Lyman School wouldn't meet any of these needs. But not returning Todd to Lyman would undermine institutional order. I arranged a job in Boston, and we helped him find an apartment. He did well. Had we done it by the book, Todd would have been brought back to court and charged as an escapee, with time added to his institutional stay. Or, as is common in some states, he would have been waived to adult court and sent to prison.

Although I didn't much like returning anyone to the reform schools, we were able to talk most of the youngsters who'd been on the run into going back. Our success at this was a sad one, since it made so little sense. It had nothing to do with better care, and even less with public safety. It was a matter of bureaucratic survival, and for the kids was more destructive than helpful.

I had tried to jolt the system by turning accepted practice on its head. A distraught parent would call, concerned that his or her youngster had just been sentenced to DYS by a juvenile court. Would their son or daughter be safe in the reform school? What educational and treatment programs did we have? Although these reasonable questions were bizarre given the traditions of our facilities, we tried to use such occasions to stimulate administrators and staff to rethink what our institutions were supposed to be. Occasionally we invited a parent to take his or her youngster on a tour, to meet with our superintendents and directors of education, to see cottage life, and to ask what services might be offered. To staff accustomed to seeing new intakes arrive in handcuffs to be routinely assigned, meeting with parents to justify programs was a new twist.

For a while I toyed with the idea of hiring nondelinquent youth, preferably middle-class teenagers, to live on the grounds and attend our schools and groups. I saw it as a way of breaking into the delinquent subcultures which tend to run large institutions. But though I'm sure we could have found willing, altruistic teenagers to help in the experiment, I was warned by our legal counsel that the insurance considerations were too much for us to bear in case of incident.

We did try the reverse—bringing reform school inmates out to visit local high schools and prep schools. I remember taking three or four Shirley youngsters over to Groton, a distinguished private prep school only a few miles down the road. Our youngsters enjoyed the interchange immensely, and it was a productive evening. Later, after we made the decision to vacate the reform schools, we did in fact find places for a small number of them in private prep schools in Massachusetts and New Hampshire. That cost less than half what the reform schools had.

10 *Anticipating the Worst*

Since Lieutenant Governor Frank Sargent had assumed the chief executive's chair when Governor Volpe was appointed secretary of transportation by President Nixon, Sargent began his first campaign for governor ten months after my appointment. It looked like a close election. The Democrats had nominated Boston's popular mayor, Kevin White, for governor, along with a young liberal legislator, Michael Dukakis, for lieutenant governor. In the race for the nomination, Dukakis had beaten another leader in the reform of DYS, state senator Beryl Cohen. That I had accepted a cabinet post with a governor who came up for election in a year was a testament to my political innocence. If you hope to have any impact on a state system, you try for at least a four-year tenure. After ten months as commissioner, my lack of job security was only too obvious.

Sargent had appointed a number of luminaries to head the various state departments—Steve Minter in the Department of Welfare, Peter Goldmark as the first secretary of the new superagency Department of Human Services, John Boone in adult corrections, Matt Dumont to devise drug programs, Milt Greenblatt in mental health. In his campaign speeches the governor regularly named the exciting and competent new people he had brought in to make state government more responsive. He didn't include me, and I knew why. By late summer 1970 I had become an embarrassment. Most of the governor's staff were recommending that he get rid of me.

In those first months I was caught up in trying to get control of the institutions. I had no intention of closing them; I simply wanted to make them reasonably humane. It had been a daunting task, and the department was in an upset most of the time. I had concentrated on such things as retraining staff, softening rigid rules, changing brutal disciplinary practices, and introducing what I considered therapeutic programs. We brought in outside experts, conducted seminars, and set up new programs in selected cottages. The Harvard studies later demonstrated that these efforts had borne fruit. The youngsters in the new, more intense, individualized programs did better, thought better of themselves, were more settled and less violent.[1] But these modest changes came at a price.

Reform school staff circulated petitions across the state demanding my ouster, along with more specific calls for a return to whiffle haircuts, inmates in state clothes, and harsher discipline. As the number of escapes and runaways multiplied, townspeople understandably wanted the inmates from local facilities to be more easily identifiable.

The escapes and commotions in the institutions assured regular negative headlines. I wasn't a plus in the governor's campaign. Though I concluded he probably wouldn't fire me immediately, no political scruples would be likely to hold him back after the election. There was also the very real possibility that he'd be defeated, and it was unlikely that a White-Dukakis administration would reappoint me. White's chief aide, Barney Frank, had been friendly to a point, and Dukakis had been supportive even though I was a Republican appointee. But given Massachusetts politics, I knew I'd be among the first to get the boot. Moreover, I didn't expect that whoever replaced me would share many of my views, much less my methods, which often seemed to cause two problems for each one solved. In my pessimism, I fell into fantasizing a worst-case scenario. What if I were replaced by Heinrich Himmler and the SS? How hard would it be for a new commissioner with the rigidity of a Nazi to undo our meager reforms? Too late, I realized it wouldn't be difficult at all.

I knew from my experience with psychiatric hospitals in the Air Force that institutionally based therapeutic communities are fragile and fleeting. Making an institution caring and decent is a full-time job. To step back even briefly is to invite apathy and violence. The problem is aggravated when the institution's inmates are captives. But making a decent institution indecent is relatively easy.

The history of mental hospitals and adult and juvenile prisons over-flows with examples of model institutions which collapsed almost as they opened.[2] It takes only a few new rules (say, new visiting restrictions, uniforms, isolation procedures, punishments for infractions, or behavioral modification coercion). To make a hurtful institution caring, however, is not so simple. Rules cannot guarantee the civility which is the essence of a therapeutic environment. You can't post requirements like these on the bulletin board—"As of eight A.M. tomorrow staff will care for, listen to, and try to understand inmates," or "Staff will question their own motives and shortcomings as they deal with these troubled and troubling adolescents"—and expect to see them fulfilled. Yet these are what make a good institution, of which there are so few, and those few short-lived. In bureaucracies with a captive clientele the pull is always away from the personal and toward the impersonal and alienating. The pursuit is less one of public safety than of convenience. Rigid rules, isolation rooms, behavioral management procedures, goon squads, threats of exile to more brutal end-of-the-line institutions—all become accepted techniques for "better" management.

Humane administrators tire of seeking the unattainable—a safe and helpful institution. Most eventually retreat to bureaucratic roles, trying to find peace in mitigating destructiveness. They withdraw to such tasks as regulating the amount of time a teenager spends in isolation, certifying that staff keep behavioral logs on inmates, and setting up point systems to measure institutional conformity. This is the way of minimum standards—better than nothing, but not much. Our reforms were in danger of going the same route. The strides we had made in that first year were all within the institutions. As the election campaign revved up and I could count my remaining days in office, I realized that I'd left everyone vulnerable. I wished I'd gotten more youngsters out of the institutions in those first months.

The idea of putting reform school inmates into the community wasn't as risky as it sounded. All of them would return to the community within a few months anyway, and our in-house studies showed that the longer we kept someone, the more likely he or she was to get into trouble when released. When I first saw the study, I concluded it simply meant that we kept the more dangerous youngsters longer. But that wasn't the case. The longer a youngster stayed in one of our reform schools, the worse he or she seemed to do when released. We were pointing our alumni up dead ends.[3]

As I looked around the department at the superintendents, directors of education, chaplains, planners, and others in leadership roles, I saw that most would be there long after I left. They could outwait and outlast me. I'd made a mistake in concentrating on making the institutions more humane. The idea of *closing* them seemed less risky.

Of Festivals and Riots

Early one morning, Jessie Sargent's secretary called. The governor's wife was interested in learning more about our department. Initially I put off any meeting because I didn't need another kibitzer. Politicians' wives are notorious for taking up causes, and this would probably be no more than a public relations exercise. But I couldn't put the governor's wife off indefinitely.

A week later I dutifully drove the few blocks down Tremont Street to a downtown Boston high-rise where Mrs. Sargent kept a small apartment office. I'd been invited for tea and conversation. It was a happy surprise. There was none of the stuffiness I had expected. Mrs. Sargent talked of the problems in the old Youth Service Board and how she'd like to be of help. She mentioned that Mrs. Van Waters, the superintendent of the Lancaster school, had already invited her to speak at the strawberry festival, an annual event held on the grounds of the institution. She wondered whether to accept the invitation. I suggested she accept.

The strawberry festival was a day-long celebration attended by friends, local supporters, professionals, and others associated with the Lancaster school. Though some of the inmates' family members hung in the background, they seemed superfluous to the events. Strawberries and ice cream were served to the visiting guests during a day of ceremonies, including a graduation conducted in the institutional chapel. As was Mrs. Van Waters' tradition, every aspect was planned down to the last detail. Model girls were selected to recite or give short speeches, whose every word was prescreened by Mrs. Van Waters and typed on index cards from which each girl read.

The inmates were impressive in their colorful summer dresses, though their contacts with the visitors were primarily as waitresses and hostesses. The scene was a re-creation of a Victorian lawn party, all the way down to the hats and the organdy. I'd been to Lancaster many times before, but this was not the institution I knew. Yet I couldn't really object. The girls were enjoying themselves, having gotten well into their assigned roles. It was a rather nice, though deceptive, tableau. The realities of the Lancaster's girls' reform school had little to do with the strawberry festival.

At the time, I was in a continuing battle with the reform school superintendents over changes in the institutions, and I was probably too concerned with being submarined. But Mrs. Van Waters wasn't above firing a few silent torpedoes herself. As I watched her take a gracious Mrs. Sargent about the lawn, threading through the laid tables, shaking hands with this dignitary or that local politician—occasionally even being introduced to an unbelievably proper inmate—I could see Mrs. Sargent being led down a primrose path in this bucolic setting.

After the pleasantries on the green, everyone retired to the chapel for the formal ceremonies and Mrs. Sargent's speech. A number of girls preceded her to the pulpit and read from their cue cards. The thanks spewed forth—to teachers, to staff, to Mrs. Van Waters, to Mrs. Sargent for all the marvelous and good things the Lancaster school had done for them. We were neck-deep in encomiums. An unsuspecting outsider might have thought he was at the finest girls' finishing school in New England. I stood off to one side, watching Mrs. Sargent's face for any reaction to what was being so well and carefully presented. She sat expressionless in the front row of the chapel. Finally, it was time for her address, but not before Mrs. Van Waters had her moment. She stood in front of the chapel and spoke movingly about how honored she, the staff, the guests, and the girls were to be visited by a governor's wife. It would be a memory the girls could take with them for life. Then she took her shot: there appeared to be some who didn't see the need for institutions like Lancaster and who failed to understand how necessary such programs were if girls were to become productive ladies. Without a glance in my direction, she stated her hope that, in conversations with the governor, Mrs. Sargent would tell him of her day at Lancaster and of the need to support institutions like it in Massachusetts. I admired Mrs. Van Waters' chutzpah. This quiet, supremely controlled woman, though approaching retirement, still wasn't about to let an outsider invalidate her work of building a model institution, epitomized in the strawberry festival.

As Mrs. Sargent began her remarks, I hoped only for damage control. She stepped into the pulpit and spoke for all of three minutes. She said nothing about Lancaster. She told the girls how pleased she was to meet them and wished them better days ahead as they went on with their lives in the world outside. Then she sat down. She hadn't taken the bait. I was dumbfounded. I glanced over at Mrs. Van Waters. Her face was fixed in a stiff and proper smile.

After the ceremonies I accompanied Mrs. Sargent, along with her secretary and the plainclothes state patrolman, out to the waiting limousine. I thanked her for her support and told her how much it meant. It wasn't what I had expected. With a woman this unimpressed by appearances, there was hope for involvement beyond that expected of first ladies. Maybe she'd be up for seeing the other side of institutional life.

I called her secretary a few days later and suggested we visit some institutions unannounced, preferably in off-hours. We arranged to meet at the Huntington Avenue Girls' Detention Center a couple of weeks later. The visit went unusually well. The girls were in the gym at their usual activities, seated in circles on the floor, conversing, playing jacks. A number were still in medical isolation. I'd put some of my own people in charge of the place, but conditions had a tendency to deteriorate whenever they weren't around. And, though it was not nearly so repressive as it had been a few months earlier, the overriding impression was one of apathy. Huntington Avenue seemed a good deal more representative than the strawberry festival.

Mrs. Sargent spent most of her time talking quietly with individual girls. This polished Yankee woman wasn't in her element among these mostly street girls. But she handled matters in a soft-spoken, competent manner. Jessie Sargent came to know, however briefly, some of the inmates by listening to contradictory stories, accusations, frustrations, lapses of language and etiquette, and a few faint hopes.

A week or so later, I suggested she meet the (supposedly) most dangerous delinquents in the department: the boys at the IJG. This was the institution the governor had vowed to clean up. Things had quieted down at the IJG, and though it had been an uphill fight, we'd made progress. I even talked publicly of the IJG as a model for how youngsters could be humanely treated in an institution. But though there were no new scandals, the staff seemed to move in new directions only grudgingly. As happens in such situations, I was bent on proving, at least to myself, that things were better at the IJG than they actually were.

I made arrangements to meet Mrs. Sargent at the institution late one afternoon. Herb Willman and I drove down from Boston. Along the way we got caught in a mile-long backup of cars on the interstate and almost missed the appointment. After a frazzling ride up the median strip, we arrived to find Mrs. Sargent waiting in her car along the road outside the main gate of the institution. I was relieved that she had waited instead of ringing the bell. I didn't want staff to know she was there. If they knew it was the governor's wife, they'd gussy things up, and I wanted her to see the place as it was lived in by the inmates. I told her I wasn't sure what we'd find. To be fair, I suppose if one visited the average family unannounced, one might come upon embarrassing, if not occasionally scandalous, situations. But our institutions weren't families, and the unexpected in them was wont to take an ugly turn.

I rang the bell on the front gate. No answer. Then another ring . . . and another. Finally, after five or six minutes, a heavy-set, ill-kempt master ambled down the sidewalk from inside the main building. He came up to the gate and let our entourage in. He was notably unfriendly and silent. I performed no introductions but attempted to make small talk with Mrs. Sargent as we walked up to the institution.

We entered the quiet stone building, the sound of our heels echoing across the hard floors and up and down the empty hallways. It seemed empty of the hundred or so delinquent boys I knew were somewhere inside, although the ambience was familiar. Here and there was a piece of crumpled paper or pocket trash; the smell of urine assaulted us from a large puddle under the doorway of the congregate lavatory.

The boys and staff were in the walled yard. Our guide unlocked a door that opened into the walled yard. As he led us into the yard, there was a commotion. Boys ran in different directions for the wall. We'd stumbled into an escape attempt. There was a lot of yelling and swearing from the staff in pursuit, with agitated shouts of encouragement and profanity from the rest of the inmates, who were ringed in the middle of the yard by other nervous guards. Though things were out of control, I was more perturbed than threatened. I noticed Mrs. Sargent's plainclothes state trooper nervously fingering the revolver inside his suit coat. Mrs. Sargent stood next to me while I tried to explain what I thought was happening—though it hardly needed explanation.

No one made it over the wall, but a couple of youngsters came close. They were dragged down, .thrown to the ground, handcuffed, and beaten. Out of the din came a steady torrent of cursing, and the would-be escapees were carried off to isolation. Their rough handling stirred up the rest of the inmates. They were shouting and shaking fists as things continued to degenerate. The guards herded them into the gym, apparently hoping to contain a burgeoning riot more easily there. Once inside, the boys began to chant "Pig, pig, pig" and stomp their feet on the gym floor. As tension built, Herb and I waded into the gym among the youngsters and tried to defuse matters by talking to individual teenagers and asking questions. We did this not so much to get answers as to let everyone save face in a scene which was growing progressively uglier. A loudmouthed youngster who had "fronted on" (confronted) a guard had to deliver on his threats. A chat with the commissioner might allow him to back away. He'd made an authority listen to him. Mrs. Sargent, meanwhile, remained remarkably cool.

After a while things settled down, and the boys were taken one by one from the gym to their cells. I suggested that Mrs. Sargent meet them individually. She went from cell to cell and talked with a number of the boys she'd seen earlier in their stereotypical stances as violent young offenders. I introduced her by name to inmates, telling her something about each and his predicament. Then I left her to chat while I went to talk with staff about the situation we'd just witnessed.

Mrs. Sargent spent the next hour or so talking through the small hinged holes in the doors, occasionally getting a guard to open a cell to allow her to speak confidentially with a particular boy. It wasn't a time for loud demands and aggressive stances. The boys whom she'd just seen cursing, shaking fists, and yelling threats were taken aback. Word got out that this interested woman was the governor's wife. The staff had apparently taken her to be a friend of mine or perhaps another do-gooder I'd imported to the central office. It wasn't a particularly fair thing to do to Mrs. Sargent, but it made for a visit she wouldn't soon forget. As we walked back through the same hallway we'd traversed a couple of hours before, the trash on the floor had been retrieved, the urine mopped up. The place was already cleaner.

We left the institution and were let out the gate. Standing there in the dusk, no one said much. I thanked Mrs. Sargent for taking the time to come to the IJG and expressed my hope that it hadn't been too upsetting an evening. She said it hadn't, adding that she didn't see how "people like that could be of much help to these boys."

As Herb and I drove back to Boston, we mused over the meaning of the night's events. I presumed that Mrs. Sargent would whisper something in the governor's ear later. Maybe it was time to leave the IJG. We had hoped to have the IJG boys in Topsfield by now, but it hadn't worked out. With no alternatives available, things were deteriorating at Bridgewater. Balancing the risk of dealing decisively with the nagging Bridgewater institution against the problems which might accompany its quick closing, I decided to take the chance.

We would have a limited time to get the boys out of the IJG. Our opportunity was tied to the aftereffects of Mrs. Sargent's visit. If we waited, we'd lose it. She seemed appalled at what she'd seen. But this was conjecture, since I didn't ask her directly. Nor did I propose closing the institution either to Mrs. Sargent or to the governor. I figured Jessie would probably agree with my actions. I could ask for her support with her husband. And, in the case of Governor Sargent, as I later learned, moral suasion was usually enough.

Before making any moves, I wanted as complete an evaluation of the youngsters as possible. What did we know about them? What kinds of services did they need? Who could go home? Who couldn't? We had no money for hiring outside clinicians. The few psychologists in our department seemed mediocre to incompetent, turning out cookbook-type reports on the juveniles they evaluated. These reports followed youngsters throughout the system, becoming a permanent part of their history, hung around their necks albatross-like and ensuring a warped consistency in the misunderstandings which inevitably followed. Obviously I couldn't depend on the reports we already had. At the time, there was still a general belief (since disproved) that a sharp clinician or a thorough battery of psychological tests could predict dangerousness. But even these questionable tools weren't available to us.

I'd recently hired Bill Madaus, a young psychologist from the University of Massachusetts who had headed an Upward Bound program which brought inner-city youth into the university. (Bill later became assistant commissioner for clinical services.) He put together an in-house team to decide which Bridgewater inmates could be safely paroled home, which ones could be absorbed into other reform schools, and which ones would have to be confined to secure settings. The team was an unlikely ad hoc combination of line staff, administrators, and older inmates from within the system, all persons who had known most of the IJG boys over the years. We included a few inmates because of my experience in the service. The Air Force had found that, though psychological and other tests were virtually useless in predicting whether a basic trainee would make it successfully through his four-year hitch, a simple peer-group evaluation taken in the fifth week of basic training was highly accurate in predicting success or failure. Since the IJG was considered the end of the line, most of the boys had previously been in one or another of the other institutions. Though they weren't nec' s-sarily the most dangerous by virtue of having committed particularly heinous crimes, they posed management problems of one kind or another in the reform schools.

Jimmy, the boy I'd first seen shackled to his bed at the IJG, had never committed a crime against a person. He had come to us as an eight-year-old for having spread rumors about the neighbors. He would walk up and down the alleys of his neighborhood on the out-skirts of Boston and paw through garbage and trash cans. If he found a whiskey bottle, he'd accuse a neighbor of having another life—of being a drunk or running around on his wife. He was an irritating enough youngster. If he had been appropriately evaluated at the start, the beginnings of serious mental disability would probably have been picked up.

Instead, Jimmy was taken to court and committed to John Augustus Hall as a delinquent. He progressed through the various detention centers and reform schools. At fifteen he was still mouthing the same rumors, getting to the same staff members where it hurt most (for example, accusing them of being closet homosexuals), and informing for the police. The pattern which brought him to us had changed hardly at all, but the ante was upped. As the reaction of the department turned more hostile and occasionally brutal, Jimmy's threats grew more scary. He became thoroughly institutionalized. On occasion, when he'd been paroled, he ensured his return to reform school by calling his parole agent and threatening to burn down the agent's house. Although his threats had never been more than verbal, he was considered a dangerous juvenile. It seemed to me that, if he was, we had had a part in making him so.

Bill's team decided that about a dozen youngsters needed to be kept in a locked setting. The rest could either be absorbed into the general populations of the other reform schools or sent home on parole. In retrospect, I can see that paroling the IJG inmates home was reckless, particularly in view of the fact that we had no additional supervision for them, but things went smoothly, and there were no incidents. Even the press coverage was positive. I took it that past scandals at the IJG contributed to the relatively calm reception. Most people were relieved that something was being done to resolve a chronic irritation.

The evaluations of the boys at the IJG took about ten days. Meanwhile, we met with Frank Ordway, the Lyman superintendent, to discuss the possibility of using a cottage there as our new secure program. Ordway was supportive of the idea. For a while we even toyed with using Cottage Nine at Shirley. Though the inmates there were now allowed to talk and move about, and we'd begun to get some minimal programming, the place still had an ominous reputation. I didn't want to move back into it—it wouldn't have mattered if it had been run by August Aichhorn himself. It still carried too much baggage.

We didn't have a model for the new secure program. I decided on Guided Group Interaction (GGI). GGI, now renamed Positive Peer Culture, was in vogue in a few training schools across the country. It was devised by Harry Vorrath, a social worker at the Training Institute of Central Ohio, the Ohio Youth Commission's facility for its most difficult delinquents. Since I'd been an occasional consultant to that commission when I taught at Ohio State, I'd come to know the model. At the time it was one of the only honest attempts to deal differently with difficult young people in state institutions. I knew that Harry was a caring person. I didn't think he'd misuse inmates or staff. Later, as I saw the model operate in our system, I had misgivings. But at the time GGI seemed the best way to get programming quickly for youngsters we were going to keep locked up.

The state employees' union representative, Joe Correia, informed the union that we'd be closing the IJG in a couple of weeks. Joe was a skilled organizer who recognized the need for change in the department. He was a man of his word and had credibility with the staff. I met with Joe, laid out our plans, and assured him that no staff would lose their jobs, but would be reassigned. Most of the other institutions were within reasonable driving distance of Bridgewater. The staff knew there was little chance of keeping Bridgewater open indefinitely, given the condition of the buildings and the agitation preceding the creation of the new department. Though there was little opposition, I don't think the staff really believed we were going to close the IJG. They were inured to missed deadlines and five-year plans. Meanwhile, Frank Ordway and Bob Brown got the cottage at Lyman in shape to accept the IJG youngsters. Harry Vorrath arrived and began training the staff in GGI.

We didn't publicly announce the IJG's closing until a day or so before it was padlocked. We quietly moved all the inmates and invited the media to tour the empty institution. The closing even got a bit of national attention, with Garrick Utley of NBC standing at the front and then fading into a voice-over on film of dank hallways and empty rooms in the broken-down old building. As I learned later, the television reality is probably the most compelling reality to the average citizen. The IJG was closed on the night it was announced on the "NBC Evening News."

We moved the dozen or so most risky youngsters (though even all these weren't unusually dangerous) to the locked cottage we had set aside at Lyman. Some had simply not been with us long enough to satisfy the courts. Though they represented a minimal risk, we knew we would be vulnerable to attacks from judges, the press, and the legislature if a youngster was seen on the street a few weeks after being committed to us. The few boys we sent to Lyman were pleased to be out of the IJG, and the Lyman staff assigned to the new program had been fired up by Vorrath. All this took place only a few weeks after Mrs. Sargent's visit. It went so smoothly that I figured it must have been a fluke. The very idea of closing down a state institution seemed reckless. Doing it quickly seemed foolhardy. But most impolitic was first to close the reform school which held the so-called hard-core delinquents. We had done it backwards. This first deinstitutionalization was a series of makeshift solutions to a crisis, and though we made it through with no serious incidents, it wasn't the way to go. In the fall of 1970, Harvard researchers summarized our first ten months. We had:

- Closed Bridgewater's Institute for Juvenile Guidance, the secure unit for the most "hard to handle" youth.
- Begun a full-scale push to bring a "therapeutic community" philosophy to Shirley Industrial School. Two-hour community meetings were held several times a week, with all staff and inmates in a cottage assembled to talk over mutual problems. Small group meetings had been introduced following seminars conducted by Harry Vorrath, outlining his "Guided Group Interaction" model.
- Completed a successful two-day conference on the therapeutic community featuring Dr. Maxwell Jones, the British pioneer in development of such communities.
- Expanded vocational training, educational programs, and an experimental tutorial program using Harvard and MIT students.

- Structured new recreational programs.
- Opened a girls' cottage on the grounds of Lyman in preparation for a therapeutic community program to begin in September (upon retirement of Mrs. Van Waters).
- Closed the farm and expanded visiting hours at the Lyman School.

But the Harvard researchers warned:

> Staff at this time was deeply divided about the central administration's goals of a therapeutic community and how it might be best implemented. . . . There was also great anxiety about job security given the new treatment orientation, and concern about the abandonment of more regimented, traditional methods for maintaining orderly routines and discipline, especially when the form and intent of the new treatment approaches were so little understood. . . . The major conflict between the school's administration and central office emerged when some of the runaways from Lyman were granted release to parole.

Staff at Lancaster were described as apprehensive over possible wholesale changes that might occur. The Harvard researchers summarized the conflicts between the institutions and the central office.

> Principal complaints by the [Lancaster] girls focused on desires for more coeducational functions and more humane considerations, e.g., an end to being locked in their rooms at night with only pails for toilet facilities. The basic difference between the Lancaster administration and the central office concerning the credence to be given to the therapeutic community concept of treatment was left unresolved and traditional treatment concepts remained dominant. . . .
>
> At Oakdale the staff was apprehensive about the new philosophy of the Boston office. This lack of sympathy for the concept of the therapeutic community was based on the rationale that young boys needed stronger authority figures and well-defined rules rather than increased freedom to make their own decisions, either individually or in groups. . . .
>
> Forestry camp was generally supportive of the new approach in central office. . . . Staff and boys maintained easy communicative relationships and the small size, varied work assignments in the community and park service, attractive surroundings and the challenge of an "Outward Bound" type of program created a social climate to which boys seemed to respond positively.[4]

Overall, I was pleased with our progress. But others saw things differently. At about the same time, Special Justice Charles Mahoney, a leader of the Committee for Youth in Trouble, which had agitated for the reform legislation, called the reorganization a failure. He cited continuing abuse and neglect of children in the institutions, imprudent and unwise spending for capital purposes, a failure of executive leadership, poor budgetary support, and gross overstaffing. I couldn't disagree. I told the *Boston Globe* a few weeks later:

> After one year on the job, it's begun to dawn on me how difficult change is: there hasn't been much. There's a facade of change. One can easily give the impression of change, but in fact, as far as the treatment of the youngsters is concerned, there's not been very much. I hadn't anticipated the staying power of this bureaucracy. There's been movement, not change.

Here's how the *Globe* summed things up:

> Dissension and division still run rampant in the Department of Youth Services where politics continues to play a more important role than the rehabilitation of delinquent youngsters. . . . Miller is not very politically oriented. But almost everyone else in the department is well versed in how to use politics to advantage. Even some of Miller's closest advisers have undermined his work behind his back. . . .
>
> Virtually alone, Miller spent a year running a holding action and trying to develop new programs for the department. No reorganization could change the personnel problems. Most of the department's 900 employees got their jobs through political connections. . . . For the majority of youth service employees, Miller's attitudes have been unacceptable. These employees have spent most of their years viewing all delinquents as hardened criminal types. It was all right to use physical brutality, as long as you didn't get caught. Long-term solitary confinement was a regular method of discipline, although it was officially prohibited. . . . When Miller arrived he called on the staff to be more involved, to take an interest in youngsters. He developed training seminars to help employees understand some of the problems and attitudes of the young people they supervised. Some employees supported Miller. But the vast majority, including men in high posts, began to undermine him. So far, Miller has not proved to be a very good administrator. He has been slow to get programs active—as much the result of lack of new top level staff and limited funding.[5]

Reforming a large state agency by concentrating on the plight of an individual youngster no doubt seemed naive. But for me, particularly during that first year, it offered hope for change along with the personal solace that, at least for this young person, I was able to do something. In this sense it was my escape. When I looked at the grand strategies being taken by my peers in other states, I was intimidated. Toward the end of that first year, I received a brochure outlining Michigan's five-year plan for juvenile corrections from reform schools to community-based alternatives. The slick public relations packet laid out the plan and projected budgets; types of programs were illustrated in the glossy pictures and elegant graphs. Meanwhile, I was preparing our own first annual report at the dining room table on an old Hermes 3000 typewriter, banging it out from rough notes and rougher statistics. My secretary, Peg Neely, put the messy text on stencils and ran it off on the rattling mimeograph machine at the back of the office.

Though we planned differently, and with some eccentricity, we had begun to redefine the issues—more a matter of symbols and gestures than of sound management policies. Fifteen years later, Michigan, with its coterie of professional human service administrators and managers, was passing some of the most repressive juvenile legislation in the nation and locking up more children than ever.

11 *Doing Least Harm: Humane Institutions*

A year after I was sworn in, the legislature finally approved funds to hire the assistant commissioners created by the reform legislation. Father Drinan had been right. They'd created a new department and then refused to fund it not so much because of any impulse to be frugal as to ensure that I was controllable before they put any further resources at my disposal. The hope had been that I'd make cosmetic changes and appoint credentialed politicos, but it wasn't happening that way. There'd been talk of de-funding my position if I chose not to resign. By now, however, I'd gotten about as stubborn as my predecessor had been. I told a somewhat startled governor's aide that I planned to stay in the position and would drive a cab at night to support myself if necessary. I would not go quietly.

But at least we finally had assistant commissioners in charge of aftercare, clinical services, education, and institutions. In anticipation, we'd frozen vacated institutional staff positions and hired Bill Madaus, the person I intended to appoint assistant commissioner for clinical services. He in turn had recommended a consultant to his program, Yitzhak Bakal, to head the Bureau of Institutions. Yitzhak was a sophisticated psychiatric social worker with a particular interest in working with delinquent youngsters. Before emigrating to the United States, he had worked in the Tel Mond youth corrections facility in Israel.

Tom Jeffers had his graduate degree in education and had been voted teacher of the year by high school students in the Columbus school system. He was later a prime mover in the successful CETA program we set up at Ohio State University. I asked him to head our Bureau of Educational Services. Though he fit the qualifications, that was not uppermost in my mind. I wanted someone who shared similar values and could be trusted. Tom was a friend. As it turned out, he probably more than anyone in the department kept me straight and saw that things were kept in perspective.

Initially I appointed a long-time employee, George O'Shea, as assistant commissioner for Aftercare, but after a couple of months he asked to resign, citing the pressures as more than he wanted to take on. He returned to another administrative position. George was well connected in the legislature, and I assumed that as my relations there began to deteriorate, he saw me as an albatross around his neck. I was eventually able to recruit Joe Leavey, who till then had been a deputy in the Division of Child Guardianship, the state's child welfare system. I'd first met Joe along with a state legislator, Phil Johnston, after the Topsfield town meeting, when they came up to offer support and condolences.

Accountability

Anyone who's tried to get help from government already knows something about unresponsive bureaucracy. State human service administrators are seldom held accountable. Since their clientele comes from the lower end of the socioeconomic totem pole, in "human service" bureaucrats are at their least responsive. A middle-class citizen trying to renew a driver's license may have to wait a couple of hours in a Department of Motor Vehicles office; citizens seeking welfare assistance or public mental health services must inure themselves to endless lines and day-long waits. The difficulty of getting any humane response from government bureaucracies increases exponentially when, in addition to being poor, the client is delinquent or criminal. In such situations, accountability even becomes inappropriate. What right does a young tough have to demand anything from those assigned to guard or treat him? The very idea is absurd. At this point state bureaucrats begin talking about responsibility to that unquantifiable entity, the public. As the word leaves their lips, bureaucrats' accountability departs from the deliberations and dissolves into career padding and political tuft-hunting. Unresponsiveness becomes integral to the rehabilitative ideology. The system uses its own intransigence to measure the client's patience and maturity.

I do not question the fact that there are dangerous youngsters who need to be held against their will, but this sad reality carries its own set of problems unrelated to crime and punishment. The unintended by-product of keeper-captive coupling is a bureaucracy which is by law unaccountable to those it holds and, somewhat oddly, purports to serve. That would be an unhealthy situation for even the most efficient manager.

If Phillips Exeter Academy, Andover, Choate, or similar respected prep schools were filled *only* with captive students ordered there by courts and forbidden to leave under penalty of longer imprisonment, the standards of even the best of faculty and administrators would shortly go downhill. Though altruism might salvage things for a while, it makes a notoriously undependable base for long-term policy.

I thought I could get over this contradiction. We would respond sensitively to each individual youngster while recognizing our public responsibility. In the abstract, these goals aren't contradictory, but in the political arena which defines corrections, they quickly become so. Control slides toward punishment, treatment turns to threats, and decency is eaten away. Society wants its pound of flesh even as it offers sympathy. The captive client must be cooperative while suffering our ministrations. If our help fails the fault is the inmate's.

In one of the most important analyses in the criminological literature, the great American social theorist George Herbert Mead posed the dilemma this way:

> It is quite impossible psychologically to hate the sin and love the sinner. We are very much given to cheating ourselves in this regard. We assume that we can detect, pursue, indict, prosecute, and punish the criminal and still retain toward him the attitude of reinstating him in the community as soon as he indicates a change in social attitude himself, that we can at the same time watch for the definite transgression of the statute to catch and overwhelm the offender, and comprehend the situation out of which the offense grows. But the two attitudes, that of control of crime by the hostile procedure of the law and that of control through comprehension of social and psychological conditions, cannot be combined. To understand is to forgive, and the social procedure seems to deny the very

responsibility which the law affirms, and on the other hand the pursuit by criminal justice inevitably awakens the hostile attitude in the offender and renders the attitude of mutual comprehension practically impossible. The social worker in the court is the sentimentalist, and the legalist in the social settlement in spite of his learned doctrine is the ignoramus.[1]

Attempts to skirt this inherent conflict plagued our reforms from the start. Since I believed that whatever we accomplished would be shortly undone anyway, I decided to do least harm and make things a bit more normal for our clientele while I was able. If along the way I could structure the department in such a way as to make it harder for any successor to beat a retreat to the old days, so much the better. Mead was right. We can't have it both ways. Some, like Roscoe Pound, recognized this from the beginning.[2] If the implied promise of the juvenile court had been realized, all of criminal law would have had to be rethought. Not surprisingly, that never happened. Those who devised, set up, and ran the juvenile court, and the juvenile corrections systems which followed, have turned from these difficult and profound implications.

I decided to emphasize the stated goals of the legislation: prevention, help, education, and training. They embodied the ambivalence to which Mead alluded. No one looking at the reform school system could honestly conclude that those goals were what it was about. The system was, above all, meant to be a threat—a "deterrent." True reform would have to ignore this tacit understanding—the unstated expectation that we would dispense punishment and call it treatment. We would do good and mollycoddle with proudly bleeding hearts. But of course we never did. The fear of an incident, the anger of a judge, the threat of a legislator, each brought its own compromise. None of them had much point beyond the need to survive a while.

Staff Training

Maxwell Jones was on my mind. His was the original therapeutic community before the term was stolen by the current crop of authoritarian gurus. Jones had run successful experiments in patient government in Scotland at Dingleton Hospital and in a small institution for the criminally insane outside London. I had never met him, but now seemed a great opportunity. I would ask his help in turning our brutal facilities into therapeutic communities.

After phoning around half the world, I located Jones in the southwestern United States, where he was visiting. I invited him to conduct a few days of seminars and staff training on the grounds of one of our reform schools. He was enthusiastic about the possibilities, and arrived in Boston a few weeks later to conduct a three-day seminar for DYS staff and administrators. The sessions were conducted in the auditorium/gym at Shirley.

Jones began with a lecture about his concept of how inmates should have some say in their own destiny, in setting goals, and in sharing some power. This was not what staff wanted to hear, though Jones's model wasn't all that radical. Only minimal power having to do with day-to-day institutional routines was shared. It seemed like a common-sense model, and I'd seen it work in various psychiatric wards.

Jones was a skilled clinician who knew the boundaries of shared responsibility in institutions with captives. His manner was direct as he worked with staff and inmates in joint meetings. This commingling of people was revolutionary enough. To have a conference of keepers and captives where either group could ask questions, object, or participate on a nearly equal footing for a few hours created a feeling of ferment and change. But things weren't very peaceful, despite Jones's attempts to keep them so.

Many staff in this first plenary session seized on it as a chance to voice their opposition as a group to any proposed changes. The inmates seemed to view the whole affair with detached and amused bewilderment. Occasionally a boy would rise to ask a simple question or make a halting comment. They were the best behaved of the lot.

But large meetings were Jones's forte. Within a few hours, he had the participants asking questions and sharing ideas for better-run and more humane institutions. Things were going too smoothly. In the middle of the discussion, an assistant superintendent stood and announced that all the boys would now have to leave the auditorium and go outside to be counted. He couldn't have timed it better. It threw me off balance. I was already viewed as too intrusive, and I didn't want to humiliate him in front of the whole department. I made no objection, but his move destroyed any fleeting idea a youngster might have had that we took all this talk of sharing and involvement seriously. Out they marched in single file to be counted while the meeting inside continued. It broke Jones's stride as well, though he was too polite to object and tried to put a good face on the fast-deteriorating situation. Then came the retaliation.

After lunch the inmates were herded back into the gym. They were barely seated when a cottage master ran down the center aisle shouting that a boy had just stolen his car. There was another hubbub as staff ran from the gym to form up for the chase. The young man was caught within half an hour and returned. By now, Jones was getting a feel for our department. It was not Dingleton or even an institution for the criminally insane. It had its own peculiar set of problems.

On the second day things settled down. Though some staff made a show of walking out—ostensibly because of Jones's earthy language, some seemed to be actually enjoying themselves. Then the familiar politics emerged. During a relatively involved group interchange, up rose George Bourque, a portly legislator from Fitchburg. George had his own agenda and a coterie of patronage employees at Shirley. He usually cut a fine figure with his white hair and booming voice. Now he was waving in the air what looked like a paperback. It was Jerry Rubin's *Do It!*[3] Apparently a student tutor had left a copy in the institution's library. It provided an opportunity for George to deliver a rousing speech about permissiveness and outsiders countenancing revolution. No wonder the inmates were in constant revolt; they were being encouraged by subversive tracts. His comments ignored the fact that virtually none of the inmates bothered to frequent the library, and the book he waved had not a single dog-eared page. He found a receptive audience among the staff, who loudly applauded and buzzed their support. I made the mistake of trying to respond seriously. But Bourque had gotten his message across: the legislator as staff protector, me as radical stranger. The next day Maxwell Jones left, stripped of the optimism he had shown on his arrival. As I left him at Logan Airport, he commented softly that perhaps his model didn't work in all settings.

We worked at creating a more humane atmosphere in the institutions—treatment programs, coed cottages, camping, and new educational programs. I hung onto the hope of salvaging the institutions and making them utopian havens of concern and care, a refuge for young people who, because of their behavior, had to be exiled. By most measures we succeeded. When we decided to close the institutions, they were among the more decent reform schools in the nation (for whatever that's worth). If we had wished to, we could have touted them as models for a different kind of Massachusetts Experiment.

Finding Allies: The Three Pauls

Much of my time was spent reconnoitering the department for anyone who shared an interest in doing things differently. I had little to offer in salaries or promotions, and the rumors that I probably wouldn't last very long were persistent. Nevertheless, we were able to put together a group of inside supporters who kept things running those first months.

Paul Dichaut, a former Navy man who'd been on the staff at Shirley for over a decade, had been a cottage supervisor and had a reputation for brooking no resistance from inmates. He wasn't above occasionally knocking a kid off the wall, but I'd also heard that he'd tired of that role and supported some of the proposed reforms in the cottages. Herb Willman arranged a meeting with Paul one rainy evening at a Howard Johnson's a few miles from Shirley. He and I arrived early and went inside. Paul drove up later, peered in through the fogged-up windows, and saw us sitting inside. He then called from a telephone booth outside and paged Herb to make sure that the coast was clear. He didn't want any Shirley staff to see him with me. Though Paul agreed to support us, I had to act as if I didn't know him when I visited Shirley. I eventually made him superintendent, and he presided over the closing of the institution.

One administrator stood apart from the otherwise bland assemblage—Paul Leahy, the superintendent of the Worcester detention center. Worcester was a breath of air, a coed facility with youngsters exuding a healthy adolescent volubility, reassuring blather, activity, and hope. A streetwise social worker and the only M.S.W. in the department, Leahy presided calmly and competently. He didn't chase runaways; he had no tombs, no silence rules, no head calls. He encouraged staff to care, and he flooded his small institution with college student volunteers. An unannounced visit was welcome. And it all worked. Although Paul was a trained social worker, his effectiveness was almost wholly unrelated to his professional training. I could never have relied solely on professionalism for the kind of concern and commitment Paul gave. The decency of the Worcester institution was a result of his charisma and personal devotion.

This was brought home to me a few years later when, as part of filming an ABC documentary on Massachusetts (never aired), I returned to Worcester. Paul was gone, and the place was frightening: a fourteen-year-old sat in a straight chair facing the wall; the silence was heavy, kids sitting at bare tables glared out angrily; the staff complained that not enough young people were locked up; and the hostility was as palpable as it had been before Paul Leahy came. Worcester had a program called the "Bouncer" program, designed to incarcerate youngsters who "bounced" out of community-based programs and to give them a taste of jail, to show how disgusting detention could be. Its rationale was deterrence, the same flawed premise that had sustained Massachusetts institutions for a century and a half. Worcester was another example of the fragility of caring institutions.[4] But Paul was a symbol of hope, the only superintendent in the department who (I felt) understood what I was about and what I wanted to do. He was respected in the Worcester community and had been able to keep the old YSB administrators at bay, running his program unmolested by the more conservative bureaucrats in the Boston office.

When I told him of my concerns, particularly that Shirley was falling apart, he offered his help. At Herb's suggestion, I asked Paul to take a leave from Worcester and run Shirley. He agreed reluctantly. I informed the Shirley superintendent that Paul would be my representative on the grounds. Paul arrived just as a front-page story appeared in the Worcester *Telegram*. A large picture of the institution behind an inset of the superintendent was topped by a headline suggesting that in the past, horrible things had gone on at Shirley. The article was the result of interviews I'd done with Eric Best, then a cub reporter with the *Telegram*. Best had done his homework and had put together an accurate story, and the Shirley staff blamed me for the negative press.

The morning the article appeared, I got a call from Shirley's assistant superintendent telling me that the story had devastated the superintendent. He upbraided me for involving myself with the press and for giving the school a bad name after years of public acceptance. I tried to reassure him that it was not my intention to make anyone a scapegoat. I doubt that he believed me. I had made moves to render the superintendent powerless to run the institution, though I couldn't legally vacate his position.

Paul Leahy arrived at Shirley with some Holy Cross students who had worked as volunteers and part-time staff at the Worcester detention center. He was to have line authority to run the institution. Understandably, the superintendent was miffed and refused to talk to Paul. Most Shirley staff followed suit. After a meeting with administrative and line staff, Paul emerged with the impression that, at best, he would be able to depend on half a dozen staff for support. Within a few days he found himself relying on the few college students he'd brought along. Staff actively sabotaged his efforts to phase out repressive practices at the school. Paul reacted by recruiting present Shirley youngsters whom he'd known in Worcester. He formed a team led by seventeen-year-old Mike Radon on which he could depend for information and for telling him who would have credibility with the inmates on the grounds.[5] Within a few weeks, Shirley was turned upside down. Some staff refused to enter the cottages, and Paul had to rely on the inmates to keep order and convey information. But the number of escapes subsided, and there were no major outbreaks of violence. We continued to develop more group programs in the cottages. But Paul couldn't stay at Shirley indefinitely. He was away from the Worcester center too much, and he worried that it might deteriorate. I had to look for other ways of keeping Shirley under control.

Paul DeMuro had joined our staff in late 1970 as a consultant. I say "joined our staff" with some reservation, since when Paul arrived from Ohio we had no position open for him. We had to give him a vacant janitor's slot at Shirley. Paul had no experience in working with delinquents short of the street-smarts he grew up with in West Philadelphia. When I met him at Ohio State, he was working on a Ph.D. in English literature. At first I asked Paul to help with planning in the central office. He evaluated all the reform schools. As things continued to simmer at Shirley, I asked if he would mind going out to Shirley and running the institution so that Paul Leahy could get back to Worcester.

DeMuro arrived on the Shirley grounds as my second acting superintendent (still being paid as a janitor). His first task was getting into his office. The superintendent was still on paid vacation, and I informed the other administrators that Paul DeMuro would be the new acting superintendent. This did not go over very well. Paul asked for the key to the superintendent's office. If there was one, apparently no one was about to give it to him, and he was told no one had it. With my approval, Paul convinced a friendly maintenance man to drill out the lock on the office door. While this was going on, the institutional chaplain showed up with a camera, took a picture, and accused Paul of breaking and entering. Incidents like these set the mood for the final phasedown of Shirley.

The Misunderstood Memo

By Christmas 1970, things had quieted down. Governor Sargent won the election, and our bad publicity subsided. We felt secure enough to send four hundred youngsters home for the holidays, and only two failed to return on time. But something else was contributing to the calm, something I hadn't noticed until it was well under way. Inmate populations were falling dramatically. At first I thought it was because the judges, in disgust over our alleged permissiveness, were sending us fewer delinquent youngsters. Boston Juvenile Court Judge Poitrast, for example, hadn't made any secret of his feelings. He wanted more disciplined institutions which kept youngsters longer.

Poitrast was on our advisory board and strongly criticized almost everything I did. I took his comments about the short length of stay young people had in DYS to be sour grapes over my opposition to his legislative request to fund his court's acquisition of an abandoned Nike missile site in the Blue Hills section of Boston. He wanted to run his own institution for recalcitrant youngsters he saw ill served in DYS. But Judge Poitrast's objections weren't simply sour grapes.

Though I'd placed a few individual youngsters in the community, I had no policy of early release. But still the populations at the reform schools were falling. I concluded that judges had begun waiving kids to adult court. Yet waivers weren't rising that much, and when we looked at commitments, we found that judges were actually sending us a few more young people than in the past. Then why the lower populations in the reform schools? Clearly, we were sending inmates home much earlier. I decided to stop the practice, since it was a political land mine.

I sent out a memo meant to stress that youths sent us by the courts should be kept longer. To avoid reckless releases of youngsters, I wrote that no youth should be considered for parole until after at least three months. The implication was that they should stay longer, probably nine months or more. I thought staff were probably releasing risky inmates early in hopes of creating incidents, and I meant the memo to be conservative, but it was interpreted to mean that every youngster sent to our reform schools *must* be paroled within ninety days or less. This wasn't my conscious intention. But I fear that my words betrayed my unconscious desire, and the staff picked up on the fact.

And yet, with the exception of Judge Poitrast, no one seemed much troubled by the early releases. No judges had written or called me.

There hadn't been any speeches about them in the legislature. There were no press conferences by prosecutors, no political columns, and no incidents. It hadn't become an issue. Meanwhile, the reform school populations continued to dwindle. I decided to keep my mouth shut. When it came time to close the reform schools, they had their lowest populations in decades.

The Changing of the Guard

At about this time another problem that had been simmering finally boiled over. Though the reform schools were quiet, Roslindale was in turmoil. Overcrowding had worsened with the placement of girls on one floor of the facility, and the staff seemed incapable of handling youngsters differently. Nowhere in the department were the traditions of the old YSB more entrenched than in the place the kids called Rozzie. In early 1971, the escape rate soared. A Boston television station began its Sunday night news with the comment that there were certain fixed ceremonies in society, among them the changing of the guard at Buckingham Palace and the weekend escapes from Roslindale. As a political columnist for the *Boston Globe* put it, "Sunday nights at the Judge John J. Connelly Youth Center in Roslindale, it's every youth for himself. While the rest of Roslindale settles down for an evening of TV, the inmates at the DYS facility start packing."[6] Doors were left open. Staff called in sick. In one case, seven youngsters were put into a single-bunk room and given a crowbar by a staff member. When they weren't out the window in an hour, he returned and asked them what was taking so long.

I appointed Frank Masciarelli, an experienced former cottage supervisor from Lyman, superintendent of Roslindale, but despite his best efforts, the staff continued their revolt. The building (originally a reform itself) added to the problem, for it was poorly designed, poorly heated, had no air conditioning, and even when calm created a siege mentality in the inmates. The recreation areas were cramped, the gym was dangerous, the outside yard was unusable because boys were forever climbing over or under the security fence, and there was insufficient space for programming. A 1970 Massachusetts Supreme Court ruling had resulted in doubling the population. Kids were sleeping two to a single room, in the hallways, and on the gym floor.

I looked around for more space. We were already using the gym, classrooms, and occasionally the dining hall for sleeping quarters. But there were two untouched areas: the chapels—a reasonably spacious Protestant chapel and a large Catholic chapel. They were used for services for perhaps a dozen youngsters an hour a week. It didn't seem right that these areas be left unused where the need was so great.

I met with Cardinal Medieros, head of the Boston archdiocese, to suggest combining the chapels and using the larger one for additional program, classroom, or living space. I was familiar with the arrangements in the military, where multipurpose chapels were the rule: Protestants, Catholics, Jews, Muslims, and others all used the same space. I had this model in mind when I met Cardinal Medieros. The meeting didn't go well. He had no intention of allowing the Catholic chapel to be used in any way other than it had been since its opening. With the Roslindale chaplain at his side, he noted that the chapel had been designated an oratory by the Vatican and was therefore untouchable for use in any other fashion. It didn't help matters when I wrote to him that it seemed unchristlike to maintain an empty chapel while youngsters lived down the hall in inhuman conditions. A few days after I had sent my letter, I got a call from the governor's office telling me to drop the subject.

As the overcrowding persisted, staff problems became even more ominous. One day a youngster from Revere happened by my office and commented that boys were being let out of Roslindale to deliver stolen goods for organized crime. After the deliveries, they returned to Roslindale provided with an alibi—"I was in detention." There were other allegations that certain favored boys were being let out to steal specific items on order for some staff. I took a statement from one youngster about his own (unreported) weekend escape from Roslindale, during which he went to a parking lot near Fenway Park and stole a set of high-tech tires from a car for a unit supervisor. The youngster gave me the date, time, description of auto, brand of tires, and staff member's name. I reported it to the district attorney's office, but I didn't have the impression they were much interested, and I never heard about the matter again.

I chalked that up to the fact that I wasn't much of a favorite with local prosecutors. Earlier I had been lumped with cop-killers by the Boston police chief because I'd sought Law Enforcement Assistance Administration (LEAA) funding for a specialized tutorial program at Shirley

Industrial School. A couple of years before I arrived, a program using the same acronym had been started in one of the adult prisons. One of the teachers (a Brandeis University undergraduate) got involved with an inmate in a bank robbery, ostensibly for revolutionary reasons. A policeman was killed. The fact that we had Harvard and MIT students acting as tutors at Shirley apparently put me among the revolutionaries in the eyes of the police commissioner even though there had never been any incidents in our tutorial program. The highly successful program, called Step, had been set up by Babette Spiegel, a committed teacher and the wife of Boston psychiatrist John Spiegel, himself a nationally respected expert on the causes and treatment of violence. But the success of the program was beside the political point.

As things worsened at Roslindale, Frank Masciarelli started suspending staff, and I began getting death threats. One bizarre incident involved Steve Delancey, a sixteen-year-old Irish boy who, along with his sidekick, Joey Bruno, had been in and out of DYS institutions and detention centers since his early teens. Late one morning, Steve dropped by my office and casually mentioned that someone was going to shoot me with a rifle in the next week or two. He said a contract had been taken out on me. I laughed, but knowing Steve's occasional involvement with adults connected to mob activity, I couldn't totally dismiss his comment: "You'd best watch your step, Miller. They're gonna kill you."

After work, I strolled over to the Golden Dome, a dank bar opposite the side entrance to the statehouse. One of our staff was at a table with some friends. He was the nephew of a reputed head of New England organized crime, and he'd been referred for his job by a ranking member of the legislature. I joined him for a beer, and in the course of the conversation quietly mentioned Steve's comments about my impending demise. He looked concerned.

"Do you want me to see if it's real, Doc?"

I mumbled, "O.K.," somewhat taken aback that he might actually be able to find out such information. He excused himself from the table, went over to a pay phone in a corner of the bar, and stood there talking for at least ten minutes before he came back to the table.

"I don't think you have to worry, Doc. The guy is a small-time punk and can't deliver. Would you like to have a driver for a few weeks?"

"A what?"

"A driver, you know—someone to pick you up at the house every morning and deliver you safe to work, and take you home at night. I can arrange it for you."

I thanked him and said I wouldn't need a driver as tactfully as possible, since he had clearly made the offer out of genuine concern.

As the summer of 1971 approached, conditions at Roslindale got worse. The building was deteriorating, and we had no funds to upgrade it. If I had requested money from the legislature to build a new detention center, I could have gotten it, since they were always in the mood to build. But I thought the place was already overused, and the majority of the youngsters didn't need to be in a maximum-security building. Besides, if we built a new, larger detention center, it would shortly be filled to overflowing. What I needed was alternative placements for most of Roslindale's population. I hadn't gotten far finding them, and overcrowding was a daily crisis. For example, every time I thought things were under control, I would stop by and be appalled. The atmosphere hadn't changed much since the first day I had walked in two years before. I had made a major error in talking the Boston Legal Assistance Project into deferring a suit over conditions at Roslindale. They had trusted me to change things and didn't want to add to my burdens during our continuing crisis. But by now every visit had become an adventure, and not the kind that has a happy ending.

One night Bobby Bolster and I went out to the facility to check on things. I passed a staff member in the hallway and, coming upon a locked door, turned around to see Bobby holding the red-faced guy up against the wall by his neck as he shouted in his face and threatened to bust his guts. As I approached, he let him down. "Jerry, the son-of-a-bitch called you a Nazi." Though I was moved by Bobby's loyalty, it was clear that things were desperate at Roslindale.

The following week, while I was working late in my office, I got a call from a supervisor saying he thought Roslindale was again on the verge of riot. I called Tom Jeffers and we drove out. The place was sweltering; the boys milled shoulder to shoulder in the cramped dayrooms. Tom and I waded in, making small talk and trying to defuse the anger. Adding to the tension was the fact that a number of the youngsters had been brought in by police late in the day and hadn't been fed. Tom called a local Kentucky Fried Chicken franchise and ordered a couple hundred chicken dinners. Fried chicken was our riot-control technique for the night. It worked, but it was hardly a long-term solution.

Summer sweated on and Roslindale still had no air conditioning. We'd submitted a number of budget requests but had been turned down by the House ways and means committee. The idea of making things comfortable for delinquents apparently rubbed the members the wrong way. While they dawdled, the place got more crowded, smelly, and dangerous. We had one slight hope of solving the problem. Two years earlier Coughlan had ordered new security windows for the whole building. He wanted to upgrade security and decided to install the latest in tempered steel, the kind which were being put in the Adolescent Remand Center on Rikers Island in New York City. I didn't want any more hardware coming into Roslindale, but the windows were a jalousie type, allowing for the passage of more air than the old slant-hinged type that came with the building. The new windows finally arrived, but they were neither escape-proof nor cooling.

It had occurred to me that if we could put staff in the buildings and rooms where the inmates were kept and move inmates to those areas where the staff were ensconced, the institutions would perk up considerably. Even the most ancient institutions seemed to manage air conditioning in the administrative offices. I decided to try a variation on this theme, submitting a budget request for large window air conditioners for the Boston central office. It was quickly approved. The day the machines arrived, we hauled them off to Roslindale and installed them in the dayrooms. It was illegal, but I doubted that anyone in the legislature or the auditor's office would care to make it an issue.

Other problems seemed beyond remedy. None of the bathrooms in the institutions had stalls around the toilets, and there were no toilet seats. When I asked why inmates had no privacy, the answer was that the boys might masturbate. This seemed a curious fear. Reform school regimens were so depersonalizing, and the reform school world so unreal, that troubled youngsters routinely grounded themselves in masturbatory fantasy. But why no toilet seats? For fear a youngster might rip a seat off and use it as a weapon. Yet how many youngsters had been sent to us by the courts for ripping seats off toilets and attacking citizens with them? It was an extremely rare offense. At Roslindale, though, the staff believed in it. We had added a new twist to the delinquent repertoire, and the fact that a toilet seat attack hadn't occurred in the memory of any staff I asked was beside the point. A threatening new reality had been created.

Meanwhile, the Huntington Avenue detention facility was prematurely deinstitutionalized when a girl locked in isolation managed to set fire to her mattress. She got out of the room unharmed, but the fire spread into the hallway. The near tragedy gave me a much-needed opportunity. I called a few legislators to come out and view the fire. The press was all over the place. Two legislators were on the scene within twenty minutes. I announced to the television cameras that we were lucky to have escaped worse and that we didn't plan ever to use the facility again. The legislators nodded their approval, thereby also giving me the nod to close it.

In fact, the fire had not been very widespread. Though there was a lot of smoke, the flames were confined to a couple of rooms in the intake area. Most of the building was untouched, but no one bothered to look closely. That afternoon we bused the girls off to Roslindale before anyone could suggest we go back in and clean up the mess. The damage to the building was later estimated by the fire department at $7,500, a small price for closing Huntington Avenue. Though we had more than our share of problems integrating them into Roslindale, most of the girls eventually went into shelter care and foster arrangements. A smaller number of girls were kept in locked detention.

Progress at Last

By fall 1971, runs had subsided and staff had given up on the more blatant types of sabotage. Bill, Yitzhak, and Tom had worked hard at setting up alternatives for juveniles awaiting trial, and they had arranged faster placement of young people committed to us by the courts. They negotiated contracts with the YMCA for a camping program for detainees. By November it looked like we might be past the worst. Indeed, the whole department was looking good. The *Boston Globe* summarized things this way: "Gone for the most part are the cruelties and regimentation of the past. . . . Hope has been substituted for fear and trust for hostility. . . . Since the Spring, Youth Services institutions have been relatively calm. Boys and girls occasionally run from confinement as they have since the Lyman School first received young miscreants in 1848. But runs no longer constitute a scandal."[7] The populations of Lyman, Shirley, Lancaster, and Oakdale were at an all-time low.

The alternative programs were now having a major effect. Roslindale's population eventually dropped from a high of 250 to a routine thirty-five. It made sense. Halfway into our reforms, an important Harvard study looked closely at the reasons for admissions to Roslindale. Why were youngsters kept in this dank institution? The results were no surprise. The seriousness of the crime did not determine whether a child would be locked up. Granted, if he had killed or raped someone, he would probably be there. But there were so few such youngsters among the thousands who went through Roslindale that their numbers were statistically insignificant. Three critical reasons emerged to explain why youth were locked up in Roslindale: (1) the juvenile was black; (2) he came from a family poorer than most; and (3) there was a bed empty in detention when he was arrested. But the Harvard studies leveled an even more damning indictment.[8] Youngsters were the worse for the experience. The greatest single predictor of whether a young person would get into further serious trouble was whether or not he was detained at Roslindale at an early age. I at first assumed that this showed our success at identifying dangerous kids— the violent, the predatory, and, consequently, the recidivist delinquent. But no such neat confirmation appeared. Youths, particularly if poor or black, were detained according to the space available. Detention at Roslindale created as much crime as it deterred.

The Harvard Center for Criminal Justice assigned five researchers to study cottage units scattered throughout the reform schools, including three cottages at Shirley, two at Lancaster, four at Lyman, and a coed program at Topsfield (then called the Northeastern Regional Training Center). They spent six weeks each in participant observation, conducting interviews, and administering questionnaires to youth and staff. The researchers arranged the cottages along a custody-to-treatment continuum, from traditional reform school custodial cottages to treatment-oriented cottages. The results were encouraging. According to almost every measure, the new treatment-oriented cottages looked better. When youth were asked, "What is this place trying to do for you?" 85 percent of the youngsters in treatment cottages indicated they were in a "place that helps kids understand the things that got them in trouble," compared with a low of 11 percent of the youth in traditional custodial cottages. And almost none of the inmates in treatment saw the cottage as "a place to punish kids for the things they did wrong," compared with as much as 78 percent of the inmates in custodial cottages. Some might question whether this represents progress. Aren't we supposed to punish wrongdoers? What about personal responsibility? What about justice? These are important objections, but they weren't my first considerations as we were winding our way out of a century of destructive traditions.

The Harvard researchers also found that whatever view the staff in our treatment cottages held of the youth, whether favorable or unfavorable, was reciprocated by the youth. The differences in staff attitudes between the traditional reform school custodial cottages and the newly staffed treatment programs, however, were striking. The researchers compared our progress in creating therapeutic settings with that of the famous California Silverlake experiment of sociologists Lamar Empey and Steven Lubeck a few years earlier.[9] They had expected the Silverlake experimental group, a highly successful alternative program set up in the community, to be more community-based than either the DYS custodial or therapeutic cottages. But the results gave us cause to think we had made more progress than we'd hoped. Though our therapeutic models were new, we were making every effort to humanize the custodial cottages, which were run primarily by older line staff.

The DYS youngsters considered our cottages and staff much more helpful than did their California counterparts. For example, 84 percent of the DYS therapeutic group and 79 percent of the DYS custody group reported that staff kept them informed about what was happening in the cottage, whereas 63 percent of the California Silverlake community group and 54 percent of the California institutional group believed they were kept informed. Ninety-four percent of DYS youth in therapeutic cottages felt they shared in decision making; only 73 percent of those in the Silverlake community felt the same. Summarizing their surprising results, the Harvard researchers had this to say:

> The youth in DYS described the social climates to which they were exposed in ways that we would consider better on three of four dimensions, while the youth in the two California facilities described the social climates to which they were exposed in ways that we would consider better on one dimension. It is possible that the differences between youth responses in the two states were largely a function of the histories of reform in the two states, and that the youth were simply making comparisons to what the respective systems were like in the past. Differences in the histories of reform in the two states would lead to differences in standards by which the youth would evaluate the social climates to

which they are exposed. On the other hand, the comparison makes sense without recourse to the notion of differential standards. . . .

We noted that the data from DYS in 1970 suggested that DYS had moved more quickly to make correctional settings more humane, and then to shift the basis of control from custodial to group decision-making. In 1970, we noted, the shift to group decision-making, in a sense part of the move toward more humane settings, was ahead of the development of treatment-oriented subcultures. After the summer of 1970 there was strong and conspicuous development of positive subcultures in many of the settings where the changes in control systems had occurred.[10]

We were on the way to humanizing the reform schools. Even the custodial cottages were looking better. But despite the progress, I hadn't forgotten my fears. Our reforms were still confined to institutional grounds. They were totally vulnerable to the attitudes of the next superintendent. The idea of closing all the institutions was still with me.

The uneasiness I had felt about whether our reforms would survive the governor's election campaign was only too firmly reinforced by an incident at Lyman. Late on a Sunday afternoon I got a call from a staff member asking for advice. A cottage supervisor in some kind of personal pique had locked two boys in a caged area of the cellar under one of the cottages and had gone home with the keys. The caller was worried that in an emergency he would have no way to free the boys.

It hit me then with the full force of conviction: our months of training, meetings, and working with staff and administrators were not going to make the difference I wanted. If things could deteriorate so quickly and easily at Lyman—an institution run by humane administrators—then all of our reforms were in jeopardy. The next day I discussed my frustration with Tom Jeffers. "They're just going to wait us out, Jerry," was his assessment. We decided to close down the whole institutional system while there was still time.

It was a proof of the mettle of Tom, Bill, and Yitzhak that they had little trouble abandoning their new babies—the model educational, clinical, and therapeutic programs being installed in the institutions. The Harvard researchers had to change their strategy, too. They had hitherto concentrated on evaluating changes within the reform schools. Just as they began to generate some exciting prospects from the new institutional programs, I decided to abandon them. They quickly renamed the model therapeutic cottages "staging" cottages—places that prepared inmates for movement into the community.

IV

The Alternative System

Look for alternatives to punishments,
not only alternative punishments.

Nils Christie

12   *Deinstitutionalization*

In the 1960s, under Governor Ronald Reagan, California engaged in the nation's first massive deinstitutionalization of patients from state mental hospitals. It was one of the few experiments where state hospital budgets were actually lowered as patients left the grounds, and its purpose was to demonstrate deinstitutionalization as a money-saving procedure. But even the conservative governor seemed unable to take on the interests which sustain state institutions. Instead, he got the worst of both worlds. The dollars "saved" never quite made it to the community, and by 1988 California was expanding old mental hospitals and building new ones. Between 1984 and 1988 seven new mental hospitals opened.[1] Much the same thing happened to more liberal state administrations which had deinstitutionalized mental health patients. Though the patients left, the monies stayed on the hospital grounds.

In the late 1970s, as special assistant for community-based programs to Pennsylvania's governor, Milton Shapp, I had the matter brought home to me in graphic terms. There stood Frank Beal, head of the state's human services, with his X-graph outlining progress in the deinstitutionalization of state hospitals over a decade. As one moved across the graph, the line representing the number of patients in state hospitals dropped dramatically, while the line signifying the number of employees on state hospital grounds surged to create an X. The graph suggested that sometime in the next century 65,000 state employees would be caring for one patient. As bizarre as this sounds, it was not entirely unlike what had happened when we closed the Massachusetts reform schools.

A study commissioned by then city councilwoman Carol Bellamy showed that, as thousands of patients were dumped from New York mental hospitals into flophouses and welfare hotels, the budgets of the state institutions increased. To fund community-based alternatives the state had to find new sources of revenue. Once again, institutional dollars did not follow the inmates to the community. Such dollars carry too much political weight to be shifted.

In this light, the question that dogged our Massachusetts deinstitutionalization, "Where will you put all the inmates?" is deceptively simple and begs the more important prior question: "Can you transfer budgets from the institution to the alternative programs in proportion to the number of inmates leaving the institutional grounds?" This issue is universally ignored in professional discussions of deinstitutionalization.[2] Only meager resources are made available to inmates sent into the community, and deinstitutionalization survives only insofar as institutional budgets don't suffer. Community-based programs are tied to whatever funds inadvertently drop from the institutional table. The institutions march on, firmly fixed in the budgetary traditions of state government.

The test for successful deinstitutionalization is this: every dollar attached to an inmate should follow that inmate into the community for at least as long as he or she would have been institutionalized. This principle requires confronting political alliances which, though they have little to do with the stated purposes of an institution in fact sustain it. It also involves a reallocation of funds from rural to urban areas.

Whatever the reasons for funding them, state institutions' continued existence is unrelated to any help, rehabilitation, or therapy they ostensibly dispense. Politics holds sway. Planning alternatives is much less difficult than dealing with the sticky politics of institutions, which must be confronted before alternatives can be addressed. But institutional politics is characterized by such Byzantine infighting that the average helping professional soon loses either direction or integrity. Few professional models for deinstitutionalization have succeeded. Those done by the book have been disastrous.

The deinstitutionalization movement in the United States was put together primarily by helping professionals—psychiatrists, psychologists, and social workers. They were clinically oriented and often ignored the political realities which undergird institutions, and they proceeded on the premise that if correct clinical decisions were made and proper community organization accomplished, the rest would take care of itself. It was a naive assumption; as a result the national deinstitutionalization movement was set on its way in a political vacuum.

As early as 1976, when it was clear that most mental hospital deinstitutionalization had become an exercise in dumping, the authoritative monograph on deinstitutionalization written for the National Institutes of Mental Health gave only a brief glance at the politics behind the fiasco. Rather, the focus was on such matters as selection of patients for community care, treatment course of patients in the community, and community resistance to patients, as though these issues were crucial to deinstitutionalization. By 1984, a special task force of the American Psychiatric Association was calling deinstitutionalization of the mentally ill "a major societal tragedy, creating a new class of society's untouchables, who wander the streets without treatment." Four years later, the editor of the task force report had become a leader in the movement for reinstitutionalization—the return of patients to state institutions posited on the belief "that the mentally ill have a right to involuntary treatment"— surely a milestone in the history of civil rights! Even more recently, we have seen our "drug czar" call for a return to orphanages.

There were exceptions. Analysts from Syracuse University's Center for Human Policy, for example, were among the few who recognized the central issues associated with deinstitutionalization, pointing to such bars to substantive change as economics and professionalism.

> Institutionalization is big business. . . . Many professionals . . . think in terms of categories and segregated services. This is the way they have been taught to diagnose and prescribe. Thus, they may not have the philosophy or the skills needed to meet the requirements of conversion (deinstitutionalization). Retraining can provide only a partial remedy; professionals do not change easily. . . . There is the brick-and-mortar, formal organization of the professions—physical and organizational elements that stand as defenses against the onslaught of change.[3]

Planning for Reorganization

In February 1971, we announced plans to implement fully the reorganization of the Massachusetts Department of Youth Services. Crucial to this was the use of Federal Law Enforcement Assistance Administration funds. Indications were that, with aggressive work, we could obtain about ten million dollars over a four-year period. To get the funds, we had to provide a 25 percent match from state resources. This involved in kind contributions of state services during the first year and about two million dollars of state funds allocated over the remaining three years. I outlined our plans to reallocate existing staff and budget, rather than requesting large amounts of additional funding.

We wanted to establish seven regional offices (based on the mental health department's regions), citing the need to establish administrative control over parole agents who worked out of their homes without supervision or secretarial help. We also committed DYS to a community-based system of halfway houses. We planned for seven such units in 1971 and an additional five in 1972. As we stated:

> The mode which we feel the Department can use best for treatment of adjudicated delinquents is that of the "community-based correctional treatment center." It consists of small residential units working with youth from a given Metropolitan area or community. There would be approximately eight to ten young people in each treatment unit. The young people would know that they would spend three to four months in the unit, then the group would be discharged, provided their adjustment warranted it. While in the treatment unit, the young people would progress through various phases. For example, the first month the group would be restricted to the house, second month some movement outside the house, third month a curfew, with more relative freedom to be in the community. There would be a heavy emphasis placed upon intensive group work and psychiatric consultation. To the degree possible, local services, schools, job placements, clinics, will be utilized. During their stay in the center the group would be responsible for such activities as preparing menus and meals within established budget guidelines. In a variety of ways, the total program will be in contradistinction to large institutional models which foster dependency in the students. The model the Department is developing will, in fact, force the group to deal with the very real day to day type problems that face all of us. As the group progresses, time will be spent with the families, schools, etc., to assist the young people in moving back into full participation with the community.[4]

We also announced other initiatives: to establish several small sheltered care facilities to keep the Roslindale detention population down and to fund privately run group homes for seven to eleven year-olds in our institutions. We also proposed construction of a small intensive security unit on the grounds of a medical school in Worcester to deal with grossly disturbed young delinquents. All but the last proposal became realities, though we later abandoned the idea of state-operated halfway houses in favor of privately run facilities.

As the first step, we contracted with a psychological consulting group for complete assessments of each of the youngsters in our institutions, with the purpose of developing an alternative program for each youth. The approach was traditional and included rehabilitation and vocational assessment, psychological testing, psychodiagnostic assessment, and neurological testing. Each evaluation took six to seven hours. Approximately five hundred youngsters were evaluated for possible placement at home or in a community alternative. Though I hoped these evaluations would help us avoid gross errors in placement, I didn't have many expectations beyond that, as the intrinsic merit of psychiatric and psychological evaluations of delinquents has always been questionable. Though the traditional psychological evaluations didn't hurt us or slow the deinstitutionalization, I would have made a serious mistake in relying solely on them. The tests were routine at the time and included the Peabody Picture Inventory (IQ estimate), the Geist Vocational test, the Jesness Personality Inventory, the Bender-Gestalt (indirect test for neurological dysfunction), figure drawing, and comprehensive background interview.

Our stance was summarized by a legislative investigative committee: "The Department does not tell the (psychologists) why a child is being evaluated. This discretion is maintained so that the testing psychologists will not be prejudiced in their evaluations or recommendations. This lack of prejudice means that tests will be more comprehensive, and psychologists will not be tempted to 'prove' through testing that one certain treatment alternative is best for the child."[5] As it turned out, the psychologists concluded that no more than a couple dozen of the institutionalized youth needed to be confined in strictly secure settings. On the basis of my later experiences in Pennsylvania, I now believe the recommendation had less to do with the psychological tests than with the fact that we'd made the psychologists aware of the wide range of alternative treatment and supervisory/monitoring programs we planned to fund. My suspicions were confirmed by later research.[6]

I saw the evaluations as providing a "cover" and professional gloss.

If there were incidents involving the youngsters we had removed from institutions, we couldn't be accused of not trying our best to evaluate each youngster professionally before placement. Community-based programs are unusually vulnerable to the anomalous incident, whereas the same harsh judgments are seldom applied to institutions. They are guiltless if an alumnus commits a crime after having been duly punished. But the first youngster in a halfway house, out on parole, or in an alternative program who commits a serious crime can seriously damage a deinstitutionalization effort. I had prepared myself for the all-too-possible backlash by compiling a portfolio of statistics and horror stories about well-known graduates of our reform schools who had served lengthy sentences. Should the need arise, I was ready to match every violent crime by a deinstitutionalized youngster with a more heinous offense by a youth who had done time in a reform school.

Shortly after I took over DYS, a seventeen-year-old shot a policeman. The headlines in the Boston newspapers blared "Youth Kills Policeman." The teenager had been released from the IJG after serving three years in various DYS institutions. The killing was the kind of tragic incident which would normally put a juvenile correctional agency on the spot. But though the press articles mentioned that the boy had been at the IJG, not much else was said. I braced myself for the inevitable telephone calls from reporters and local television stations, the critical editorials, the hard questions as to what had gone wrong in our treatment of this young man. But there was only one call, and the reporter wanted to know only how long the boy had been with us. He had served his full time and was not released early. No one seemed concerned that he was an IJG alumnus. I concluded it was because we'd been properly punitive. This adolescent, sent to us for car theft, had become an institutional management problem. We had dealt firmly with him and given him discipline to rival the stuff of the strongest speeches. If this delinquent got in further trouble, the fault must lie with him.

But if this boy had been in an alternative program, even for a few days, and then killed a policeman, our department would have been held totally responsible. Cries of "Permissiveness" would have drowned out all rational accounts. But the more basic question went unasked. How could we have taken in an adolescent in his midteens for car theft and after three years in our institutions have sent him out to murder a policeman? Hadn't we made him more dangerous?

The psychological evaluations gave each youngster the luxury of having qualified professionals spend hours thinking over his or her case. That was something new for our inmates, and it probably flattered most of them. If nothing else, we might get a placebo or Hawthorne effect—the attention being therapeutic in itself. I don't mean to imply that thoughtful evaluation isn't necessary to a proper deinstitutionalization strategy. It clearly is. But traditional evaluations are seldom helpful in planning deinstitutionalization. They are even less helpful when the inmates are young offenders easily classified in those more hurtful categories which fall toward the so-called characterological end of psychiatric and psychological nosology.[7]

Certain youngsters are at more risk for repeating their delinquencies. If one bases the estimate of risk on a youth's previous record, particularly offenses characterized by gratuitous violence, that is enough legally to justify intensive supervision. But even then the assessment is less the decisive factor than the alternatives available to supervise, assist, monitor, and negotiate. Unfortunately, when we were ready to move kids out of institutions, few diagnostic regimens were fit for the kinds of alternatives taking shape in our thinking.

Then another curious thing happened. As soon as the psychologists began showing up at the institutions, incidents began to increase. Slow, methodical evaluation wasn't feasible when the very process of evaluating youngsters individually hastened the deterioration of the institutions. As we judged each youth's suitability for alternatives, we were in a race with institutional staff, administrators, and local legislators who worked just as assiduously to stop us. The longer the evaluations dragged on, the more unstable the institutions would become. We went in on a crash basis, working nearly around the clock, interviewing kids into the night and over weekends, and placing youngsters outside of the institutions as soon as each evaluation was completed. By quickening the pace, we kept ahead of the increased intake from the courts, and the institutional populations continued to fall.

Budget Politics

Having gotten budget approval in both houses of the legislature for our first community-based programs, I waited for the final version of the budget to come back from conference committee. Early one evening, as

I headed across the parking lot behind the statehouse, I saw the chief aide to Senator James Kelly, the chairman of the senate ways and means committee, walking down Beacon Street carrying a huge sheaf of papers. I commented on his heavy load. He replied, "It's the new budget." It had just been approved by the conference committee, and he was taking it over to the printer. I said I was pleased to see it, since our first community-based budget was in it. He replied, "I don't think it's there." I said, "But it must be. Senator Kelly gave me his word." The aide laid the bulky tome across the hood of a car and thumbed his way to the DYS budget. Seven hundred thousand dollars had vanished. I was livid. It meant that when the federal funds gave out, we would have serious problems paying our bills for the new group homes. Why had the budget item vanished?

A few weeks before, I'd been asked by a legislator on the conference committee to fire an employee who'd been referred by one of his political rivals. I hadn't done it, and now I assumed that the legislator had taken his revenge by making our community-based budget disappear. Senator Kelly's aide took the budget book back across the street, and the $700,000 reappeared the next morning, clearly added with a different typewriter. Senator Kelly had honored his commitment. Thanks to him, we got the group homes which, but for a chance meeting in a parking lot, would have been lost for the year.

Though by now we'd decided we might be able to close all the reform schools, we didn't have enough money to do it. I'd gotten some new line items through the legislature, but these hadn't yet threatened the institutional budgets, to which the legislature remained tied. Indeed, in May 1972, after we had closed all but one reform school and had placed all the inmates in the community, the legislature still refused to allow us to transfer money from the institutional budgets to a community-based budget. They fully funded the salaries of those institutional staff who remained on the grounds of the empty reform schools.

Our LEAA funds were short-term and could only buy us time. They could provide a financial cushion as we moved the remaining reform school inmates out, but there wouldn't be enough funding to cover the former inmates for more than a few months—and nothing to handle the new intake. During the breathing space provided by federal funding we'd have to build our alternative system into the state budgetary traditions. Short of some windfall in state revenues, there was no way to accomplish this through normal channels. To succeed in our deinstitutionalization, we'd have to take the money from the institutional budgets, and that was like a declaration of war.

The state's fiscal policies, bent on sustaining legislative control over jobs, worked against change. The legislature assigned monies to each specific budget category—personnel, travel, operations, and so forth. The DYS budget was tailored to fit institutional needs. Certain amounts were set aside for food, staff, utilities, maintenance, and the other specifics necessary to a smoothly running institution. Transferring money from one account to another involved an extremely complex series of special approvals and waivers. Everyone got an oar in— administration and finance, the personnel office, the comptroller's office, and various legislative committee members. I had almost no power to transfer old funds to new programs. I had no authority to transfer any staff person without special approval from a variety of statehouse bureaucrats and politicians, many of whom were friends or patrons of the very staff members with whom I was trying to deal.

With LEAA funding I began hiring 03s—the state budget category for consultants—to help plot out directions for the department. In doing this I managed to avoid both civil service complications and legislative interference by hiring individuals first and then creating their roles. If I had tried to get legislative approval for a new state-funded staff position before the fact, the sharks would have circled for a piece of the kill. In that case the new person would probably not be someone I needed or wanted. If I didn't hire someone referred by a legislator, it was likely to be taken as both an insult and a reason to come after whatever reform the new position represented. But through the 03 account I was able to hire most of my team.

We set up a planning unit and I hired Arnold Schucter, a thoughtful and aggressive human service planner. Arnold was exactly what we needed at the time. I could roll out an idea in the morning, and by late the same day he would have it in a formal proposal, with citations from the literature. Arnold had his own connections on Beacon Hill, primarily with Al Kramer, an aide to the governor. I always had the impression that I was eminently expendable in Arnold's eyes. Indeed, he had on occasion told his staff so. I never expected or demanded Arnold's loyalty, but at least we were headed in the same direction.

Late in my administration, Arnold wrote a planning document which a postaudit committee happened to find. It gave them the great "Aha!" which proved I was on some sort of anarchist mission. They quoted from Arnold's paper, "One of the great challenges to our society in the remainder of the 20th century is to dismantle state government agency by agency, and distribute the responsibility and financial resources to new mechanisms for the organization and delivery of human services."[8] It still makes sense to me.

I used the 03s in a variety of ways. Formal job titles and classifications meant very little. I wanted to use talents and assign tasks as necessary. I had a person in a janitor's position, Paul DeMuro, running Shirley, an architect handling public information, and a couple of bright Princeton grads doing planning for the department while working out of CETA positions at minimum wage. Mine was not an approach which would endear me to state government.

But state government responds to certain kinds of pressure, even when artificially generated. If I could depopulate the institutions by creating sufficient alternatives for those youngsters we moved out, and if I could keep them in the community long enough, there was at least a chance of tearing something loose from the budgets of the empty institutions. This would cripple the institutions. But it would also make returning young people from the community to the institutions more difficult. It was a risky strategy, but ultimately it worked. I followed an axiom I'd learned in the military—it's easier to seek forgiveness than permission. That attitude greatly upset a hostile postaudit committee of the legislature, which was formed too late to stop us. The committee reported:

> It was the preconceived idea of DYS that, once the group home program had been instituted with federal funds, state funding could, of necessity, be obtained even though approval for the closing of institutions and the transition to group home care had never been sought from the Legislature by DYS. It was the intention of DYS, likewise, that state funds, which had been appropriated for personnel at the various departmental institutions, would be used for group home payments once the institutions were closed and the services of those employees were terminated. This indicated a total unfamiliarity by the DYS hierarchy with the laws of the Commonwealth relative to appropriations, personnel, and civil service.[9]

It's a good description of what we did. Contrary to the committee's conclusion, however, I knew the laws of the commonwealth reasonably well. But I'd also been reluctantly educated in the traditional politics of the Massachusetts legislature. Had I done it the way the committee wanted, no institutions would have been closed and no alternatives begun.

At first I tried to get approval from the governor's department of administration and finance to tap the institutional budgets to fund community programs. I thought we could effect savings of a few million dollars in operating costs and so wouldn't have to request new community-based monies from the legislature. Though I didn't see deinstitutionalization as cheaper, I hoped our proposal would sweeten the pot. Instead, it had virtually no effect. There was no interest in saving money. There was, however, near panic that I might get discretionary control of the institutional budgets. I should have anticipated the negative reaction on the basis of an earlier meeting with house ways and means committee members regarding capital outlay, where I had returned five million dollars the legislature had previously approved to spend for new buildings on institutional grounds. My action had been met with disbelief and anger.

Our strategy of using federal funds to move youngsters into the community eventually paid off. By keeping the institutions empty, we made it politically risky for local legislators to tout continued funding and staffing of their favorite institutions. At times I thought we would be criticized by the legislature for running fully staffed institutions with almost no inmates, but apparently that could have gone on indefinitely. I had no authority to transfer staff members. Unless they volunteered for a community-based assignment, they could stay at the empty institutions as long as they liked, and most did. I've since concluded that a fully staffed institution with no inmates can be a rather nice place. Meals are served on time, the grass is well cut, the flowerbeds are maintained, the floors are buffed, and the bucolic atmosphere is left undisturbed.

But something had to give. Unless we could claim institutional staffs and budgets for alternatives, our community-based strategy would founder. If we ran out of funding, I resolved to send youngsters directly home rather than return them to institutions. I hoped the legislature would give in before I had to do that. We rode the edge of that crisis for a few months, from time to time paroling juveniles home within days after the courts had sent them to us.

The problems associated with tapping institutional budgets were skirted when Speaker David Bartley put in a substantial additional community-based budget for us. Bartley, a decent and practical man, placated the legislature while continuing his strong support for our initiatives. But it simply postponed the day of reckoning.

One of our first attempts to use institutional resources for alternative programs came in late summer 1971. We'd found a relatively obscure paragraph in our legislation which stated: "When funds are available for the purpose the Commissioner of Youth Services may . . . establish, on land under the control of the Department of Natural Resources, or upon other sites approved by the Commissioner of natural resources, forest or farm school camps to which children placed in the care of the Department of Youth Services may be sent."[10] The governing phrase was "available for the purpose." We had no specific funding for a new forestry camp. If I could attach an alternative program to an existing budget, however, I could probably stretch the meaning of the legislation to cover it. I decided to create an annex to the Shirley Industrial School and the Westfield Detention Center, which became the Middlefield Forestry Camp. Funds to support it came from institutional budgets. It provided a short outdoor experience for some of the seven to twelve-year-olds from John Augustus Hall. We knew it would have a limited lifespan, but it opened new opportunities.

Our biggest break emerged from a series of stormy negotiations with the Department of Administration and Finance. I was reluctantly given permission to freeze vacated positions of institutional staff who retired or resigned and to transfer the monies attached to the empty slots from personnel to purchase-of-care accounts, so that every time an employee left, our dollars for community options were increased by the amount of his or her salary. Since the annual turnover rate in the department had reached nearly 20 percent, and personnel was the largest item in the institutional budgets, the new policy had the potential to provide significant funding for our fledgling community-based system.

We identified other sources of federal funding, for example, Title IV-A. This legislation wasn't specifically meant for delinquent youngsters, but rather for services to children of the poor. I saw it as a potential source of funding for our community-based alternative programs. Using the Title IV-A measures, we evaluated the young people in our institutions and found that 80 to 90 percent were at or below the poverty level and technically qualified for Title IV-A funding. Although the Title IV-A legislation specifically forbade funding children in institutions, as soon as we put our youth in community alternatives, we qualified them. It was probably outside the intent of the Congress, but it seemed technically legal. The question whether the state wished to use its limited Title IV-A federal funds for our delinquents was another matter. It didn't. It wanted to use them for more "deserving" youth populations (child welfare and school problems). But we had created a situation where the state had little choice, and we got the money. By the time the federal government objected a year later, it was too late. We were in the community and no longer needed Title IV-A funds.

State-Run or Privately Run?

One of our problems was that we had only a limited conception of what we needed to replace the institutions. Where would we send the reform school alumni? Could most go home? If they did, what other services would they need? How would we fund the alternatives? And, perhaps the most crucial question of all, Who should run them?

At first we had only one alternative in mind, the halfway house. I chose this model not because I was that conversant with it but because it was the alternative which had been touted by the late Robert Kennedy. I tried to weave his comments into my speeches around the state and into my testimony before legislative committees. I thought the Kennedy support of halfway houses might make our proposals more palatable, coming as they did from a native son rather than an outsider.

The department planned to staff and run its own halfway houses. The fact that the houses were state-staffed and state-run might make it easier to get them into the community. We'd also be more likely to get the support of the legislature if we expanded the number of state employees to embrace community programs. We would retrain institutional staff and assign them to state-run halfway houses. It was a naive plan, and if we had gone the route of relying on state-staffed and state-run alternatives, our reforms would have been dead in the water.

There were certainly alternatives to the halfway house. Joe Leavey educated me to one, the group home. Its concept derived from child welfare rather than corrections. The idea embodied what I'd been trying to get across about the youngsters in our reform schools—that it would be more productive to see them as adolescents in need of caring supervision than as delinquents suited for incarceration.

Group homes presented a whole new set of possibilities. As distinct from correctional halfway houses, group homes were developed for dependent and neglected children, and they were privately contracted, nonprofit facilities. None was staffed by state employees. As our emphasis shifted from state-run halfway houses to privately run group homes, purchase of care became our focus. We asked private agencies to develop programs for the youngsters in our reform schools and detention centers, and we sought out small, noninstitutional, individualized programs for the damaged youngsters in our care. This was entirely new for a state juvenile correctional agency at the time, at least on the scale we envisioned. But we also wanted nonresidential ideas.

We circulated statewide a request for proposals to create alternative residential and nonresidential programs for reform school youth. We asked nonprofit agencies to submit proposals along with cost estimates. We didn't specify any single treatment method, since I believed that a variety of options would enhance our ability to meet the needs of the youngsters, who didn't all come from the same mold. The response was overwhelming. We were inundated with proposals from child care agencies, universities, art schools, YMCA's, private and religious charities, psychiatric and drug treatment programs. We welcomed them all. If the institutional budgets could have been freed, we would have had hundreds of people interested in working with our reform school youth. Our request for proposals had opened doors kept closed for a century. It was a lesson as appropriate for mental health, retardation, children's services, and adult corrections as it was for our department. Most states have still not learned it.

We asked the private agencies to do something other than re-create traditional correctional ideology in the community. We wanted the full range of youth services which we, as a state youth corrections agency, had never given. We would judge performance strictly, but our measure wouldn't be control or efficient management alone. Rather, we would look to the ability of the program to individualize treatment and to provide unconditional care for each youngster. Fear of recidivism was not what was driving me, because I knew we couldn't do much worse than we had. If we failed to lower recidivism, we would at least fail showing our best, not our worst.

As programs took shape, we had serious problems in monitoring their performance, but what we lost in adequate management, we gained in creativity. It's not that one can't have both good management and creative programs. Over the past two decades, however, as I have watched the creation of many inauthentic and destructive community-based programs nationally, I've become convinced that there is an inverse ratio between primary emphasis on management and the program quality. I think it has to do with the captive status of the clientele. Captive, delinquent young people are not easily managed without suffering.

We found ourselves breaking new ground almost daily. There were no mechanisms in Massachusetts government for setting daily rates or per diem payments to specific contracted programs. There was no rate setting commission (that came later). Though we eventually got the Department of Administration and Finance to agree on the funding mechanisms, we had to devise our own crude rate-setting procedures as we went along. We used a simple formula, dividing the projected annual budget by the number of youngsters the program intended to serve daily to establish the per diem rate. With large established agencies, we set per diem rates with payment to follow as youths were placed. For small new agencies, we used LEAA monies for start-up grants. Funds were often insufficient, and our problems were exacerbated by a state bureaucracy that didn't always honor its commitments to us. The state was also slow in paying its bills, and the same cash-flow problems continue to plague state-funded child care and contracted mental health agencies in most states today, because community-based programs are seldom fixed in state budgetary mechanisms. This is in contrast to state institutions, where the money comes in regularly, on time, and, given their questionable results, too abundantly.

Our tardiness in paying bills was a particular hardship on the smaller new agencies which, deprived of sufficient start-up funds, found themselves with a cash-flow crisis in caring for youngsters they had already accepted. Some agencies took out bank loans with our letter of intent as collateral. Others teetered on bankruptcy. I was soon acting out a monthly charade—blustering around the offices of the Department of Administration and Finance, threatening to blast it in press conferences, to call in the governor, to resign. The tirades would usually free a particular check and stem an agency's crisis for a month or so, but it was no way to run an agency.

As things got more desperate, we resorted to less traditional ways of honoring our commitments. Gardner Jackson (whom we'd hired to take on the thankless task of keeping our finances straight) and Joe Leavey came up with a new strategy. The defunct YSB had a board and allowance account which occasionally allowed a youngster a few dollars upon release from a reform school. This account remained in place when the new DYS was created. We also had tacit authority to transfer other department monies into this account. Though the account had seldom been tapped for more than three or four hundred dollars a year, we realized it had potential. To help the account realize its potential (and keep the agencies afloat), we had kids from group homes come into the central office along with staff members. We wrote individual board and allowance checks to each youngster who, in our presence, would endorse his or her check over to a group home staff person. Through this means, payroll was met, food purchased, and electric bills paid. It was an unusual procedure, but it worked for those frantic weeks while we ran from state office to state office trying to find a smoother way to generate checks for the emerging community-based system. Within a few weeks, the board and allowance account grew from a few hundred dollars to a quarter million.

We made errors of judgment in deciding which community-based programs to fund. Some didn't work out at all; some were incompetent; a few were dishonest. I expected that at least 20 percent of them would fail for one reason or another and the contracts would be terminated. Theoretically, this would free the same percentage of our annual purchase-of-care budget for other programs and approaches. It would make the system more competitive, ensuring that the state's money went to the most productive, and it was really a rather conservative approach. But we found ourselves supporting programs which were on the edge financially and all too often had limited administrative and fiscal resources to manage their money. Sometimes they worked out, and new agencies, embodying new concepts, were created and thrived. An example was the Key program, which started with half a dozen youngsters and grew to be a national model, providing quality community supervision to hundreds. Other agencies didn't fare so well and eventually folded. This was a major criticism of the postaudit committee, which pursued me after I had left the state. I saw the fact that a certain percentage of community-based programs closed down after a year or so as a measure of our accountability.

Staff Resistance

Recognizing that state institutions exist as much to dole out state jobs as to provide care was essential to reducing staff resistance to closing them. Joe Correia, the union representative, became our director of personnel. He worked long hours meeting with staff supervisors, cottage parents, and stewards, reassuring them that their jobs were not in jeopardy and discussing opportunities for them in the new community-based system. In many ways the new system was more attractive. It would be safer and more interesting work than sitting in an institutional cottage facing thirty or forty hostile teenage delinquents. But it was difficult for most staff to make the transition from the familiar to the unknown. Though many institutional staff continued to go to work every day (waiting for the inmates to return), as our contracting with private agencies grew, staff warmed more to the idea of reassignment to alternatives. We arranged for some state employees to work for private, nonprofit agencies while retaining civil service status and benefits. Through this mechanism we lowered per diem payments to the private agency in proportion to the number of state staff it absorbed. But most alternative programs didn't want our staff, preferring to screen and hire their own employees.

At one point we offered employees the option of taking a youngster home as their full-time job. They could collect their full salary and retain their state benefits. We had only a couple of takers. Our employees tended to be older, and the changes we wanted went beyond simply learning new management techniques. We wanted staff to become advocates, to question their own motives, and to hold themselves accountable for services to the youth in their care. Many of our employees could not have done this even if they had wanted to.

The Press

I worked continually to build public support for my program through favorable presentation in the press. It was simpler than many might think. The key was to make the routine goings-on of reform school life a matter of public record and to begin to chip away at the stereotypes most citizens had of reform school inmates. I made it department policy that any member of the press could have access to any building, room, annex, or facility of DYS and could talk with any youngster, provided the kid consented. There were no restrictions on visiting hours. Reporters would be welcome at any reasonable hour. Lengthy stories about our problems and individual kids in our care began to appear in local papers. By opening the doors we were less prone to "attack journalism." Facts kept intruding to neutralize other agendas.

Early in my administration, Adam Yarmolinsky had introduced me to Tom Winship, editor of the *Boston Globe*, and I made it a practice to meet periodically with the editors, usually bringing along a couple of ex-inmates to answer any questions. When we had incidents—fires, escapes, talk of riots, and rumors of rape—I invited the press to meet with those involved. When escapees returned, I asked reporters to sit with them and try to find out why they had run and often, who had assisted them. Ernie Posey was a good case in point.

I had been hearing rumors that staff at Roslindale had resumed beating inmates, so I mentioned it to the superintendent, but he couldn't nail down anything specific. Staff denied any problems, as did inmates. The rumors were second- and third-hand, usually from kids who had left Roslindale and occasionally stopped by the central office to chat. I needed some help chasing down the rumors. Ernie Posey, a Harvard undergraduate associated with Phillips Brooks House, had stopped by my office to volunteer his services. Ernie, who was twenty, looked about sixteen. I proposed that he volunteer to be admitted to Roslindale as a delinquent and spend a few days there. He agreed. We made up a phony admission order and delivered Ernie to Roslindale in handcuffs over a holiday weekend. He spent four days there.

During his short stay, Ernie watched while a staff member held a twelve-year-old's head under water in the toilet. A fourteen-year-old was dragged by the legs over a urine-soaked floor, his T-shirted chest used as a mop. Other boys were beaten, hit about the face, and carried off to isolation. Ernie himself was hit in the face for reading a book "in an unauthorized area." I suspended the staff involved for a few days, but civil service procedures didn't allow me to do much more than that. I also gave Ernie's report to the *Boston Globe*. It provided much-needed information to the general public.

Probably the greatest benefit we got from welcoming the press was the dilution of public stereotypes. Clearly no one wants a thief, an armed robber, a mugger, a chronic incorrigible, or an otherwise disturbed delinquent running loose in the community. If our deinstitutionalization was going to work, we had to flesh out the definitions of *delinquent*. We didn't have to distort, hide, or otherwise dissemble about the kids' crimes. The public needed to know more, not less, about the youngsters in our care.

Confidentiality in juvenile justice, more often than not, works against the best interests of juveniles and ill informs the public. The idea of making juvenile records public is nothing new. Prosecutors and police routinely call for juvenile court records to be dragged out before judges and juries in adult courts. What's wanted then, of course, is a history of offenses. But that's not enough. We insisted that people know more than that. If the public was to avoid stereotyping, they needed to know a young offender's accomplishments, background, and family disasters. They also needed to be made aware of the record of the child welfare and education systems and of alternatives previously made available in each youngster's life. Unfortunately, this seldom happens. It's easier to tear a young offender from his or her moorings, particularly if we're bent on punishment. I hoped we could break into this conspiracy of ignorance. We would insist that the public see, hear, and know our youngsters.

It was another variation on Mead's insight that the more one knows another, the more difficult it is to be punitive. We would show youngsters' faces, tell their stories, reveal their secrets (often of their own abuse), and lay out the uncomfortable meaning of their lives—all hitherto forbidden under the guise of protecting children's rights. The average citizen can be unusually forgiving, even of the chronic delinquent, when given an opportunity to know the young offender behind the narrow legal label. The more we confine young offenders to their legal definitions, the more understanding is impoverished and treatment warped. In this narrow context, reform schools make sense. They are indeed designed for thieves, robbers, and assaulters. Institutionalization confirms the label. It's one reason why so few middle-class youngsters end up in reform schools.

Judges, police, prosecutors, and probation officers usually realize that there is more to the average middle-class delinquent than the crime alone suggests, even when it is a heinous crime. Because this teenager is more apt to resemble their own brother, son, sister, or daughter, they tend not to institutionalize the middle-class offender. History, personal accomplishments, school associations, friends, sports interests, health problems, and psychological trauma all become intensely relevant. The offender's role is stretched enough to give the definers a personal frame of reference. They don't have to be imaginative to be just. The label "delinquent" loses some of its hold.

I usually took youngsters with me wherever I went to speak—on television shows, radio talk shows, PTA meetings, Kiwanis, Rotary, Lions,

League of Women Voters, Unitarian Universalist seminars, and Holy Name Society breakfasts. I'd stop by the reform school or detention center nearest wherever I was scheduled to speak and pick two or three youth at random. I didn't screen youth for their opinions, trusting that, given the chance to talk about their situation, they would come through. Though I usually brought along a black youngster or two, I also, very deliberately, chose one boy or girl who looked as if he or she might be from a suburban white high school. It stimulated the compassionate juices of the mostly white middle-class audiences, who might otherwise ignore the possibility that their own children could land in reform school.

Occasionally staff would handpick inmates who were known escape risks and have them waiting in the front office to accompany me. Apparently they hoped for an embarrassing incident.

One of our most ambitious attempts to undo stereotypes came in June 1971. One of the few decent things at Shirley was the food service program. The dining hall chef, Nick Hidriotis, was an unusually committed and kind man who took pride in helping boys assigned to his kitchen to learn the restaurant trade. Though only a few of these inmates went on to use these skills in running restaurants, Nick's kitchen was an island of concern in an otherwise empty institutional existence. We decided the best service we could do Nick and the program would be to bring them into the legislature. But instead of using the occasion to showcase an institutional program, we took the opportunity to show off the dozen or so boys. The idea grew, and we ended up bringing in approximately fifty youngsters from the various institutions for a lobbying day in the legislature.

Nick's boys served a free buffet luncheon in the state house for a hundred legislators and four hundred state employees. Each reform school boy and girl wore a badge with the name and district of his or her state representative. After lunch, they visited their legislators' offices to talk about themselves and their situations. It was particularly educational for those lawmakers who were wont to make speeches about hardened young offenders in need of harsher incarceration. For a few hours, at least, they shut up. Particularly compelling were the eleven and twelve-year-olds from John Augustus Hall. We lost three or four kids that day—the possibilities of the situation were too much for them to resist. But they soon came back. The legislative day was a great success.

Slowing Down

We had vacated Bridgewater's Institute for Juvenile Guidance in September 1970 with no incidents in the community, no angry speeches in the legislature, no marches, no threats, and no staff sabotage. Within its own limited terms, it was a success. At the time, the fact that we had so few community resources and almost no provision for long-term aftercare hadn't been a major consideration. The bulk of the IJG boys were approaching their seventeenth birthdays and would shortly become adults by law. They wouldn't be our legal responsibility. At seventeen a young offender was no longer subject to DYS unless we chose to keep him or her under our supervision until age twenty-one. The old YSB had hung on to no more than two or three cases a year, so we took it as a given that our responsibility for the inmates would end when they turned seventeen. Since most of the IJG boys were well over sixteen, we wouldn't have to supervise them in the community for very long. It was a narrow, callous view, and it would have been entirely proper to institute long-term aftercare past age seventeen. But given that all we had for care were reform schools, and they probably did at least as much harm as good, there was a valid counterargument for our getting out of these adolescents' lives as quickly and completely as possible.

So, despite the smoothness of the process, the IJG deinstitutionalization was hardly a model. The methods we used to classify the IJG inmates were likely to backfire if we used them in closing other institutions. This wasn't because the IJG evaluations weren't as reliable as any, even though in most cases they rested on a congeries of unscientific impressions and gut reactions. But they were demonstrably unprofessional and would have been hard to defend if one of the youngsters had committed a serious crime upon his release. Even though things went smoothly, I wasn't sure it had been more than a happy accident. I decided to move more deliberately the next time, through some consensus building of employees, administrators, local communities, and legislators.

The legislature's Joint Committee on Post-Audit and Oversight understood what I had been up to at the IJG and correctly identified the problems associated with our later, consensus-building approach to deinstitutionalization:

> The closing of the Institute for Juvenile Guidance at Bridgewater in September, 1970 provided DYS administration with a future direction in which to aim its as yet unsubstantiated rehabilitative goals. . . .

Shortly thereafter, the Industrial School for Boys at Shirley was selected as the second target in the dismantling of an institutionalized system which had been in operation for over one hundred and twenty years. . . . An attempt was made during the first three months of 1971 to close Shirley, through the gradual removal of all of its inmates. This attempt was unsuccessful and was accompanied by a large number of escapes (68), staff and inmate unrest, several fires of suspicious origin in the administration building, and vocal displeasure by the residents of the town of Shirley, culminating in a protest meeting in the Governor's office.[11]

When we went to a nine-month strategy to remove the youth from Shirley slowly, the number of incidents mounted. There was another surge of runs and the number of teenagers sent to us by the courts grew exponentially. While we were trying to shut the place down, the court was trying to pack it fuller than ever. Having planned our community programs on the basis of previous years' commitment rates, we were soon caught in an unanticipated crisis for lack of alternatives. Later we saw the same pattern following the closing of Lyman: court commitments to DYS of thirteen to fifteen-year-old boys (the ages normally assigned to Lyman) rose dramatically. Immediate pressure to reopen the school was brought to bear on us. We refused and for an uncomfortable few weeks sent young people directly home after their commitment to us. In a state which richly merits its reputation for political hardball, these changes in commitments were no accident. It recalled a comment of the British psychiatrist Ronald Laing, who said that we have a word for those who think they are being persecuted when they aren't, *paranoia*. But we have no word for those pathetic souls who are being persecuted and refuse to acknowledge it.

Consensus politics had brought about the reform legislation. A strong constituency for the reform of DYS had developed in the waning months of the Coughlan administration, and though many of these individuals and groups supported my efforts, I was expendable. I'd been appointed to implement the legislation they had conceived and moved through the legislature. Most, I think, saw reform as a matter of slowing the patronage and bringing in qualified professionals. I saw it as something more and had taken their legislation further than they planned or wished.

Some groups stuck with me—particularly the Massachusetts Committee on Children and Youth (MCCY) and the Massachusetts Council on Crime and Corrections. Ceil DiCicco, the executive director of

MCCY, worked primarily with the legislature. She was one of those middle-class women who have been the backbone of reform in children's services and prisons. She kept me informed of legislation affecting our department, and she gave early warning of mines laid along the statehouse corridors for the likes of me. "Jerry, you didn't pay enough attention to Representative ——" or "Judge —— had a private meeting with the Ways and Means chairman about your budget." I can't say I looked forward to her calls, since they usually meant another round of meetings with this or that lawmaker or committee chairman, often with understandings regarding jobs for constituents or funding for local programs. But little as I enjoyed her calls, they were invaluable.

Legislation was filed to head off virtually every reform I might envision, and though periodically the legislature adjourned, it never left town. When lawmakers weren't in formal session, they were wandering around making deals directly or through their aides. In fact, the efforts of DYS staff with political connections to undermine change seemed to peak when the legislature was not in formal session. Of course, at those times there was more latitude for private meetings with local reps. As soon as the legislature reconvened, I could anticipate bills to allow juvenile parole agents to carry guns, unexpected capital outlay proposals for new buildings, and the perennial measures to allow juvenile judges to set time and sentence youngsters to specific reform schools.

The department's most abiding support came from the League of Women Voters. Evelyn Bender, their lobbyist on Beacon Hill, suffered me patiently, and she was always there to help bail me out in the legislature. I kept her informed of our problems and plans. When we had a rush of escapes, I made sure she knew about the sabotage, the youngsters, and the stories of what was going on in the system. From her, the information percolated throughout Beacon Hill.

Sam Tyler, head of the Massachusetts Council on Crime and Corrections, was routinely supportive, particularly during the tumultuous legislative hearings chaired by Representative Robert McGinn in the months before my departure. Sam and John Hough, a young writer, had led an early attack on the patronage-laden county training schools. When things seemed downright hopeless, I could always walk over to their office and regain my perspective as I listened to them joke about their latest discovery at some training school: "Jerry, the superintendent has two degrees—one in embalming, and one in massage."

But the strongest support came from less neatly definable groups. I can't recall turning down a speaking invitation—Lions, Junior Chambers of Commerce, Rotary, Business and Professional Women, Holy Name societies, B'nai B'rith, college and high school classes, commencements, radio and television talk shows, and anyplace else where someone might listen. Never having run for public office, I can only surmise that the experience is much the same for a politician. I found it hard to repeat the same things so often in banquet halls, service clubs, pizza parlors, gyms, and church basements across the state. Some of the encounters were funny. For example, after preparing a formal speech for a local men's service club, I arrived to find three middle-aged gentlemen seated at a Formica table in the front section of a busy Italian carry-out. It turned out to be one of the better meetings. The realization that I had the good wishes of such disparate groups of people helped me during the many crises.

13 *Community-based Alternatives*

Where Are All the Kids?

"Where are all the kids?" was the first question I had when touring the reform schools. It was the last question I heard three and a half years later, and it plagued the reforms long after it had been answered. My original question was meant as a goad—why were the inmates so invisible in these bucolic surroundings? I knew the answer. They were somewhere inside. If I didn't find them in vocational shops, classrooms, or locked in cottages, they would appear in sullen groups of ten or twelve, herded two by two along the narrow sidewalks bordering some institution road, staff trailing a few yards behind, often in cars. But after the reform schools were closed, the question took on a different meaning. Where were the kids? Were they shipped off to adult prisons or sequestered in institutions in other states? Perhaps they had only left for a while and then had been quietly dragged back and locked up again. But no, they were gone. Therefore, the closing must have been done recklessly. Any other possibility was inconceivable.

At first we paroled most inmates home. The fact that I headed the state youth parole authority made this relatively easy. But there were limits to this strategy. The judges objected, and if a parolee hurt someone, the blame would be laid at my door. Besides, many of the kids couldn't go home or wouldn't do well there without additional community support services. I wasn't wedded to the idea that every juvenile had to return to his or her neighborhood. Some didn't want to go back: she too firmly the family scapegoat; he too easily cast by peers as the local hood. For others, the best hope lay in the chance for a stable life elsewhere. But most would go back to their communities whether or not we wanted it, even when they went to uncaring homes and dangerous neighborhoods. We had no convenient Australia, nor was it our place to engage in forms of juvenile transportation.

We had tried new therapeutic models in some cottages, and they seemed to be successful in their limited task. There was less violence, the kids seemed happier, an atmosphere of normalization created a better milieu for treatment and education. But institutional preconceptions governed even the best therapeutic cottages. When we started them, we had almost no funds for contracting with community-based agencies. We were confined to what was available: institutional buildings, institutional staff, and a few outside consultants. At their best, the cottages resembled traditional child welfare group homes. At their worst, they began to look like some of the more frightening therapeutic community models.

The early agitation in the institutions didn't help matters. Badgering by staff and politicians had skewed my judgment. Rather than adopting the more reasonable programs, I looked first to those which would look more structured, less permissive, and better disciplined. I was drawn to models which, though presented as wonderfully caring and humane, were at their core rigid and authoritarian. My version of the Faustian bargain was to gain control at the expense of understanding.

As our first step in establishing state-operated halfway houses, we acquired a state-owned house in the Hyde Park section of Boston, only a few blocks down a back road from the Roslindale detention center. Hyde Park House stood in seductive contrast to ratty Rozzie, with its endless shunting of inmates, occasional violence, and general apathy. The neat house had open doors, a comfortable living room, food cooking in the kitchen, and well-behaved boys sitting with their tutors, and it was proof we could find institutional staff willing to try new models of care.

Hyde Park House was put together by Pat Tague, a former priest who'd been a client in a respected therapeutic community in Rhode Island. Like almost everyone else, he had connections in the department and the legislature. His uncle, Mark Burke, was the man who'd been my first guide around the statehouse, and who now occupied the steward's position at Roslindale. When Pat was referred to me, I checked with the director of the Rhode Island program and found out that Pat knew their model well, though he'd perhaps left prematurely. The recommendation was lukewarm, but Pat's interest in starting a therapeutic community program, something we very much wanted to do, was convincing. His program was our first, and we were able to set it up through administrative action alone. I didn't have to wait on the legislature for funding and contract approvals. Pat enlisted Peter Castignaro, a young cottage counselor from Lyman, to join him. The program seemed well structured, well planned, and well supervised. It could start taking youngsters immediately.

From the beginning, Hyde Park House fit the bill. We could have our cake and eat it, doling out control as therapy and psychological assault as discipline. What's more, we could not have been accused of permissiveness. (The Hyde Park model is the one in vogue throughout the United States today for treating adolescents involved in drugs.) Youngsters were expected to conform themselves to authority at all times, to lay out their problems, to assume responsibility for their own actions, and to disown whatever excuses they might have found in their backgrounds. House government and group therapy sessions were held a number of times a day. There were chores to do, individual tutoring, and a consultant psychiatrist. Supporters and critics alike were impressed. After we took in the drug-dependent son of a Boston police detective, it became a favorite charity of policemen, who helped raise funds for programming and recreational equipment. It all sounded fine, but the hard edge got brittle as time passed.

One day I made a swing by the house after another depressing trip to Roslindale. My quick stops by had become a ritual of reassurance for me, but that one was no such thing. While sitting at the kitchen table talking with Pat over a cup of coffee, I glanced into the next room. A boy was sitting on a chair with a sign hung around his neck, something to the effect that he'd been unwilling to deal with his problems. I was embarrassed and sensed that Pat felt the same. I asked the boy why he was wearing a sign. His answer was that he was dealing with his problems. He approved of his discipline. Though the measures were less stringent than in Cottage Nine, his response was uncomfortably reminiscent of my encounter with Doug in the tombs. I said nothing.

A week or two later, I got wind that youngsters were occasionally sent upstairs to sit in a closet as punishment for not "getting with" the program. Again I looked the other way. The staff sensed my ambivalence and stopped using the closet and signs, at least when I was around. The sad fact was that I wanted so much to be able to endorse this first alternative that I was willing to overlook problems I would have pounced on at Shirley or Lyman. I justified the inaction by telling myself I didn't sufficiently understand therapeutic community treatment models. After all, I told myself, most of my professional peers were already recognizing them as offering the best hope for rehabilitating delinquent and drug-involved youngsters. But it was a weak defense.

Some people didn't much like Hyde Park House. Tom Gallagher of the *Boston Herald-Traveler* was one. Hoping to turn him from writing carping columns, I took Tom out for a noontime lunch and conversation with staff and boys. He came along reluctantly but seemed impressed. As we left, he thanked me and said he intended to do a positive article on the place. The next afternoon, he was on the phone shouting that the whole visit must have been a setup. I'd tried to con him. He couldn't be more specific than to say that the kids had probably been rehearsed. The place was too impressive. There was no appeasing Tom, and as we talked, our argument deteriorated into name-calling. I was disappointed, but not too much, since I knew he disliked me and what I was doing. I thought his outburst was just the old Gallagher reasserting himself. But it was more than that. Tom was right about Hyde Park House—although probably for the wrong reasons.

Similarly, Leslie Stahl, who was then a news reporter for a Boston television station, came out to do a feature story. She also seemed impressed by the boys, the staff, and the program. But her story on the following evening's news was generally critical. I called her and complained that she hadn't given us a fair shake. But she too was right. Neither Gallagher nor Stahl could articulate what lay behind the uneasiness. It seemed to have more to do with the too-perfect demeanor of the boys than with the ideology. Ironically, they probably saw Hyde Park House as too permissive, too idealistic, not recognizing the dangerousness of the youth, instead of the opposite. To them it didn't seem a tough enough substitute for reform school. Hyde Park House continued to take kids throughout my tenure. Though the harsher aspects of the program were eventually modified, it was closed by Joe Leavey, who succeeded me as commissioner.

The experience with Hyde Park was a testament to the fact that there were no ready-made treatment programs for delinquents coming out of reform schools. In its own way that was a blessing. We had to make our own. Had there been approved models of professional community-based programs, such as those currently touted by the American Correctional Association, we would have used them—and effectively undone our reforms. Correctional bureaucrats see the reform school as integral to a spectrum of services for delinquent youth. Every youngster apparently should retain the right to his or her own institutionalization. The practical effect, had I followed this route in Massachusetts, would have been a system of rebuilt reform schools side by side with a new cluster of state-staffed mini-institutions called "community-based" and scattered throughout the Commonwealth to serve newly defined groups of delinquents allegedly in need of restrictive residential rehabilitation. Twice the number of youngsters would be under state control.

Treatment: Who Needs It?

We had decided to get out of institutions before we had thought through the alternatives. But the decision didn't seem foolhardy. Our reform schools were as great a threat to public safety full as they were empty. We wanted to do the least harm. The hard truth is that adult and juvenile penal institutions have minimal impact on crime. If most prisons were closed tomorrow, the rise in crime would be negligible.

Years later, the conservative writer Charles Murray would argue that sending a child to reform school has a "suppression effect" on later delinquency.[1] Though Murray's study was the subject of controversy with reference to its methodology, a reanalysis of Murray's data by criminologists of less rigid conservatism revealed that he had lightly passed over the most startling implications of his own data. Youths sent directly home did about as well as those incarcerated for a year or more.[2]

But conservative analysts like Murray seem forever fated to be detached from the stuff of their studies. Anyone who has felt an institution, smelled its corridors and cellblocks, heard its din, or spent enough time with an inmate to know him or her well cannot come away thinking it does anyone much good. The only value it has is its potential to incapacitate or deter; and virtually all the research, including

Murray's, shows institutions to be a small deterrent. Locking up offenders has minimal effect on crime rates. Incapacitation works only when it is so massive as to challenge the nature of a democratic society. In fact, correctional institutions probably stimulate the very behavior they claim to treat. For example, in an exhaustive cohort study of violent delinquents, a group of respected Ohio researchers concluded: "Our most important single finding emerges from the analysis of the impact of the court's disposition on the intervals between future arrests. . . . This interval, measured in 'street time' (the actual number of months during the intervals between arrests when the offender was free to commit an offense), diminished dramatically after each commitment to an institution."[3] The Rand corporation, which gave us the term *incapacitation*, has more recently suggested that correctional institutions may produce criminals and that incapacitation as the major tenet of crime control is a questionable social policy.[4] In a Justice Department study, Rand suggested that prisons probably encourage crime among their alumni. The word *criminogenic* was used in describing prisons in the first draft. It was excised from the final product at the insistence of the government funders of the project, apparently because it flew in the face of administration rhetoric on the effectiveness of imprisonment.

Long before these computer-generated truths came to light, however, DYS had concluded that it wasn't doing anything particularly risky in closing reform schools, even if no alternatives were available. But it would have been a gratuitous insult to the courts had we not set up an alternative method of control and treatment. Unlike many of my civil libertarian friends, however, I didn't believe that the only thing we could do for these youngsters was to minimize the damage. At the least, community-based treatment could assist these young offenders in developing skills needed to negotiate their difficult family and community environments and to avoid self-destructive miscalculations.

Twenty-five years ago, the respected American sociologist Erving Goffman wrote a seminal article, "On Cooling the Mark Out: Some Aspects of Adaptation to Failure."[5] In discussing therapy, Goffman used the metaphor of a professional con game. The con artist, having taken the mark's (victim's) money and disappeared, employs a confederate to approach the victim just as he or she recognizes his or her predicament—the sudden embarrassing illumination "I've been had." The confederate calms the victim down. He suggests, for example, that perhaps something has delayed the con man (for whom the victim waits on the street). Perhaps there has been a misunderstanding, a misperception, or instructions not clearly understood. The con man's confederate emphasizes the futility of the victim's situation, the problems in reporting such matters to the police, and the potential for embarrassment. Meanwhile, the con artist gets out of town.

Goffman saw the role of the helping professional as similar to that of a con artist's confederate. The chronic young offender is likely to have been "had" in terms of family abuse, economics, a violence-laden environment, and limited opportunities. The therapist diverts attention from these issues by redefining the game as, for example, the need for the client to assume personal responsibility for his or her own plight, to learn self-discipline, to set limits, and to try again for mostly unattainable goals. As Goffman puts it, "The psychotherapist is in this sense, the society's cooler. His job is to pacify and re-orient the disorganized person; his job is to send the patient back to an old world or a new one, and to send him back in a condition in which he can no longer cause trouble to others or can no longer make a fuss. In short, if one takes society, and not the person, as the unit, the psychotherapist has the basic task of cooling the mark out."[6] "Cooling out the mark" is the ruling ideology among those who work with delinquent youngsters. I didn't want our alternatives to be a variation on that theme; I wanted them to validate each youth's personal experience. Though I recognized the need to control the youth's crime or violence, I wanted to give due consideration to and respect for each one's life history, with the hope that we, the definers, would occasionally reconsider the ways in which we dealt with delinquents.

In this sense the question of whether our alternatives worked was not primary. Solutions in this field are inevitably dangerous. Programs which "work" by some standards can cause more problems for the larger society than those which "fail" but tell us more about an offender and his world. I saw cutting recidivism as a happy side effect of the more crucial task of understanding the roots of a particular youngster's illegal behavior.

Although I had spent most of my professional life in psychiatric settings and was at home with some of the more traditional psychiatric settings for our youngsters, I didn't believe that these approaches were particularly effective. However, the better psychiatric programs still left patients with some sense of dignity and worth. This was probably because the patients who could afford such care were people of means. Though the psychoanalytic model was of limited effectiveness in treating delinquents, it still stressed the importance of life history, even if narrowly conceived within orthodox theory.[7]

I placed a small number of our most difficult youngsters at the respected McClean Psychiatric Hospital in Belmont, Massachusetts. Most of them had been sent to us for murder or other crimes of violence. McClean had a tradition of humane, individualized care of the kind that the wealthy deviant and mentally ill traditionally demand. At McClean one didn't hear the allegations of patient abuse which dogged the state hospitals or state facilities for the criminally insane. I always felt it was because the relatives who paid the bills for McClean's patients would not tolerate a family member being knocked off the wall. If that happened, they would remove the patient to another private setting and take the family's money with them. My wife was a chief psychiatric nurse at McClean, and I was aware that the hospital had a few well-to-do patients who had committed horrible crimes but, because of their station, were given psychiatric treatment instead of prison. It seemed to me that if any of DYS's charges had to be locked up, it might as well be in a comfortable place with an interesting clientele. Even if the treatment were only minimally effective, at least our more serious delinquents would not be so mistreated as would be likely in the state institutions.

Besides, the private mental health system has provided a convenient alternative for teenage delinquents of the middle and upper classes for a century. And on its own narrow terms, it seemed to work, at least in diverting recalcitrant youngsters from a system which usually dragged its clientele ever deeper into crime.

The first two youngsters we sent to McClean had different problems. One was an openly gay youngster who had been victimized at one of our training schools; the other, a fifteen-year-old who had killed his grandmother with an ax. They both did well at McClean, and I never regretted sending them there.

But there were occasional problems. A later referral, Nino (a street kid from East Boston), gave the doctors at McClean more problems. Though he was occasionally unruly and had been diagnosed as near psychotic, he was a continual management problem, unwilling to take the therapy seriously. One day I got a call from a supervisor at McClean who had attended a ward meeting about Nino. They concluded that he needed a more structured setting, and they recommended that he be transferred to the adult prison at Concord. It struck me as particularly out of character that this group of sophisticated helpers would prescribe an adult prison as the best option for a troublesome teenager. I called the director and informed him that should McClean find itself unable to treat Nino, we would of course remove him to one of our reform schools, which by then were reasonably humane. In such an event, however, we would feel compelled to remove the other youngsters placed at McClean as well (a small number, but providing a not insignificant income to the hospital). It must have been the first time in its history that McClean had recommended prison as therapy. I figured it had to do with Nino's lower socioeconomic class. McClean kept Nino, and the issue never came up again.

Another alternative was the newly chic drug programs, which would later become a national ideology. Matt Dumont, head of the state's drug programs, had embarked on a project of supporting so-called therapeutic communities. These were peer-group, confrontative residential programs initially run by ex-addicts and later peopled with professional social workers, psychologists, and psychiatrists. The idea was new at the time, having come to public notice through Lewis Yablonsky's well-received book *The Violent Gang*.[8] Yablonsky outlined the Synanon model developed by a young ex-alcoholic, Chuck Dederich. Synanon was the granddaddy of hundreds of programs which sprouted up across the country in later years. The Syanon model called for a new, ultimately threatening kind of "therapeutic community" based on group pressure and self-revelation. It seemed a good enough idea, but it eventually led to the kinds of authoritarian enclaves of brainwashing and true-believerism which characterize many contemporary drug-abuse therapeutic communities. A number of these new programs were willing to accept delinquent kids coming out of reform schools. We even began one of our own, run by an alumnus of one of the private programs and other state staff. It was deceptively simple, unusually reassuring to administrators, visitors, and politicians, and one of the bigger mistakes of my tenure.

What models did we eventually follow? Our community programs ran the gamut from tightly programmed, highly supervised treatment models with most services, for example, education, counseling, and job training given within the confines of the house, to programs with minimal supervision, attendance at local schools, and so on. We contracted with respected and established child-care groups like the New

England Home for Little Wanderers, You Inc. in Worcester, and Downeyside Homes in the Springfield area. Downeyside Homes was headed by Father Paul Engel, a local priest who'd pioneered family group homes for youngsters caught up in the child welfare system.

We also contracted with dozens of less traditional groups like Libra Inc. (an ex-offenders group), the New England Arts Academy, and Genesis II. Some worked; others didn't. The Libra contract gave us many problems later, and the house was eventually closed.[9] A psychiatrist and psychologist came to us with a proposal to start Genesis II, a group home across the border in Maine, for six or eight youngsters with drug problems. After I left the state it evolved into Elan, a controversial drug treatment program for more than three hundred youngsters—and not the kind of program I felt proud of having any part in generating. Many of these programs were begun because we were willing to fund the model. Others had existed before but had not dealt with delinquent youngsters. But among the dozens of newly found or newly created community-based programs, a few turned out to be integral to successful deinstitutionalization.

Subsequent research showed that some programs were highly effective in lowering recidivism among ex-inmates. They weren't the programs we had planned at the beginning, nor were they the most professional models. The more effective programs often sprang up as a makeshift response to a particular youngster's crisis. One such model was the Community Advocates Program (CAP), later renamed Key, Inc. It was conceived by two university students, and it began as a summer alternative for a few youth from the reform schools.

In summer 1970, I got a call from Scott Wolfe, a junior at Harvard. He knew of my attempts to reform DYS and had talked some fellow undergraduate students at Phillips Brooks House into fashioning a summer program for a few selected youngsters who'd been committed to DYS. Scott hoped to offer on-campus tutoring and a cultural enrichment program for a few ex–reform school kids from the Cambridge-Somerville area, which borders Harvard. At a time when we had few alternatives, the students' interest in helping us out was welcome. We contracted to pay out-of-pocket expenses, though they donated the bulk of the resources. The program ran through summer 1970 and ended with the opening of fall term. The kids went over to Harvard during the days to be tutored, exposed to literature, and taken out on field trips, to rock concerts, and to museums.

Generally the program went well, though an occasional youngster got into minor scrapes with the law or stole money from open wallets and purses left on desks by too-trusting students. That alone would have ended many a university's involvement—"the ungratefulness of it all." But the Phillips Brooks students saw it as a challenge and looked to adjust the program. By now they had come to know their charges well and had a better view of what might be needed to keep them out of trouble.

That fall, Scott and his brother, Bill, a sophomore at Clark University, came up with a new idea. They proposed a more intensive program in which students would work with kids in their homes, be available to their charges in the evenings and on weekends, and would be allowed to take a youngster into their own apartments or homes if things seemed to be getting out of hand in the youngster's own home. They would assign university students to work with youngsters one to one, each putting in from ten to thirty hours a week with his or her youth. The students would be paid a modest hourly wage and would get class credit for their efforts.

I hammered out a loose contract with the Wolfe brothers, who were still in the process of creating a nonprofit entity. Within a few weeks they were recruiting and training undergraduates from Boston, Worcester, and Cambridge. They began taking kids returning from the reform schools. As we ran out of group home slots, CAP became our overflow agency. CAP offered something less than a residential group home but more than simple parole. Within a few months the Wolfe brothers had set up a nonprofit ice cream parlor in East Boston and a pizza-delivery service, both run by the youngsters, which catered to university dorms at Clark and Holy Cross universities. The receipts went into wages for the juveniles.

CAP also got caught in the middle of our problems in getting the Department of Administration and Finance to honor our contracts. There still were no uniform ways of setting rates, and the checks weren't being generated on time. In order to open the ice cream parlor on schedule, the Wolfe brothers used the trust fund their father had set up for them. At the opening festivities, Mr. Wolfe approached me and asked whether it was likely his sons would be reimbursed by the state for the $30,000 they'd already spent. It was the first I had heard of it, and I was taken aback at how far out on a limb Scott and Bill had gone. I reassured him that the state money soon would be there and apologized for the delay. The state's dollars were freed a couple of months later. The CAP program proved to be one of the most effective in lowering recidivism among its clientele. As Key, Inc. it grew to be the largest nonprofit organization in Massachusetts giving on the street services to delinquent youth. Key presently supervises approximately five hundred delinquent Massachusetts youngsters in the community.

We also used established models of adolescent treatment. The late Al Trieschman, a nationally respected child therapist took a number of our youngsters into his wonderful Walker Home in Needham. Walker was an intense therapeutic community with a Freudian cast. It had stood the test of time as a decent and humane program for disturbed and abused youngsters and was much in the tradition of Bruno Bettelheim's Orthogenic School near the University of Chicago campus.[10]

Dare, Inc., in Boston had run a halfway house program for a few young delinquents before I came to the state. The director, Jerry Wright, was at first supportive of our efforts to create community programs, but he grew less so as deinstitutionalization progressed. Aside from the fact that he thought I let youngsters manipulate me, he was particularly perturbed when he realized I was going to close *all* the reform schools. For a number of years he had stood outside and berated the YSB for its brutal institutions, but he had also come to depend on the threat of reform schools to motivate kids to stay in halfway houses. Wright was concerned that, without the backup of reform schools, his youngsters might walk out the front door.

My response was, "So what? Find another way to keep them." This approach upset a number of treatment programs. Threats are the life-blood of juvenile justice. First comes the threat of institutionalization. Then, when a kid gets to the institution, he finds that the whole place is held together by harsher threats. If you escape, you must go to the hole. In some states, they might transfer you to adult prison with its threats— also delivered on—of rape and assault. To what effect?

Given the average delinquent youngster's life history, for threats to work they would have to have consequences so draconian as to betray the very nature of help. Things would end up looking like something out of the Dark Ages—threat upon threat, violence upon violence, payback upon payback—each round escalating. The cumulative effect would be staggering.

By late 1971, it was clear we could close most or all of the institutions. It was such a drastic and unthinkable action that the opposition seemed unable to respond in any focused way. Though staff had been relatively effective in causing us problems in the legislature while we were trying to humanize the reform schools, they had no strategy for fending off their closing. Perhaps this was best exemplified by the occurrences one night at the Shirley Industrial School.

We seemed to have made enough progress at the school that I thought it an appropriate time to symbolize where we were headed and what we rejected. I located a few youths who had been confined for long periods in the tombs and Cottage Nine. We gathered them with a few staff on the second floor of the now-deserted building. Each boy was given a sledgehammer and invited to beat down the cement walls of the small isolation chambers.

As we were about to begin the ritual, one of the staff mentioned that a state senator, Joe Ward, was on the grounds addressing a local men's club in the school dining hall. I went up and invited Senator Ward to join us in the demolition, suggesting that he might want to take a few whacks at the walls himself. Press and photographers were present as the senator joined in. It was a strange moment, since he opposed the closing of Shirley and had spoken out against our earlier attempts to change the discipline procedures at the school. To me it was a sign that, at least for a while, the momentum was with us as we moved to leave the institutions entirely behind.

I eventually settled on one expectation for the youth leaving our institutions: "We are assigning you to a program we hope will best meet your needs and keep you out of trouble. But if you don't think it's working, call us. We will reconsider matters. We're not here to prove a particular program works for you. If you impulsively leave a program, let us know. We don't care if you move through a dozen programs a year so long as you keep in touch and out of trouble." This was anathema to program administrators. We were letting young toughs manipulate us. But we stuck by our resolution, and it worked. Young people called or came into the central office by the dozens to negotiate and redefine their community programs. I later found some solace in a study done by a Harvard researcher who found that those youngsters who picked or found their own placement or program did significantly better than those forced to stay in placements they believed were no good for them.

Despite our financial problems and ad hoc administrative tactics, by the end of 1972 we had contracts with approximately 175 different private programs. Kids were placed in universities, private prep schools, Outward Bound programs, specialized foster care, in a wide range of group homes, in their own homes with supportive family services, in art schools, in military schools, in therapeutic community drug programs, and wherever else a program might develop in response to the needs of a troubled or troubling teenager for whom we were responsible.

14   The Myth of "Violent" Teenagers

We had our share of violent youngsters: Al, who axed his grand-mother; Billy, who raped and killed a seventy-year-old woman; Harry, who in a holdup shot his victim in the head for eight bucks; Mark, who sexually assaulted and killed a seven-year-old boy. But, horrific as the crimes were, their perpetrators were rare in our system, even among those sent us for violent crimes.

Violent juvenile crime was a major concern of the public in Mas-sachusetts. Not only in the state, but across the nation, violent crime had steadily increased during the fifteen years following 1956.[1] Rob-bery, assault, and rape had tripled. As is the case whenever crime increases, most of the increase was attributed to an explosion of juve-nile crime. But did the attribution fit?

Violent crime in the United States has always been higher than in any comparable Western country, and rises and falls in juvenile crime usually have followed the same patterns as adult crime. Though there has always been a disproportionate amount of crime among young males, particularly in the eighteen to twenty-five-year age range—and though older juveniles (sixteen and seventeen) commit more crimes than younger adolescents, there have never been self-contained dra-matic increases of violent juvenile crime which did not parallel in-creases in adult crime. Juvenile crime rates follow adult crime rates, only a bit less so.[2] Unfortunately, one would be hard pressed to argue this to a public primed to believe that juvenile crime is a runaway horse. Think back to the national obsession with New York street gangs and the Dracula killings in the 1950s, the Chicago street gangs of the late 1950s and early 1960s; the Philadelphia gang violence of the 1970s; and the Los Angeles juvenile gangs of the 1980s. Certainly, from time to time, there are unusual explosions of violent crime. But much of this is related to increases in the number of adolescents in the population. It isn't always clear at the time what's going on, or whether more juveniles are actually involved in violent crime than was previously thought.[3]

Though it makes up an extremely small percentage of all violent crime committed by juveniles, it is generally agreed that the most reliably reported crime is murder. Homicide rates in the United States nearly doubled between 1958 and 1972, from 4.5 homicides per 100,000 to 8.5 per 100,000. But even this unsettling surge of violence wasn't unprecedented. Homicides more than tripled between 1900 and 1914, from 2.1 to 7.3 per 100,000, and reached a high in 1933 of 9.6 murders per 100,000. As with adult homicide, the juvenile murder rate was also higher in the 1930s and 1940s than in the early 1960s.[4] The major rise in homicides occurred between 1965 and 1970, followed by a drop between 1973 and 1975 and a rise in 1980. The national homicide rate for 1990 exceeded the 1980 rate.

In June 1988 a national newspaper, *USA Today,* ran a series of pro and con articles on whether the death penalty should be invoked for juveniles convicted of murder. In the lead article in favor of the penalty entitled "Executing Juveniles Is a Social Necessity," the head of the conservative Washington Legal Foundation began, "Nearly 20,000 murders are committed by juveniles every year, and that number is not reflected in the number sentenced to death."[5] The fact that the statement was grossly inaccurate is less compelling than that a widely read newspaper apparently didn't question the figure before printing it on the editorial page. To be sure, many inaccuracies end up on editorial pages, but in this case, the outrageous figure of 20,000 juvenile murders was taken as unexceptional.

In 1990, for example, slightly over 23,000 murders and manslaughters were reported in the United States. Of the 20,000 persons arrested for these crimes, approximately 2,000 were juveniles.[6] Even this figure is inflated, however, since juveniles tend to get involved in such incidents in groups and with peers. A single offense often yields multiple arrests of teenagers. In addition, due to police overcharging, charges made at the time of arrest are often lowered later, if not completely dismissed. That leaves something like 1,200 juveniles across the United States who are tried annually for murder or manslaughter. Of these, probably no more than 500 will be convicted of murder in a court of law. This is 2.5 percent of the figure which appeared, unquestioned, on the editorial pages of *USA Today.*

This kind of gap between the myth and the reality of juvenile delinquency hounded me from the beginning in Massachusetts. Each year we received no more than five or six youngsters convicted of murder. That number has remained relatively fixed for the past decade. Some years there would be as few as three; other years, as many as seven. For a while, I thought juvenile murderers were being sent to adult prisons, but they weren't. We got virtually all those under seventeen who had been convicted of murder. Then I concluded that the small numbers might have to do with the fact that juveniles in Massachusetts were subject to adult trial at age seventeen. In thirty-eight states and the District of Columbia, the juvenile court retains jurisdiction till age eighteen.[7] In eight states, including Massachusetts, juvenile court jurisdiction is kept until age seventeen.[8] In four states, sixteen-year-olds are handled as adults.[9] These differences alone didn't explain the small numbers of Massachusetts adolescents arrested for murder, for when seventeen-year-olds were included in the statistics, they usually accounted for no more than two additional murders per year.[10] But homicide is a relatively rare crime. What about the other violent offenses juveniles commit?

About 25 percent of the young offenders sent to us were committed for crimes against persons.[11] However, when these "crimes against persons" were distilled, few actually involved physical violence or even the threat of it. Nationally, about 4 percent of the arrests of juveniles are for offenses classified as violent. Violence, however, covers a wide range of behaviors. For example, a recent crime survey of victims indicated that there was no physical injury in 72 percent of offenses classified as violent and committed by juveniles. In those violent offenses in which injury did occur, it wasn't serious enough to require medical attention in 93 percent of the cases.[12] A study of 811 Columbus, Ohio, youths with at least one violent crime on their records showed that 73 percent had neither threatened nor inflicted significant physical harm during the commission of those offenses. The same study followed a cohort of over 50,000 youth from birth to adulthood.

Of this group, only twenty-two youngsters committed two or more aggravated offenses in which physical harm was threatened or inflicted.[13]

Juveniles seldom use weapons in committing crimes. In M. E. Wolfgang's cohort study of Philadelphia boys born in 1945 and living in the city between their tenth and eighteenth birthdays, weapons were used in only 263 of 9,934 offenses known to police.[14] A 1978 New York City study showed that weapons were present in only 17 percent of juvenile offenses classified as violent.[15] A later victim crime survey revealed that juvenile offenders used weapons in 27 percent of violent offenses, though guns were present in less than 5 percent of those incidents.[16] With the exception of purse-snatching, most truly violent juvenile crime is confined to peers, with young males far more likely to be victims.[17]

I looked assiduously for those few violent youngsters who provided the rationale for our reform schools. They were the symbol which justified the ritual of institutionalization. But despite the fact that they provided the political rationale for the whole system, they weren't so easily identified, particularly if one knew them and their offenses in detail (though I'm told that some of my successors had less trouble locating this elusive group). Youngsters defined as violent made up about 25 percent of our reform school populations. When the details of each case were known, however, less than 5 percent of the juveniles had clearly demonstrated personal violence directed at another. Here one is subject to the war stories which drive juvenile corrections: the tale of the youngster involved in a particularly lungeous and brutal act. Such juveniles exist. But while they may provide the stuff of nightly television crime news stories, they don't represent the average youth in a reform school or detention center, even one for violent offenders.

Visiting other state youth correctional systems, I felt uncomfortable hearing administrators carry on about the new violent breed of delinquents filling their institutions. I couldn't understand it. Either we had dramatically fewer dangerous youngsters in our system than they did, or I was grossly misinformed about those who peopled our institutions. It was neither. As I got to know them better, it was clear that my peers in other states knew the inmates in their institutions only dimly. They were acquainted with few personally and were uninterested in the events and circumstances which surround each offense and which are so incompletely, and usually inaccurately, represented by a rap sheet. The fact is, the number of inmates in the average youth corrections system who have a propensity for personal violence has always been extremely small.[18]

And all too often, state administrators are flagrantly dishonest. While they hop from convention to convention bemoaning the dangerous delinquents in their youth institutions, their states are simultaneously binding over or waiving hundreds of nonviolent teenagers to adult criminal courts and adult prisons. Maryland routinely waives between eight hundred and a thousand youngsters into the adult system annually. Virginia, the same. (Recently, in preparing background in the case of a juvenile convicted of murder, I learned that, on the day of his sentencing, there was only one youngster in the whole Virginia juvenile reform school system of approximately one thousand youths who had been convicted of murder. The half dozen or so Virginia juveniles who commit murder each year must be shuttled into the adult prison system.) The pattern of sending large numbers of juveniles to adult prisons prevails in most state systems. Yet these same states also maintain large reform school systems for (presumably) serious juvenile offenders too dangerous to be in the community.

Those who run the juvenile justice system gain by defining young offenders as more violent than facts dictate. It's a kind of no-risk heroism for all concerned—judges, superintendents, institutional staff, therapists, police, and probation officers. It encourages the posturing and strutting of the I-told-you-so crowd, who make sure that, no matter what happens, no one will be accountable. This is the correctional equivalent of the old psychiatric diagnosis of "latent schizophrenia," now called "borderline personality." If the patient improves, it can be chalked up to the therapist's skill at treatment. If, on the other hand, the patient deteriorates, the therapist looks even more sophisticated, having predicted it all along. In this world it is to no one's advantage to destigmatize labels, except for those who are labeled. The process by which we label delinquents is more crucial than are its labels.

I eventually got to know personally the fifty or so most dangerous youth in the department. Though some had committed serious violent crimes, most were repeat property offenders who consistently placed themselves and others in potentially dangerous situations. A few were considered dangerous to themselves because of repeated escapes from detention facilities or runs from community programs. After we closed the institutions for the most violent, the number of dangerous youngsters in need of secure care, interestingly enough, decreased. We'd been defining juveniles according to the numbers of beds available for locking up the dangerous ones. Certainly there is a need for special handling of truly violent youth. But these few kids are often hidden in piles of lightweight offenders, like needles in haystacks.

As we closed the reform schools, we set up regional offices throughout the state to develop community-based options and to take responsibility for placing youngsters in their own communities. But each regional director had a few young offenders who were seen as in need of secure treatment or care. Aside from McClean Hospital, we had only one locked and secure program for juveniles, the Andros program. It was a privately run program for putatively violent youngsters.

Andros was begun in February 1972, through a contract with the Human Resources Institute, a private psychiatric group, and the Boston Mental Health Foundation, another private agency. We housed Andros at the Roslindale facility, since its population had fallen to fewer than fifty juveniles. The contracts allowed the psychiatric groups to hire people of their own choice and to bring in qualified mental health consultants. In its first months, it was run by professional social workers, psychologists, and psychiatrists under contract with the Human Resources Institute.

The Andros program combined psychiatric models and the then-popular therapeutic community residential programming. ("No sex. No violence. No narcotics.") It was designed to handle thirty-six youth. During his first thirty days, no youngster was allowed off the grounds. Then gradually, through group and individual counseling, he could progress to supervised group outings, individual off-grounds trips, and unsupervised weekend passes. As he approached his parole date, he was required to lead and direct other youths who were lower on the achievement scale. There were daily mandatory community group counseling and therapy sessions. After morning groups and lunch, the residents had a choice of activities, though each had to choose one: swimming, basketball, occupational therapy, tutoring, or lectures on various subjects. Free time was available for recreation, calling or writing home, and small-group discussions. Each youngster received a cash allowance based on his progress and the geographic location of his home to cover expenses for home visits.

Compared to Cottage Nine and the IJG Andros was a breath of fresh air. It was relatively short-term (the average youngster stayed in it no more than three to six months), it was active, and it treated its residents with unusual respect and concern. But Andros also exemplified one of the central contradictions in running effective therapeutic programs in corrections: unless one plans to institutionalize the clients and maim them psychologically, they must be brought into the local community as much as possible from the very beginning. That leads to runaways and escapes. The idea of a completely secure and therapeutic program soon becomes a contradiction in terms. The two aspects don't mix well. Despite the fact that Andros was supposed to be our secure program, in its initial stages a large number of its clients went over the wall.

During one early six-month period in which 118 youth had been in the program, fifty-seven residents were absent without leave. Of these, eleven left the program four or more times. Though some left from the theoretically secure building, most ran from group outings or failed to return on time from weekend or extended passes. But even among these (putatively) most dangerous youth in the state, of the fifty-seven who went AWOL fifty-two returned. Thirty-four came back on their own, ten were returned by family or police with no new charges, and eight were returned with minor new charges. Though it was a generally humane and professional program, Andros had poor security, so the program brought in a new director, Andrew Vacchs, who recruited and supervised his own staff—many of them ex-offenders. Andy was a driven, highly involved person who worked around the clock handling this most difficult population of youngsters.[19] After he took over, escapes stopped. In one remarkable incident when a youngster did escape, Andy's staff were waiting inside his home as he crawled in the window. The earlier escapes from the Andros program had never, for some reason, become a major issue, nor were there any major incidents associated with them. Part of the reason was that staff were not predisposed to run to the phones every time a youngster left. That was one of the major problems in the state-run programs, which by tradition, predilection, or statute must immediately report every runaway as though it were a major crisis—which, unfortunately, it then became.

Andros was soon filled with youngsters considered too dangerous for more open community-based programs. We had no other place to put them. The routine response would have been to develop additional secure programs, and my successors eventually did so. I took another tack. If we define youngsters as dangerous according to the number of beds we have for dangerous youngsters, why not set a limit on the number of beds? If the theory held, we could limit the number of dangerous or violent youngsters. If we had had a maximum-security institution for three hundred, five hundred, or a thousand violent delinquents, the necessary number would have been found and labeled. We would sift things down to that relatively irreducible group of violent youngsters who, no matter what the facilities available, would fit the definition. As soon as one does this, much of the rationale for secure care falls away.

I set an arbitrary number of thirty-five. In Massachusetts we would have slots for no more than thirty-five dangerous youth in secure care. I arrived at that figure based on the numbers of juveniles in our system who had been sent to us for violent offenses—including murder, rape, armed robbery, and aggravated assault—not simply every youth charged with such a crime, but only those in which a close reading of the circumstances of the offense clearly demonstrated a propensity for personal violence toward the victim. It made a big difference. We allocated a few of the thirty-five slots to each region in the state. If the secure slots allotted to a specific region were filled, the regional director had two options: to negotiate with another region for any empty slots they might have or to declare one of the dangerous youngsters presently occupying a secure slot as no longer dangerous and in need of secure care, releasing him to an alternative.

The plan sounded risky, but it wasn't. There were no major incidents and no apparent increase in violence among other youngsters who were supposed to be deterred by the knowledge that their "violent" peers were being locked up. What we risked in prematurely releasing a potentially dangerous juvenile was more than compensated for in holding within bounds the pervasive process of overdefining too many youngsters as "dangerous" and keeping them in that status—a procedure having less to do with public safety than with minimizing bureaucratic or political risk.

Secure care is seldom therapeutic, but one can minimize the harm. The joining of therapy with coercion is contradictory. Given the behaviorally coercive models of treatment in most secure treatment units, I took a perverse comfort in the fact that they didn't work. The implications of being able effectively to force a person to change are as ominous as they are helpful. Though I'm convinced that one can run small, effective programs for violent and dangerous youngsters—even for a while in secure settings—when genuine and lasting changes occur they have little to do with coercion.

15   Side Effects:
The County Training Schools

My Dear Mr. Miller, [the letter began]

You cannot imagine how happy and delighted are the people of Massachusetts when they learned this past week that you are about to pick up your bags and depart from our beloved State. I can predict that there will be dancing in the streets.

Governor Sargent put a blemish on his record when he first brought you here. It is hard to understand how you fooled so many people posing as a great Administrator for Juvenile Delinquency. Your Youth Service Board is in a state of chaos as the result of your way of doing things. Instead of closing the training schools, you should have first cleaned up the mess that you created, namely your Youth Service Board. Some of your employees have been involved in bank robberies, rapings, car thievery, and you name what else.

You squandered millions of taxpayers' dollars when you established these half-way houses, and there isn't a Chief of Police of any City or Town in the State who is not delighted because of your leaving.

I have been told that you spent four years in the Maryknoll Seminary, and that you were phased out. If so, why did you not list this item amongst your many qualifications?

I am going to ask Governor Sargent to have the Massachusetts National Guard Band serenade you off at Logan airport, the day that you depart.

Very truly yours,
William J. Donovan
Essex County Commissioner[1]

By most measures one would have said that we should have left the county training schools alone. Our timing could not have been worse. We were just getting our own equilibrium as a department after months of tumult. Things were considerably more relaxed. Incidents were at the lowest point since I had taken over the department, and a generally good atmosphere was beginning to prevail in the reform schools. Our changes in the reform schools made the problems in the county schools more glaring. Our kids were bona fide delinquents—burglars, car thieves, occasional assaulters, addicts, and rip-off artists. The county schools held school truants. Complicating matters was the fact that, having made our institutions for true delinquents relatively stable and decent, we had now decided they were superfluous.

The county training schools had been around for half a century. They were bastions of county patronage and, through state reimbursement mechanisms, were tightly woven into the convoluted patterns of the legislature. A twelve- or thirteen-year-old boy could find himself locked in a county training school, often for years, because of his failure to attend a local elementary or junior high school. But the county training schools weren't accredited. The true reason for their existence—to provide patronage jobs for friends and relatives of county commissioners—was clear from a simple scan of the staff résumés. The superintendent of one of the schools had degrees in massage and embalming. The superintendent of another came to his position after a stint as a pie salesman. What they had in common was having worked in the campaign of a county commissioner or otherwise endeared themselves to a local politician or state legislator.

When the Youth Service Board was created in 1948, it was given the duty of annually inspecting the county training schools, a duty that came over to our department at the time of the reform legislation. The inspections were perfunctory. YSB administrators or staff made only an annual courtesy tour, and their inspections yielded little beyond support for more funding of the schools and recommendations for occasional new programs, building repairs, and staff expansion. After my first visit to the Middlesex County Training School, I decided a courtesy call would no longer suffice.

A large percentage of our youngsters were county school alumni who had moved on to state reform schools. It would be easy enough to find out how they'd fared in the county schools, and I decided it might be useful background for our formal visits to the county schools. At first I tried to use volunteer students from Harvard Law School to interview them. With the help of the head of the law school's Center for Criminal Justice, Jim Vorenberg, we recruited a group of student volunteers and sent them out to interview DYS boys who had spent time in the county schools.

Based on the few private conversations I'd had with some of these boys, I expected the Harvard students to be able to document the scandalous conditions in the county schools. But though there were hints of some unsavory practices in the county schools, the boys were evasive, and their allegations were vague. The investigative reports were arid, devoid of passion, and onerously legalistic. Despite the radical rhetoric at Harvard Law in the early seventies, the students were uneasy with these mostly white kids from poor and blue-collar backgrounds. Things might have gone better if the kids had been black.

After I had set the Harvard students to work, I appointed a special blue-ribbon commission headed by a respected former Republican state representative, Mary Newman, to assume the inspection task assigned our department by the legislature. I asked the commission to visit the schools and to file a report summarizing their findings. We provided staff backup. Meanwhile, Sam Tyler and John Hough of the Massachusetts Council on Crime and Corrections (MCCC) were un-covering a trove of patronage, padding, and incompetence. Because of their corruption alone the schools deserved to close down. But in redoing the interviews with the boys, we uncovered a new series of scandals.

We had expected the corruption, but we were surprised at the amount of abuse left unadmitted to the Harvard students. I discussed the situation with a staff person who'd recently begun working out of the Boston office. She was an unusually attractive young woman who, despite her easy manner, was more than a little hard-nosed and taken with her role as an investigator. We assigned her to travel around the state interviewing former county school boys.

A few weeks later, she came back with names, dates, persons, places—a series of obscene incidents which, as I read them, I knew sounded the death knell for the county training schools. Why was this young woman able to get information unavailable to the law students? Her success at uncovering the scandals in the county schools was partly due to a more sensitive interviewing technique, and I fear that part of her success was for other reasons, which I preferred to ignore. She was an attractive, accepting, and not unseductive young woman who was open to hearing the stories and concerns of these teenage boys. The implications were obvious. The next question was whether the boys had fabricated the stories. We subsequently learned that, though there may have been an occasional embellishment, the allegations held up remarkably well. She had interviewed the boys individually in our reform schools and detention centers or on parole in their own communities. She was able to get corroboration—identical incidents told by different boys giving names, dates, places, and graphic details.

The Newman commission filed its report in April 1971, characterizing the young inmates as "truly children in bondage, with fewer civil rights than any other group in the Commonwealth, even including inmates in our state prisons." The language was strong, but the commission was tastefully civil, skirting the less savory allegations. Chester Atkins, then a state legislator, filed legislation to establish alternatives for youngsters being sent to the county training schools. The MCCC set a goal of 50,000 cards or letters to be sent by citizens to county commissioners in opposition to the continuation of the schools.

Because of the sacrosanct nature of county patronage, the likelihood that the legislature would take on the county schools was small. I had attempted to interest the leadership in the issue to no avail. In frustration, I had all the interviews with the boys—their allegations of being handcuffed to poles, forced to do push-ups over an open sewer, having to rub their own feces on their faces, and other abuses—reproduced in a large report labeled "CONFIDENTIAL" and hand-delivered to the governor, the speaker of the House, and the senate president. I attached a note indicating that I would hold a press conference the following day, outline the allegations, and call for civil and possibly criminal action, should no other action be forthcoming.

Though I received no response, before the end of the day the speaker and the senate president held a joint press conference and announced that they were appointing a special committee to look into all children's services across the state. Hearings would be held regarding the county schools. The politics of the situation was finessed by the speaker, who agreed simultaneously to appoint a special committee headed by Representative Robert McGinn, a legislator from Hampden County and a strong supporter of that county's training school, to investigate our department. I went ahead and leaked the county training school report to the papers. It undid the relative calm and led to a raucous series of hearings and investigations. As the *Boston Globe* noted in an editorial, "Youth Services on the Mat," "No less than four committees of varying energy and commitment are studying the Department of Youth Services. And a few weeks ago Senate President Kevin Harrington and House Speaker David Bartley called for the establishment of a fifth group, in the form of a blue-ribbon commission, to study all the state's youth services."[2]

As the county schools' hiring practices and programs were brought to the light of day, the schools became a political liability. Reform-minded legislators, led by Representative Charles Flaherty, had a field day. The testimony about how people were hired and what jobs they performed at the schools was the stuff of a Jimmy Breslin novel. A newcomer to politics, Paul Tsongas, won a county commissioner's seat with, among other things, a pledge to close the Middlesex County Training School.

Even under these pressures, though, the schools crumpled very slowly. The one in Hampden County hung on the longest. We funded a street academy in Springfield, the city that gave the school most of its youngsters. In juvenile court, through aggressive advocacy for truants, we were able to convince the local judge to sentence them to this new alternative program. The county school's population fell, and by the time its annual budget came up for approval by the legislature, the school had only one student. Predictably, the legislature funded it for another year.

The county training schools were finally closed because we had vacated the state reform schools. The fact that Massachusetts no longer locked up true delinquents made it impossible to institutionalize ersatz ones, but the reverse would not have been true. If the schools for truants had been closed first, it would have had no meaning for the inmates in the reform schools. By directing our reforms toward the more serious delinquents, we guaranteed better care for less serious delinquents. But taking on the county training schools brought on a new attack from the legislature which didn't end until I left the state.

16   Backlash

The Massachusetts Experiment is often attributed to a period of craziness in liberal Massachusetts. No doubt times were different. But they were different in other states as well, and none took their delinquent youth out of the reform schools. Though Massachusetts had a reputation as a hyperliberal enclave, when it came to state politics, it could be as conservative as any. I recall walking up the steps of the statehouse while sign-carrying state prison guards marched back and forth demanding the ouster of John Boone, the commissioner of corrections. "Boone the Coon" was their chant. John, a quiet black man who had formerly headed the District of Columbia corrections department, had been appointed by Governor Sargent to lead the system in a progressive direction. He was eventually forced from office, but his presence exposed another side of "liberal" Massachusetts for all to see. And his troubles diverted some attention from ours.

The backlash against my appointment began with my swearing-in and never stopped. When the department wasn't being formally investigated by the legislature, it was being privately pursued by others in hopes of a scandal or at least some missteps. Everyone had something to say—juvenile judges, professional groups, administrators, correctional experts in other states, and town selectmen. It was all very democratic. Even many parents of reform school youth couldn't stomach the idea that their boy or girl might do better living with another family in specialized care than being stashed in a reform school. It revealed too many of the ambivalences which the rituals of institutionalization cover so well. Some of these people even lobbied for a return to "humane" institutions. I should have caught a glimpse of things to come when a consultant child psychiatrist with the department requested that I reopen the isolation rooms at one of the reform schools in order to motivate a recalcitrant boy for treatment.

Similar issues emerged around a number of community treatment programs for youngsters with drug dependency and addiction. These programs had a policy that, if a client failed to cooperate, he or she could be dumped out onto the streets or sent back to reform school. I refused to allow this in the drug treatment programs, and some programs made accommodations. We stopped using the rest.

For the first two years, the political opposition never quite got their act together. If they had, we would have been stopped. Though we were often disorganized nearly to chaos, our critics were in even worse shape, largely because so many staff were politically appointed. Jobs were the issue, and it was every man for himself. In one sense the legislative investigations were a continuation of the commotion which had brought down the old YSB. Though the rhetoric then had to do with halting abuse, the reality was that Coughlan didn't have enough vacant staff positions to keep the legislature at bay. Many staff had outlasted the tenure of their original sponsors. Another five hundred or so new positions for distribution would probably have saved the YSB. Creating the new department hadn't lessened the pressure for patronage jobs as much as many had hoped. If anything, it increased it.

The real purpose of legislative investigative committees was usually unrelated to their stated one. I concerned myself less with published mandates than with the relationships members had with institutional and administrative staff, state employees' unions, contractors, local judges, and prosecutors. It took more than a little fancy footwork by Speaker Bartley to support our reforms while simultaneously responding to legislators keen on bringing back the old days. He effectively controlled committees through the shrewd choice of a chairman or vice chairman. Only toward the end of my tenure did things get out of hand. By then, even the speaker was ready to throw in the towel, though with some regret.

Four months after my arrival, Bartley appointed a seven-member special committee to investigate conditions at Shirley. It came in response to complaints by local legislators and centered on our problems in halting escapes. In the first months of 1970, escapes from Shirley grew almost tenfold, from 19 to 180. The speaker picked a friendly representative, Jack McGlynn, to head the probe. He calmed the committee members by using my reassurances that no jobs would be touched during the reforms.

Simultaneous with the filing of the committee report came word that Attorney General Robert Quinn was going to investigate our purchase of the Topsfield facility. Bartley then joined in with a request to pursue an investigation. The Joint Senate-House Committee on State Administration was asked to make a thorough evaluation of the DYS. The speaker again appointed Jack McGlynn cochairman. The committee contained a number of lawmakers who would later go on to greater political prominence: George Keverian, Jack Backman, David Locke, and Clifford Marshall. As I looked over the membership I didn't see many potential supporters. But McGlynn controlled the agenda from the committee's first day. And Ken Trevett, who had been Jack Backman's legislative aide, was chosen as the committee's staff person. Ken spent hours with us acquainting himself with our problems, goals, and hopes. He also summarized the committee's visits and meetings, and compiled the final report.

Keeping the committee friendly took an occasional favor of the kind that I would publicly deplore but privately come to know as the substance of Massachusetts politics. Periodically I would be asked whether we might hire this or that person in order to keep a particular committee member supportive. Other things being equal, I'd usually make some kind of arrangement. The committee held hearings and visited facilities for a year. Their final report was a ringing endorsement of the reforms, and it was released to coincide with a particularly vicious attack from another group of legislators.

Some investigations seemed ideologically motivated: an opportunity to wave the "law-and-order" flag. But they often turned out to be politics as usual. A major investigation was led by Senator Francis X. McCann of Cambridge, in his role as chairman of the legislature's Special Commission on the Causes of Violence and Crime. I was a member of the same commission, though in these circumstances I was not present in my role as member. The focus of the investigation was going to be my department. McCann had strong support from the new senate president, Kevin Harrington. Though McCann hoped to run the commission like a legislative committee, his control was less than total. Paul Quirk, head of the state association of child-care workers, delivered a petition to the speaker—signed by six hundred workers in fifty community-based children's agencies—supporting me. The *Boston Globe* called for a check to find out whether other statutory members of the commission attended meetings—these included persons skilled in penology, sociology, and psychiatry. Most of these statutory members had neglected attending the previously infrequent meetings. But with the publicity, they began showing up.

I always had the impression that the dour McCann probably did his best work after hours. He had an inside track to most of my critics in the department, and his hearings gave them a public platform. McCann subpoenaed them, put them under oath, and asked the questions they'd rehearsed in prior private meetings. The practice of using subpoenas had an additional purpose—menace. Periodically a portly man would appear at my office door or travel to my house thirty miles outside Boston to serve a subpoena demanding my attendance at a hearing in a room one hundred yards from my office. I called McCann and told him a subpoena wouldn't be necessary; a simple call or memo would suffice. My suggestion fell on deaf ears. Subpoenas continued to flow. The process also generated income for patronage subpoena servers, who collected a fee (plus travel and expenses) for each service.

One afternoon McCann invited me over to his office in the Senate, and he spread out before me drawings for a large youth prison—a detailed architectural plan on which someone had clearly spent a fair amount of money. It was a reformatory—buildings, security systems, fencing, and all the accoutrements conjured up by the formulas of modern corrections—an early version of what later came to be known as the "new generation" prison. No doubt it would come with a large influx of newly hired uniformed staff. If I had pledged support for such a facility, the investigation would have been halted. The new facility would almost certainly have moved quickly through the senate with the necessary millions of dollars attached. I deferred a decision.

McCann's hearings never developed a clearer focus than was given by allegations of permissiveness, hiring unqualified staff, or ignoring established procedures in starting new programs. The hearings drifted off with no clear conclusion. I figured McCann had decided to drop the matter. But I was wrong. He had been testing the waters, and he would return a year later to throw out his nets as senate chairman of the Joint

Committee on Post-Audit and Oversight. A committee staff member told me they planned to have me in jail by the time they finished.

Investigations were clearly a way of life, so I tried to keep myself in a state of mind that would hide my frustration at exercises less and less concerned with improving the effectiveness of the department. I had some basic belief in progress. If we did our best and our programs seemed to work, others would support us. But the reality was nothing like that. I got some sense of the poisoned atmosphere one noontime as I walked down Tremont Street in downtown Boston. From across the street came a yell, "Miller, we're gonna flush you down the toilet." I didn't recognize the balding, middle-aged man shouting at me. I asked the staff person walking with me if he knew who the man was. He was a Boston city councilman—someone I'd never met, nor, it seemed, would care to. But there he was, on a crowded downtown street, yelling wildly for all to hear. But Boston pols aren't stupid, so there mustn't have been much political loss of face in such gratuitous insult.

Even routine legislative business contributed to the noxious atmosphere. Take the House ways and means committee chairman, Joe Early, who, though conservative on law-and-order issues, didn't use his authority in a hurtful way or expect trades with every budget conciliation. No, he left the dirty business to the vice chairman, George Sacco, a legislator from Malden.

For George, no passage came without its toll. Though he had friends in the department and occasionally referred individuals for hiring, it was mostly a matter of style. Hiring a person he referred didn't much placate him, since he might change his mind a month or two later and demand I fire the same person because of some arcane political twist in his district. I finally decided my best course was to avoid contact, since it seemed to draw me into things I didn't handle particularly well. But such ostrichlike behavior ill fitted a department head. I developed an appreciation for Coughlan's dilemma, having caught myself up in the very things I had offhandedly condemned a couple of years before. I got some sense of how strongly George felt when, a couple of years after I'd left Massachusetts, I returned to Boston to attend a conference. I picked up *What's in Town* magazine, and there, winding its way through the restaurant ads and showgirl pics, was a long article by Sacco denouncing me and the deinstitutionalization of delinquent youth in Massachusetts.

The most severe backlash came in response to our taking on the county training schools. The investigating committee was headed by Representative Robert J. McGinn, who had been the prime supporter of the Hampden County school. The McGinn hearings almost brought down the reforms. Emotions on both sides got so out of hand that for a time it seemed as if there were no way out. Committee members had shown up at Westfield and had confronted a number of the young staff and consultants I'd hired to institute new educational and treatment programs, calling one of them an "uppity black bastard." Ironically, Westfield was one of our better facilities, with a variety of exciting new educational programs brought in by young graduate students from the University of Massachusetts. Many sported the long hair, bell-bottoms, and other informal attire of the day. On the basis of reports I'd received from Larry Dye, a graduate student at the University of Massachusetts who had started the new Westfield programs, the hearings seemed likely to run out of control. The students were generally cooperative and polite, but the committee members smelled blood.

Formal hearings were held in Boston, and at first the press didn't cover them. I was relieved, since they were among the most vitriolic I'd seen. Tommy Sheehan, the politically well-connected department counsel, offered to set up a meeting with McGinn to set a quieter, more amiable tone. We arranged to meet one afternoon in a carry-out shop near the capitol. The meeting seemed to go well. Though we disagreed on some things, we agreed that we shared many of the same goals. Predictably, even this meeting showed up in the *Herald* the next day— where we were described as smoking a peace pipe. I found the article interesting not for its content but for the fact that the details had been so accurately leaked. Peace, however, was not to be.

Though McGinn's committee had authority to study the Westfield center, he soon cut a wider swath, subpoenaing students, consultants, wives, girlfriends, children, parents, and acquaintances. Accusations of loose living and free love were routine. At one point the committee demanded that a University of Massachusetts student who was living with his girlfriend produce a marriage license. Old line employees obliged the committee with rumors, allegations, and tidbits of possible scandal. One of the chief informers to the committee was a former Roslindale employee I had suspended for waking certain youth at 6:00 A.M., making them duck walk up and down the hallways, and then beating them up.

Early one afternoon, Bill Madaus called me from the statehouse and told me he thought I should come over. A DYS parole agent was testifying before McGinn's committee. I was less perturbed by this than by the fact that the agent was from the other side of the state, nowhere near Westfield, the purported focus of the investigation. This hanging jury committee was aggressively widening its mandate to take on the whole department.

I hurried over and stood in the back of the hearing room as the parole agent read from a boy's DYS file, which lay open on the table in front of him. The room was ringed with reporters and television cameras; the committee had prepared well for the show. The parole agent droned on about a teenager on his caseload, calling him "one of the major dealers in heroin on the South Shore." I handed a note to a McGinn aide asking if I might be allowed to respond. A few moments later he came back and told me I wouldn't be allowed to testify.

I couldn't contain myself. I shouted that the committee had no mandate to elicit testimony unrelated to the Westfield center. McGinn yelled out, "I'm being intimidated by the commissioner of youth services."

I replied that the committee members were "racist and bigoted—a bunch of frauds."

"Leave this hearing!" was McGinn's loud retort.

"The days of McCarthyism are gone!" I shouted back.

"Leave! leave!" screamed McGinn, this time joined by Representative James Grimaldi of Springfield.

The sergeant at arms was ordered to eject me. As I was being hustled out of the hearing room, McGinn appeared to collapse. He pulled himself together and left the room, saying he felt ill. There was concern that he was suffering from a recurrence of a heart condition. When a committee member suggested that the session be terminated, Ed Budelman, a young University of Massachusetts psychologist I'd hired to head residential care, shouted from the back of the hearing room, "What's the matter, did the cameras leave?" It was not one of our finer moments.

The statehouse physician examined McGinn and said he hadn't suffered a heart attack but had been "emotionally disturbed." He gave him a mild sedative. When McGinn returned from the doctor's office, he told waiting reporters, "I'll bury Miller if it's the last thing I do. He's a nut. He belongs in an insane asylum." I wasn't in much better shape. As I hurried away from the hearing room, David Nyhan, the statehouse reporter for the *Boston Globe*, came up. He looked worried and asked if I knew McGinn might have had a heart attack. I blurted out, "Good!" By the time I'd walked the block and a half to my office, the viciousness of the afternoon's events hit me. My comment to Nyhan was unforgivable. The center wasn't holding. Before that day, even when things seemed most bleak, I'd been able to retreat for a while—long enough to regain my reason. Now I'd lost that and taken a bad turn. I'd also put Speaker Bartley in an untenable position by insulting the legislature. He had to back McGinn.

But the committee was a loose cannon, and that was a problem for the speaker. He'd appointed it. The governor's office called me at home to tell me that the governor continued to support me and that I needn't back away. It was lucky that the flap had occurred late in the week, as most legislators had gone home and wouldn't be back until Monday. No immediate action could be taken on the House floor.

The speaker, while publicly demanding that I make an apology to the legislature, sent word to me through his aide, John Eller, that a coalition of reformers and human service professionals had approached him to propose my immediate ouster. They would testify that, though I might have accomplished some things, I'd gone much too far, too fast. They were unwilling to come out publicly on their own, however. Indeed, the person who contacted the speaker for the group had led the search committee which selected me as commissioner. Eller told me Bartley's response would probably hinge on whatever public support I could muster by the following Monday. I spent the weekend calling individuals and leaders of citizens' groups I'd spoken to over the previous three years, asking them to contact the speaker's office.

Meanwhile, McGinn moved in the legislature for formal power to conduct a statewide investigation of the department. But by the time the motion was on the floor for a vote, things were cooling down. The *Boston Globe* published an editorial highly critical of the McGinn hearings, the governor made his support clear, and the League of Women Voters stood fast in its support.

Simultaneously, Jack McGlynn rushed to release the long-awaited reort of the Joint Committee on State Administration. Though it had been completed a couple of months earlier, it hadn't been put in final form. It was readied hurriedly and released the day before the House was to vote on McGinn's motion. The committee report endorsed the phaseout of the reform schools and praised the community alternatives as "more humane, less expensive care for juvenile delinquents."

The speaker kept the McGinn committee's mandate confined to investigating Westfield. McGinn apologized on the House floor for saying I belonged in a nut house. The following day, I publicly apologized for disrupting the hearings and calling the members bigoted. I suggested tempers had gotten out of hand and invited McGinn to meet again. I thanked the speaker for his help during the crisis, noting that McGinn had what he wanted—the right to investigate Westfield, while I had what I wanted—no expansion of the committee's mandate.

The truce lasted about three weeks before the hearings again deteriorated. After an hour or so of angry exchanges, McGinn said that the committee had gathered enough information to seek indictments against me. He announced that he was forwarding the matter to the attorney general or a grand jury. McGinn's vice chairman, James Grimaldi, added, "Somewhere along the line, Mr. Miller, you will get chopped up. Residents don't want halfway houses in their areas."

The hearings moved to focus on the Project Joe program at the University of Massachusetts, the nonprofit organization which had placed the last hundred youngsters from Lyman. The project was headed by Larry Dye, who was clearly a target of opportunity. Despite the fact that he was finishing a Ph.D. at the University of Massachusetts, he made no secret of his having been an inmate in the California Youth Authority. I explained that working through private, nonprofit agencies gave us more flexibility in allocating staff and spending funds for individual youngsters. McGinn replied that we could have done the same thing with state employees. I snapped, "If we went through the state, we would have to get jobs for your friends and relatives." Civility had once again fled from the hearings.

Then it became clear that McGinn was being fed information from my own office. In one particular case, I had discussed an internal memo which listed specific kids whose placements had not worked out. A couple of their names had been misspelled because of typos by a secretary in my office. McGinn requested information on the very same youngsters, misspelling their names the identical way. I hired a Boston attorney, Michael Keating, to represent me at the hearings.

Staff reappeared like ghosts of Christmas past. Father Bergeron, the former chaplain at Shirley, showed up at the hearings to urge the governor to remove me "for the good of the youth he is supposed to be serving." He went on to criticize the idea of creating small community settings for reform school youth, and what he saw as letting the youngsters themselves decide if they were ready for parole.

Meanwhile, the House ways and means committee refused to approve the federally financed salaries of our newly created regional directors. Suffolk County (Boston) District Attorney Garrett Byrne, whom I'd never met or spoken with in three years, made public a letter he had written to me, but which I hadn't received, demanding stricter supervision of youths in the department. He called for a long-term juvenile detention center.

After half a year's uproar, the McGinn committee brought forth a twenty-three-page report. The indictments had fizzled, and the report sang a familiar plaint—we were too permissive with delinquents. The committee alleged a serious lack of discipline and supervision: "Children practically run some institutions. Children with serious criminal records are being placed back on the streets." The matter of the county training schools—the motivation for the investigation—was hardly mentioned. But, despite the flimsiness of the report, the hearings had hurt us badly, and the ordeal convinced me that my days in Massachusetts were numbered. My wife and I both liked the state and had hoped to stay, eventually living somewhere along the North Shore. But now I knew it would be impossible. Besides, in those final months, she'd been getting obscene telephone calls; their content established that they came from someone in my office.

A month or so later, I was asked by New York's mayor, John Lindsay, to come down and discuss possibilities in the city's corrections system. I had spent a day at the new Adolescent Remand Center on Rikers Island. It hadn't yet been filled with young offenders, and Lindsay had invited experts from around the country to advise him how to make the place productive. I suggested he tear it down. If organized crime or a cabal of subversives had sat around a table and plotted how to create crime and mayhem on the streets of New York, they would have come up with the programs and architecture of the Adolescent Remand Center. The huge facility could only alienate, embitter, and contribute to the deterioration of youth in the city.

Lindsay was a compelling and engaging person. I thoroughly enjoyed the meeting. He offered me a position on his staff to work as his liaison with the corrections department. It would have been a considerable increase in salary over my $25,000 position in Massachusetts. But it came with no line authority. Although Lindsay said I could, in fact, call most of the shots in corrections from the mayor's office, he had no plans to make changes in the top positions in the department. I decided against joining his staff.

I was also called to Washington to meet with Secretary of Health, Education and Welfare Elliott Richardson to discuss my heading the Office of Youth Development and Delinquency Prevention, but his offer was set aside when President Nixon appointed him attorney general.

In late November 1972, I was approached by a representative of the new governor-elect of Illinois, Dan Walker, and asked to join his cabinet. I didn't really want to leave Massachusetts and turned him down twice. Peter Goldmark heard of the Illinois offer, called me over, and asked me to stay. He said the governor agreed. I was as flattered as I had been at our first meeting three and a half years before. I half-heartedly suggested that I'd stay if the governor would appoint Boston Juvenile Court Judge Frank Poitrast to Superior Court—not so much a promotion as a way to get him out of my hair. The governor wasn't able to do it. I was told it was because such an appointment was reserved for others closer in spirit to the administration. I understood this and realized I'd set an impossible condition. But I knew I wouldn't survive long into the next year in Massachusetts. It was only a matter of time. With the demise of the McGinn committee, Senator McCann was starting up a considerably larger, better funded postaudit committee to investigate DYS. Its cochairman was Gerald Lombard, the legislator with the defunct Shirley school in his district. It was time to go. In January 1973 I accepted the Illinois job.

Aftershocks

In 1970 the National Conference of State Training School Superintendents had quietly hired a former reform school superintendent, Frank Manwell, to look into the closings of the Massachusetts schools. He had filed three separate reports, all critical. Apparently, no action was to be taken on the report until I had left office. Six months after I left Massachusetts, it was reported that participants in the fiftieth annual meeting of the National Conference of Superintendents of Training Schools and Reformatories (NCSTS) had voted fifty-eight to two to censure me for my role in closing schools in Massachusetts.

By then I was a pariah among most fellow state juvenile corrections administrators. I had committed the unforgivable sin of agreeing to be an expert witness for San Francisco's Youth Law Center and the Men-

tal Health Law Project in their suit against the Texas Youth Council—
Morales vs. Turman. I'd spent a week or so touring Texas reform
schools, where I saw kids beaten, tied, locked in isolation, forced to run
till they dropped, hauling dirt from one pile to another and back again,
gassed and maced while locked in closetlike cells, and chased by blood-
hounds and shotgun-toting guards. Texas members of the NCSTS had
retaliated by voting in favor of my censure.

A few weeks after the NCSTS meeting, I was invited to be a panelist at
the New Orleans meeting of the National Council on Crime and Delinquency (NCCD)—to debate representatives of the NCSTS and defend the
Massachusetts deinstitutionalization. The ballroom was packed with
close to four hundred corrections experts. At a table in the front sat a
middle-aged woman facing a huge reel-to-reel tape deck. I thought she
was probably from National Public Radio, there to record the debate.
But the machine was motionless, and the operator sat silent during
the presentations of my copanelists. As I rose to respond, she flipped
switches and donned earphones. I was flattered. I shouldn't have
been. She was there to record my remarks for Texas Attorney General
Mark White, who was defending the state in Morales vs. Turman.

I took the opportunity to vent my feelings about the so-called Manwell Report, criticizing "those who root around and sneak around,
sleuths with the sick mission of disparaging anything humane in treating delinquent youngsters." My language matched the disgust I'd
experienced while touring the Texas institutions. I suggested that those
trying to undo what we had accomplished in Massachusetts would
soon find their own repressive reform schools overwhelmed by the
movement we'd started. It was a naive and grandiose statement. No
way would what we did in Massachusetts be allowed to happen in most
other states.

Seated next to me on the platform was a member of the censuring
board of the NCSTS. He denied there'd been a censure and delivered a
prepared speech about Don Quixotes on impractical missions, characterizing those in NCSTS as the Sancho Panzas of juvenile justice, putting
things right step by step. I replied with a reference to Dante's *Inferno*:
"Abandon hope, all ye who enter here." From the audience came a
cacophony of applause, catcalls, and boos.

Senator McCann's and Representative Lombard's postaudit report
didn't appear for another year. True to tradition, committee members
leaked tidbits during the months before its final publication. The phones

were particularly active between members of the committee and Illinois politicians. An article appeared in *Boston Magazine* entitled, "Boston Smoke for a Chicago Fire," laying out the machinations between members of the postaudit committee and members of the Illinois legislature. But after $300,000 was spent for five staff members to investigate what we had done, the postaudit pretty much drew a blank. The language was strong, and the criticism of my style was well taken. There were indeed many administrative problems. We had opened community programs and moved youngsters while skirting the usual administrative mechanisms of government. Funding for many of the community-based programs had fallen short. Staffing of new programs was often ad hoc. Specific programs were started without previous legislative approval. And now, others had to pick up many of the pieces. But we'd set a new system in place—one which wouldn't be easily undone—and the committee knew it.

In the end, the postaudit report amounted to little more than a temper tantrum. Senator McCann summarized his feelings, "The condition of the division is the result of Miller's scatterbrained propositions. His concept that we didn't need institutions had no rhyme or reason." Cochairman Lombard said, "Miller closed the institutions and the young offenders are roaming the streets."

I worried that people might jump on a bandwagon to reopen the reform schools. Superior Court Chief Justice Walter H. McLaughlin, brother of the former Boston police commissioner with whom I'd had an altercation, called DYS a shambles. "There's no sound place for detention. . . . They laugh at the judges because they know there is no place where we can put them. You cannot threaten the youngster with depriving him of his freedom. They don't fear punishment." And perhaps most disappointingly, my staff, having ridden out my tenure, swung over to what appeared to be a new winning side. By 1974, Herb Willman, then director of administration, who'd been so helpful much of the time, risen to Director of Administration, told the *Boston Herald*, "The department went through a pretty horrendous three years under Miller." But succeeding commissioners straightened up most of the administrative problems I'd created. Joe Leavey took most of the flak and got very little credit, but he managed to keep things in equilibrium while he reestablished relationships with the legislature and the judiciary.

The last major assault on the reforms came in the late 1970s, under the conservative governor Ed King. He entered office supporting the death penalty and calling for harsher handling of juvenile offenders. King created a Governor's Task Force on Juvenile Crime made up primarily of police, judges, and prosecutors, and with Harvard's James Q. Wilson as the resident ideologue. The task force held hearings throughout the state, eliciting testimony from selected local officials, police, and judges, all of it aimed at building a case for harsher and more stringent handling of juveniles. It recommended more use of locked facilities, longer sentences, and more ease in trying youngsters fourteen and older as adults. But it was too late. The money had left the institutional grounds. Youth corrections was largely in the hands of private, nonprofit agencies who delivered services to the youth. The old system couldn't be resurrected without grave political consequences.

17 *Results: After Almost All Is Said and Done*

What did we accomplish? Was the state any safer after our reforms than before? How many returned to DYS or went into adult jails and prisons? What was the impact on youth crime rates? These questions have remained central.

Recidivism

The concern with recidivism was curious for a field not particularly given to claiming accountability for the high failure rates of its alumni. But there was an internal consistency to the questions. It was the logic of the pilot project. If the Massachusetts reforms prove successful, other states will emulate them. It sounds reasonable, but it had little relevance in the byzantine world of corrections. Whether a pilot project succeeds or fails has almost no influence on policy. Images and posturing are stronger cards. Sadly, the ghost of a Willie Horton or the packaging of Scared Straight boot camps is what matters.

In evaluating juvenile correctional programs across the nation in the late 1960s and early 1970s, Robert Vinter's University of Michigan researchers found a disturbing pattern. Although they saw many promising programs on early site visits, by the time the research teams got around to a second or third visit, many of these programs had vanished. Not only did they have no effect on the larger youth corrections system, they were methodically starved out of existence through such mechanisms as time-limited funding. Less effective models (primarily institutional) remained firmly fixed in state bureaucracies and budgets. Pilot programs were irrelevant as a reform strategy.

But closing all of a state's reform schools was too total to be dismissed as a pilot program. Though it continued to be described as an experiment by most correctional administrators, so long as it survived, it couldn't be easily ignored. In this light, sound research was crucial, if only to establish a written record of the reforms before their inevitable demise.

Despite the fact that some of the most famous studies in the literature on delinquent behavior derived their samples from youngsters under the YSB,[1] the agency knew very little about how its alumni fared after release from institutions. From time to time some visiting graduate student would do a recidivism study, but the methodology tended to be flawed and the findings contradictory. The research and statistics arm of the department also tried to keep occasional recidivism figures. But again the findings were incomplete.

When I first met the superintendent of the Shirley Industrial School, he presented me with a study touting a 5 percent recidivism rate among released boys. Ninety-five percent success seemed impressive, but a closer look undid the rosy conclusions. The Shirley researchers had counted only those boys returned to that institution as recidivists. Since Shirley held the oldest boys in the department, most were released shortly before or upon reaching legal adulthood. Later charges were likely to show up only in adult court, with recidivists placed on adult probation or sent to adult prisons or jails. The offenders weren't returned to Shirley; therefore, they weren't counted.

Lyman had less reassuring figures. An in-house study found that the longer a boy stayed at Lyman, the less likely he was to make it on the street. The earlier he was released, the better his chances of success. This dovetailed with a later, more sophisticated study of Lyman alumni by the respected psychologist William McCord. McCord and his associates compared matched samples of Lyman alumni with boys released from a therapeutically oriented private residential program. Predictably, the Lyman boys repeated their crimes at a demonstrably higher rate. McCord's findings as to long-term patterns of delinquency among the two samples were particularly enlightening, and anticipated later research findings in Massachusetts.[2]

Though there were then, as now, questions as to whether it is possible to rehabilitate young offenders, there was, in fact, credible research suggesting that appropriate alternatives could cut recidivism. The University of Southern California sociologist LaMar Empey[3] had documented an appreciable drop in repeat offenses among delinquent youth placed in community care. Empey's findings came with no magic bullets. The majority of youth still reoffended within a year, but they offended less often and less seriously than before intervention.

The idea that an effective delinquency treatment program should allow some flexibility for a youngster who was, in fact, winding down his or her career of illegal behavior seemed unacceptable. Routine incarceration at least incapacitated the young offenders for a while, and, during that lock-up time, stopped all delinquent acts on the street. But the practice could be likened to rehospitalizing a pneumonia sufferer at the first sign of a cough. It's a costly and dangerous overreaction.

The Harvard Studies

Early research by Harvard's Center for Criminal Justice had concentrated on the politics of change, inmate attitudes, staff perceptions, and the quality of care in the treatment cottages we'd set up in some of the institutions. Though the recidivism rates of these institutionalized youngsters were also studied, it was three years before anything definitive could be said, and recidivism was not the primary consideration in the studies.

When we moved unexpectedly to close the institutions in 1972, the Harvard researchers shifted their focus to recidivism; that is, to DYS alumni placed on probation after reappearance in court, recommitted to DYS, or incarcerated in county jails or state prisons. The subsequent studies would have been even richer if the researchers had maintained their original emphasis on the quality of care being provided in our programs. In fact, the quality and the integrity of treatment programs became the determinants of whether recidivism increased or decreased among youngsters in community alternatives.

Though enough time had passed to follow the recidivism rates of a control group of 1969 reform school youth, results on the experimental group of youth we'd placed in alternatives in 1972 and 1973 were slow in coming. Periodically I would call Lloyd Ohlin or Bob Coates and ask what the data were showing. "Things seem to be going in the right direction" was the usual reply. I took this to mean that the youth in alternatives were getting into less trouble than those from the reform schools.

The first solid figures didn't appear until 1975, more than a year after I'd left Massachusetts to head the Illinois Department of Children and Youth Services. As a courtesy, the Harvard Center sent me an initial draft of their findings. A few pages into the complicated material, I slumped back in my chair. Recidivism hadn't gone down. Statewide, it had increased slightly, particularly among girls. At best, our four years' effort had been a washout.

I mulled over the depressing news for a couple of days before calling Lloyd. Though I didn't expect much encouragement, I wanted some clarification of the sometimes confusing figures, graphs, and tables. Lloyd's response surprised me. The results hadn't seemed to discourage him. I concluded he probably didn't care much which way things turned out. Researchers have to be objective, and it was unfair to expect otherwise. As he discussed the draft paper, however, I realized that my first reading had been too pessimistic. Lloyd felt that the study provided significant support for our reforms.

The crucial finding had to do with the differences in recidivism between regions in the state. The slight statewide rise in recidivism rates was attributed to a national pattern of rising crime rates in 1972–73, the years from which the sample of youth in alternative programs was drawn. When crime rates increase, so does recidivism. In addition, we'd diverted a large number of younger offenders to the Department of Welfare's Division of Child Guidance during those same years, leaving us with older youth convicted of more serious offenses—a group more prone to recidivism. Of more consequence to the Harvard researchers were the modest, but solid, drops in recidivism in certain regions of the state. An intriguing pattern had emerged which appeared to be tied to our regionalization efforts. The report put it:

There were seven administrative regions in the reformed system. Regions II and VII were the regions that pursued the reforms most aggressively. This was evident in efforts to provide a large number of diverse program options, so the special needs of each youth could be more nearly met. Region V, on the other hand, hardly changed at all from the traditional approach before the reforms. The results are dramatic.

Regions II and VII are the only two regions where recidivism went down, and Region V shows an exceptionally large increase. The decrease in Region VII is on both criteria. The increase in Region V is also on both criteria.[4]

The conclusion was relatively simple. Recidivism dropped where: (1) the regional offices developed a diversity of programs from which to draw in dealing with each individual youngster; and (2) the alternative programs had therapeutic integrity joined with strong "community linkages."

Success in lowering recidivism depended upon the quality and the diversity of the alternatives. Where programs broke their institutional tether, recidivism went down. When alternatives fostered isolation or duplicated institutional regimens in the community, the youth did poorly. To my chagrin, Bob Coates suggested we'd been too faint-hearted in implementing our reforms. We hadn't gone far enough. As the Harvard report said, "For the state as a whole, it is clear that the reforms did not go nearly far enough . . . we saw that there was an alarming amount of variability in the program scores on social climate, extent of community linkages, and quality of community linkages."[5]

The conclusion hardly seemed to justify the extensive research effort. A diversity of good alternative programs lowers recidivism. A narrow choice of poor programs does not. Though we hadn't done as well as we should have, the fault was in the implementation rather than the concept. Recidivism dropped where we did things right. If all the regions of the state could create enough quality options, most of our delinquent youth would make it in the community. And the researchers had looked at youngsters drawn from a sample at the very beginning of the deinstitutionalization, when we were most vulnerable and still building the alternative system. If backsliding could be held in reasonable check, the deinstitutionalization stood a chance of success.

In succeeding years, despite political pressure to return to the institutions, DYS continued its community-based emphasis. Even the administration of the right-wing governor Ed King was unable to return kids to reform schools. The reasons had less to do with any commitment to alternatives than with new political alignments, which had been created by funding a wide variety of private, nonprofit agencies. Once these agencies had the money, they weren't about to give it up easily. Many were too powerful for the legislature to challenge. The money couldn't be taken back. Reopening the institutions would require DYS to double its budget, running the community-based programs side by side with reopened or new institutions. The state was in no condition to absorb this kind of fiscal shock, and as a result, the new system was left alone.

Later Patterns

As the community programs stabilized, more signs reinforced the early conclusions of Ohlin, Coates, and Miller. Between 1978 and 1988, there was a dramatic drop in the number of youth appearing in Massachusetts juvenile courts. Arraignments fell 34 percent, from 28,000 to 18,000. At first the drop was attributed to the passing of the baby boom, which meant that there were fewer teenagers around. But the percentage drop in arraignments was nearly three times that in number of juveniles. The juvenile population fell only 12 percent during the same period, from 718,599 to 627,487.

Juvenile arrests statewide also decreased at a faster rate than did the juvenile population, and the number of youth waived for trial in adult court fell to an all-time low. In 1989, while states like Maryland and Virginia each tried up to a thousand youngsters in adult courts, and Florida waived nearly four thousand youth to adult court, Massachusetts tried a total of twelve youth in adult court.[6] This demonstrated another important fact. Massachusetts was handling its most serious young offenders in a primarily community-based system. And the system appeared to represent minimal risk to public safety. As NCCD research revealed, in any given year, youths under DYS jurisdiction represented approximately one percent of all arrests in the state. According to the NCCD, "Few of the offenses committed by DYS youth involved violence (less than ten percent)—the majority of their crimes are minor property offenses." Massachusetts ranked forty-sixth of the fifty states in reported juvenile crime. Things weren't going all that badly in the state which locked up the fewest teenagers of any in the nation.

One of the most interesting phenomena emerged in the Massachusetts state prisons. The percentage of adult inmates who were alumni of juvenile corrections fell from 35 percent in 1969 to 18 percent by 1985, although the number of youth under commitment to DYS remained at about two thousand on any given day during the same period. The drop in alumni entering state prisons couldn't be attributed to fewer youngsters' being in the system. But whereas in 1969 virtually all the DYS alumni in state prisons came from reform schools, after 1973 only a minority had spent time in "secure care." The same kinds of youth were being handled differently. It seemed reasonable to conclude that Massachusetts might be breaking into the familiar subculture of delinquency which characterizes a certain segment of harder-core youth in states still wedded to reform schools. Though this supposition awaits a controlled study, the available figures are encouraging.

In late 1989, the NCCD completed a three-year follow-up of 875 Massachusetts youths who left DYS in 1984–85.[7] The findings closely paralleled the conclusions of the Harvard researchers. Three years after their first community placement, approximately 12 percent of the DYS youth had been recommitted to the department (usually for continued supervision in the community), 10 percent were incarcerated in county jails, and 2 percent were sent to state prison. Seventy-six percent were still maintaining themselves in the community, free of DYS supervision. This relatively low rate of recidivism approximated the rate found by the Harvard researchers in the most successful regions of the state in 1974. It suggests that, as the community-based system diversified and grew, it dealt more successfully with youth who would otherwise have been institutionalized. As the NCCD study noted, "The overall re-arraignment rate for the 1985 DYS group equalled the regions with the lowest recidivism rates in the earlier Harvard study. This finding suggests that recidivism rates have improved as DYS came closer to its stated goals of reform—a rich diversity of community-based services permitting youth normal experiences in school, work and family settings."[8]

What about rearrests and reappearances in juvenile courts? Neither, in itself, is an adequate measure. Arrests of youth from certain socioeconomic classes and races is a pretty random event. Elliott and others found, for example, that approximately one-third of all youth residing within a Southwestern urban juvenile court's jurisdiction were referred to the juvenile court for a delinquency or status offense before their eighteenth birthday. Forty-seven percent of all males and 21 percent of all females had juvenile court careers.[9] Wolfgang, in his Philadelphia cohort of youth, found that as many as one-third of all black youth were arrested at some time in their teen years. One study of young black males in California suggested that seven out of ten would be arrested at some time.

Half the DYS youngsters in Massachusetts were rearrested at some time during the NCCD's three-year follow-up. This rate, however, was lower than rearrest rates in comparable states in which reform schools remained the backbone of state youth corrections. In California, for example, 70 percent of youth released from state reform schools were rearrested within twelve months, with over 60 percent being re-incarcerated within thirty-six months. In contrast, of Massachusetts youth in community-based programs who were subsequently rearrested, only 24 percent were recommitted to DYS or incarcerated in adult prisons within three years. The NCCD study further suggested that rearrests in Massachusetts were for less serious incidents than those of youth in California.

Looking at it conservatively, one can see that deinstitutionalization posed no measurable threat to public safety, as things were no worse than in states that relied on incarceration. More positively, the reformed Massachusetts system contributed to a safer community. Massachusetts had shifted the bulk of state institutional budgets to private, nonprofit agencies. New treatment and supervision models had sprung up across the state. Destructive correctional programs were terminated; something that is still unheard of in corrections nationally. But most important, a major state's youth corrections system and, at least for a while, the public's perception of the youngsters relegated to it, were altered.

The problems didn't disappear with the reforms. Every year legislation is filed to bring back the reform schools. I have little doubt that one day it will succeed—probably in the wake of a publicity campaign over a tragic incident. Youngsters will continue to do things around which politicians can vie to prove their "toughness"—to send more juveniles to adult court; to deny the department power to place its charges in the community; to demand more stringent handling of delinquents. Policy is impervious to facts where television bites reign supreme.

In response to these kinds of spastic pressures, the current Massachusetts DYS has done many things I would not want to claim. Too many young people are in "secure care."[10] No youngsters wander the halls of the central office conversing with and otherwise annoying administrators. As the department has become professionalized, the hurtful side effects which inevitably accompany certain behavioral and medical models when they are practiced on delinquents have re-emerged—the reintroduction of isolation rooms in some of the small secure settings (this time to "set limits") and the use of psychotropic drugs to control recalcitrant youngsters—as ways to avoid having to deal with the sources of their "unreasonable" demands.

In keeping with the style of Governor Michael Dukakis, the DYS substituted smooth management for advocacy. Though in the short term sounder management was necessary, it now seems perilously close to becoming the raison d'être of the department.

In pursuit of fiscal control, the department has cut back on the number and variety of alternatives. Whereas I preferred to risk looser control by encouraging smaller, often financially unstable programs to apply for state funding, my successors have moved to ever-larger contracts with fewer but admittedly more stable agencies. The rationale is that a few large agencies can provide the same range of services as a mixture of less established and more innovative small agencies. Indeed, this strategy has settled things down considerably and will continue to work for a while. But ultimately it will prove to be an error. Competition will be driven away, and the large private agencies will become vested interests. This is a mixed blessing. Large, politically powerful private agencies are at least a counterbalance to state employees' unions and to legislators endlessly on the prowl for the kinds of patronage and influence which traditional institutions provide.

It was inevitable that things would move in this fashion. The reforms had to be integrated into the routines of state bureaucracy. I couldn't have done that. I had alienated too many in state government to expect their support in stabilizing matters. To the credit of succeeding administrations that has now happened, but at a price. Some time not far off someone will have to shake up the reformed system as roughly as we did the institutional system. But for a while we established a new model which dealt individually, and usually sensitively, with a category of youngsters unaccustomed to such concern. We also demonstrated that, if well implemented, the new model could work better than what it replaced. Sadly, its survival will not be based on results, but will be a matter of chance, of happenstance, of politics and mood.

V

Ponderings on Criminals and Criminologists

18 *Of Psychopaths and Allopaths*

Having commanded Adam to bestow
Names upon all the creatures, God withdrew
To empyrean palaces of blue
That warm and windless morning long ago.
And seemed to take no notice of the vexed
Look on the young man's face as he took thought
Of all the miracles the Lord had wrought,
Now to be labelled, dubbed, yclept, indexed.

Before an addled mind and puddled brow,
The feathered nation and the finny prey
Passed by; there went biped and quadruped.
Adam looked forth with bottomless dismay
Into the tragic eyes of his first cow,
And shyly ventured, "Thou shalt be called 'Fred'."

Anthony Hecht

Nearly every correctional reform uses diagnosis as its first step. If we can name what's wrong, goes the myth, we can treat it. But labeling is also crucial to culling the good from the bad; the wicked from the elect; and, ultimately, "them" from "us." The progressive Maryland Juvenile Services Administration Department began its reform in the late sixties by creating the Maryland Children's Center as a model classification and diagnostic facility. Every child committed by the courts across the state was sent there for classification. But the diagnostic program failed, and the classification facility was closed. It was an old story. Despite the new diagnostic regimen, the treatment for youngsters continued to be either institutionalization or referral to an overburdened probation system. In such a narrow world of options, individual diagnoses were superfluous.

In Massachusetts, diagnosis had come to be so irrelevant that a disgruntled psychiatrist wrote "Mary had a little lamb" seventy-five times in his diagnostic study of a youngster, and no one noticed. "Cookbook" dicta were the rule, and youngsters ended up classified

according to the needs of the system—age, sex, size, and manageabil-
ity. It was a classic example of treatment (or lack of it) driving diagnosis.
Let me give another.

A few years after I left Massachusetts, I joined Governor Milton
Shapp's staff in Pennsylvania. Shortly after I arrived, sixteen-year-old
Bobby Nestor hanged himself in the adult prison at Camp Hill. He had
been sent there through a quirk in Pennsylvania law which allowed
juvenile courts to sentence juveniles to adult prison without benefit of
adult trial. There were four hundred of them at Camp Hill, most confined to cells twenty-three hours a day. The rationale was "dangerousness." Boys sent to Camp Hill were diagnosed as antisocial and sociopathic and classified as too difficult and dangerous to be handled in the
state reform schools.

Bobby had come to Camp Hill by a circuitous route. His parents had
found some marijuana in the pocket of his jacket and called the police,
who advised that he be arrested and detained for a few days to frighten
him. While in juvenile detention, he met an older teenager, and they
escaped together, stealing a car along the way. They were quickly
caught, and because of the new charge and his incorrigibility, the court
ordered Bobby to the Camp Hill prison, describing it to the parents as a
special school. The boyish-looking sixteen-year-old was immediately
subjected to sexual pressure from older inmates, culminating in his
rape and suicide. (There were unresolved questions as to whether he
had been murdered.) News of his death appeared in a nearly hidden
notice on the inside pages of the *Harrisburg Patriot* as just another
inmate suicide. When I heard of Bobby's death, I drove across the river
from the state capital to Camp Hill. After a records search and a series
of interviews with other youngsters and staff, we put together a report
on the events leading up to this boy's tragic death and took it to the
governor. He'd been concerned about the juveniles at Camp Hill for
most of his tenure, but his staff had been unable to find a way to deal
with the problem. It took Bobby's death to provide the impetus for
removing juveniles from the Camp Hill prison.

Juveniles had been routinely sent to Camp Hill for years, usually to
serve an average of three years. But previous efforts to get juveniles out
of Camp Hill always hinged on a classification and on diagnostic procedure. A year before Bobby Nestor died, Governor Shapp assembled
a group of experts to devise a way to get juveniles out of Camp Hill.
These probation officers, youth workers, judges, psychologists, psy-

chiatrists, and social workers reclassified the inmates. Based on this classification, they recommended that three hundred inmates be transferred to a special locked institution on the grounds of a state hospital for treatment. The panel also proposed that most of the remaining hundred boys be placed in state reform schools. About a dozen inmates were diagnosed as being fit for return to the community on parole. Ninety-five percent of the juveniles in Camp Hill were classified as needing maximum or medium security institutionalization. The plan had yet to be implemented.

Following Bobby's death, I proposed to the governor that we look at the problem again. Politics were a first consideration, and I prevailed on him to pressure the attorney general, who at the time was appointed by the governor, to declare the practice of juvenile courts' sending youngsters to Camp Hill unconstitutional. After a series of meetings with a reluctant attorney general and accusations by his aides of bringing undue, if not frankly dishonest, pressure on him, I got a favorable opinion.

But before we could go back to the juvenile courts with alternative sentencing proposals for each youngster, another classification or diagnostic process would be necessary. I selected a group of professionals not unlike those who had assembled the year before—psychiatrists, psychologists, social workers, family therapists, educators, probation officers, and correctional counselors. These experts, some with national reputations, did not need or want interference. Obviously we could not instruct them how to diagnose the youthful inmates. One might expect that their conclusions would have been similar to those of the previous group, but this time something quite different happened.

Before we brought in these new diagnosticians, we paid them to attend a series of orientation meetings designed to acquaint them with programs we were considering for the Camp Hill juveniles if they were released. The full spectrum of real and possible options was described, from Outward Bound and wilderness camping programs to group homes; from halfway houses to hiring advocates for youths; from foster care to specialized monitoring, where the monitor would be paid a full salary to look after an individual youth; from vocational and educational programs to residential and nonresidential drug treatment programs; from house arrest to small residential treatment programs for emotionally disturbed youngsters; from day treatment to small, locked, secure programs for juveniles who were at risk of committing violence.

In addition, these professional clinicians were assured that no youth would be moved from Camp Hill prison unless he could be placed in the precise program recommended. Whereas earlier diagnosticians had been left only the choice to institutionalize or to parole, the new group had a wide range of options to consider. The outcome differed dramatically.

The new diagnoses of the Camp Hill youths were nearly the opposite of those formulated by the earlier group of experts. Ninety percent (360 boys) of the Camp Hill inmates were seen as fit for some form of community placement. Only 10 percent (40 youth) were diagnosed as so dangerous as to be in need of being locked up. Once provided an array of options between extremes, the experts had diagnosed the inmates in a thoughtful, graduated manner. They felt at less risk if they recommended something other than prison. The conclusion was obvious. The treatment options in the mind of the diagnostician determined the diagnosis of the person being evaluated. This is the reverse of what we commonly assume happens in diagnosis and classification of offenders. We assume that we measure the delinquent against medical, psychological, and sociological criteria and prescribe treatment accordingly. In fact, the theory-diagnosis-treatment flow runs backward. The diagnostician looks first to the means available for handling the client, then labels the client, and finally justifies the label with psychiatric or sociological theory. Diagnosis virtually never determines treatment; treatment dictates diagnosis. The task of the diagnostician is to validate the means of handling already available. The implications are overwhelming. It seems that if we are to make progress in understanding and controlling delinquents, the treatment options must be guaranteed before any diagnosis is made. Unless this is clearly understood, diagnostic and classification procedures will only mislead us and label youngsters to fit organizational needs. When clinicians routinely label a youth "antisocial, in need of institutionalization," they are more likely to betray their lack of imagination concerning less restrictive options than any particular insight into the young offender's character.

Other professions understand these relationships better. British architect Michael Forsyth comments that, just as composers are greatly influenced in what they write by the places in which their works will be played, so architects of buildings for music are heavily influenced in what they design by their own visions of the musical purposes the buildings will serve.[1] This is precisely the relationship of psychiatric and social work professionals to the correctional institutions in which they work and for which they design classification and treatment models. In the diagnosis of delinquents we are closer to the conceptions of contemporary architects than to those of behavioral scientists. As in the view of the American architect Louis Sullivan, form must follow function. Theory and, by implication, diagnosis, follows its embodiment in service. But the service is as much determined by bricks, concrete, and local politics as it is by scientific fact. "Form follows function" can be translated to "theory follows practice," which turns diagnosis on its head. A 1983 study of classification of delinquents came to a similar conclusion: "The less resources, the more punishment was seen as beneficial for the youth."[2] When the person making the diagnosis is aware of a variety of alternative or noninstitutional options for treatment and handling, he or she gives less extreme, less rigid, and less restrictive diagnoses. Wanting this, diagnosis becomes more judgmental and punitive.

Sorting Sociopaths

Diagnosing offenders is too often a political action. Liberals prefer diagnosis to treatment. They are willing to observe and prescribe—so long as they need not touch. Whatever contact is necessary is reserved for hired guns—helping professionals—who do it only on their own terms, carrying their attenuated view of the problem back to their employers. Contrariwise, conservatives are poor, even shallow in their diagnoses. But their elitist ideology allows them the certainty to be quick with global prescriptions which seem to make common sense. These characteristics make liberals impotent and conservatives dangerous. In both instances, personal responsibility is diffused to the point of irrelevance. I would rather forgo a sophisticated (albeit valid) psychiatric diagnosis for a delinquent given by a clinician who takes no responsibility for implementing the treatment—if in its place, I can have an assessment, "He needs a job" from someone willing to find him one and take him to it each day.

Diagnosing the errant is a time-honored pursuit. From the medieval monks' *Malleus Maleficarum* (Witches' hammer) to the *Diagnostic and Statistical Manual* (DSM-III) of the American Psychiatric Association;

from the "possessed" youngster of the seventeenth century to the "rabble" of the eighteenth; from the "moral imbecile" of the late nineteenth century to the "constitutional psychopathic inferior" of the early twentieth century; from the "psychopath" of the 1940s to the "sociopath" of the late 1950s, the search for diagnosis continues. With the growth of professionalism, the number of labels has multiplied exponentially. Psychology, education, psychiatry, social work, medicine, anthropology, and sociology, each brings its own set of nosologies. From the "reaction to adolescence" to the "compulsive delinquent"; from the "dyslexic" delinquent to the delinquent "reacting to depression"; from the "unsocialized aggressive" delinquent to the "socialized aggressive" delinquent; from the "bored" delinquent (by reason of high IQ), to the "bored" delinquent (by reason of low IQ); from the delinquent working through unresolved oedipal problems to the delinquent as a product of child abuse; from the antisocial delinquent to the drug-addicted delinquent; from the delinquent in the chaotic family situation to the delinquent subject to "superego lacunae" deficits in family socialization; from the delinquent "unresponsive to verbal conditioning" to the incipient "sociopath" unresponsive to electric shock; from the "criminogenic" family to the "born criminal," the theories and labels proliferate. The search has been futile both in predicting delinquent behavior and in shaping public policy for effective treatment, despite our admittedly greater knowledge of delinquent patterns, family constellations, and community environments. In a familiar reprise, we are once again hearing the classifications of earlier ages: "evil," "malicious," and "genetically influenced" youth. In this sense, there is truth in Chapman's characterization of the helping professions as "latter-day Lombrosos whose social function is to provide the scientific explanations required by the culture."[3]

The British anthropologist Edmund Leach characterized this process as a procedure whereby we bolster the maintenance of the existing order against threats which might arise from its own internal contradictions. Labeling reassures us that the fault lies in the warped offender and takes everyone else off the hook. Moreover, it enables the professional diagnostician to enter the scene or withdraw at will, wearing success like a halo and placing failure around the neck of the client like a noose.[4]

In spite of all this, a particular diagnosis is not necessarily invalid in its own terms. Though it may reflect particular interests and biases, it often touches upon important elements in the makeup and behavior of a delinquent youngster. The issue, however, is one of the relevance of the diagnosis. Diagnosis of young offenders cannot be conceptualized outside the demands of a frequently irrational juvenile corrections system. Labeling is not aimed primarily at understanding the offender or his or her situation. It must serve the purposes of smooth management while leaving unchallenged the public stereotypes of the delinquent. Diagnosis is too often antithetical to the interests of a particular youngster.

Here follow the characteristics of the psychopath as outlined in the classic study by psychiatrist Hervey Cleckley:

1. Superficial charm and good "intelligence."
2. Absence of delusions and other signs of irrational "thinking."
3. Absence of "nervousness" or psychoneurotic manifestations.
4. Unreliability.
5. Untruthfulness and insincerity.
6. Lack of remorse or shame.
7. Inadequately motivated antisocial behavior.
8. Poor judgment and failure to learn by experience.
9. Pathologic egocentricity and incapacity for love.
10. General poverty in major affective reactions.
11. Specific loss of insight.
12. Unresponsiveness in general interpersonal relations.
13. Fantastic and uninviting behavior, with drink and sometimes without.
14. Suicide rarely carried out.
15. Sex life impersonal, trivial, and poorly integrated.
16. Failure to follow any life plan.[5]

Now consider this as a list of survival skills in the average American prison or reform school. You had best be charming, free from delusions, show no sign of nervousness, be untruthful when conditions warrant, watch out for sincerity, mask remorse, occasionally fight, exhibit poverty of affect, be unresponsive in interpersonal relations, avoid suicide, hide love, have an impersonal sex life, and, given the vicissitudes of your situation, eschew anything resembling a life plan. If the family therapist and anthropologist Jay Haley was correct when he described state mental hospitals as hothouses for schizophrenia, surely correctional institutions nurture psychopathy in the same fashion.

Other professionals take a different tack. Referring to the newer term *sociopath* as outlined in the *Diagnostic and Statistical Manual of Mental Disorders* of the American Psychiatric Association, Alan Stone, Professor of Law and Psychiatry at Harvard University, has this to say:

> The invidious aspect of the testimony about sociopaths and their future dangerousness has to do with the racial and social implications of the diagnosis of sociopath as defined by DSM-III rather than with the ethics and expertise of the particular psychiatrists. The diagnostic criteria for antisocial personality in DSM-III might apply to . . . many black men who have grown up in inner cities. Those criteria include the following characteristics when manifest before age fifteen: 1) truancy, 2) delinquency, 3) running away from home, 4) thefts, 5) vandalism, 6) school grades below expected, and 7) repeated sexual intercourse in a casual relationship. The existence of only three of these factors is sufficient to establish the disorder in this age group.
>
> Over age eighteen, manifestations include 1) inability to sustain consistent work behavior, 2) lack of ability to function as a responsible parent, 3) failure to accept social norms, e.g. holding an illegal occupation (pimping, prostitution, fencing, selling drugs), 4) inability to maintain enduring attachment to a sexual partner, 5) failure to honor financial obligations, 6) failure to plan ahead, 7) disregard for truth, and 8) recklessness. If there is a pattern of at least four such manifestations the diagnosis of sociopath is to be made.
>
> Whatever scientific value the diagnosis of sociopath may have, there can be little question that the urban poor and racial minorities will be swept into this diagnostic category. DSM-III may well introduce . . . racism.[6]

Given the bias of the tradition, it would probably be better to avoid psychiatric, psychological, and social work labels. But they persist, whether grounded in science, common sense, prejudice, or myth. Ultimately, they have meaning only in a world which demands them, creates them, and carries out the actions which flow from them—a world of political posturing and militant ignorance, not a world which respects either effectiveness or humane impulse.

The fact that labels attached to captives by correctional bureaucracies derive neither from scientific fact nor cohesive theory seems to have no impact. Contemporary commentators even revel in flying from such considerations. A curious comment of the conservative writer James Q. Wilson exemplifies this attitude. "When confronted with the assertion, 'Crime and drug addictions can only be dealt with by attacking their root causes,' I am sometimes inclined, when in a testy mood, to rejoin: 'stupidity can only be dealt with by attacking its root causes.'"[7] Such an attitude saves us the messiness of knowing too much about delinquents, their families, their lives, their opportunities, their backgrounds, or their experiences. Another's life experience can be rather easily dismissed as irrelevant. But critics like Wilson need not worry. Root causes are low on the national agenda. Our efforts are directed at validating what we are already set to do, since we are more concerned with fueling the engines which drive bureaucracies than with issues of crime and punishment, treatment and deterrence.

Compounding the problem is the fact that, when dealing with the delinquent poor, diagnosticians have untoward power to make their definitions stick. From Lombroso to Wilson and Herrnstein, this has been a primary task of forensic psychiatric diagnosis.[8] One interesting exception has been the feminist analysis of women offenders. For the most part it stresses *common* experiences between women offenders and nonoffenders.[9]

And what of those who understand delinquency and crime as the quintessential human condition in the context of original sin and evil? If this view is granted, the predisposition to evil lies as much in the heart of the definers as the defined. The complex problems which accompany a delinquent's brush with the law are too easily dismissed, the offender too easily fit to a Procrustean bed, limbs hacked or stretched according to national mood or political demands. It seems to me that the greater responsibility rests with those who have the greater power. Those who have risen in the meritocracy have a greater duty to be merciful than those at the bottom and, therefore, are more responsible for their inability to be so. A look at the average prison or reform school population suggests that too much original sin has been heaped on the heads of the poor and of minorities.

I sent an early version of the manuscript for this book to a friend on the faculty at Yale. With kind words, he suggested his publisher. The editor called me a few days later and asked that I send along the manuscript. It sounded as if it might be of interest to them. After a couple of weeks, the editor telephoned me. She said that she liked much of the book but felt it needed another kind of publisher, probably one with a wider market than the primarily academic audience to which her company catered. Then she added a comment that rocked me a bit: "You may have some difficulty with this book, though. It's too compassionate for the times." I took this to mean I was out of touch. At best, the experiences and views I had outlined belonged to another era. At worst, they were wrongheaded and naive.

One seldom sees oneself as particularly naive. I'm certainly no Rousseauian given to positing an innate goodness of man. I hadn't intended my writing as a commentary on the human condition. At times I have been only too aware of the question of the evil in the doings of my fellow human beings, particularly in the past decade, as I have returned to my clinical roots and worked with a wide variety of violent young offenders.

The teenager who killed his father, stepmother, and ten and eleven-year-old brothers, who now sits on death row in a Southern state; the young man who raped, sodomized, and tortured two young women (with fishhooks through their breasts), while their bound and gagged husbands were forced to watch; the myopic fourteen-year-old schoolboy who shot his mother in the head and, while the life slowly drained from her, went dutifully to his English, math, and social studies classes, returning home to check on her death agonies as she crawled from bedroom to bathroom and back again, and finally expired in a runway of coagulated blood late in the second afternoon after the shooting; the young woman, now on death row, convicted (probably unjustly) of having set her house on fire and killed her two infant sons in order to collect a $10,000 insurance policy; the fifteen-year-old who killed his mother and eight-year-old half-brother ostensibly because he had been told he would have to leave home if he got bad grades—all these are individuals I came to know as I tried to make sense of their actions while keeping alive some faint hope for their future.

And occasionally the impossible happens—a young man who, having killed his father, is sent to us for treatment. He must deal with the complicated meaning of his violent act, never to be undone, and in the process he must weather the suicidal ghosts which haunt his wrestling. This exercise would have been denied him had he once been sentenced.

Not infrequently, as I've wound my way through the unspeakable acts and tried vainly to unwind a sense-dulled youth, I've felt the too palpable evil which hovers over and finally chokes a life so twisted that it can find affirmation only in bringing pain to another. But acknowledging an evil act and knowing the capacity for evil in a human being are not the same as labeling a person evil. That is much too simple and is the most naive of conclusions; it is an unforgivable sin which by its nature closes the door on redemption. My purpose has not been to excise human responsibility, overlook the demands of justice, or deny personal accountability. I have tried to nurture hope.

I think of the hundred-pound teenager who killed two others and now awaits sentencing as an adult—a piece of fresh meat to inmates who, outside prison, wouldn't consider abusing him sexually—and I try to find ways to delay his sentence, cajoling and manipulating with a faith grounded in the incompetence of the system, gaining time while fashioning some alternative for the court to consider, and winning a melancholy prize—he is sent to a caring treatment facility until he can grow big enough to survive assault in the twenty years of prison which will follow his rehabilitation. I thought of all these things when I recalled the editor's comment that all this was "too compassionate for the times"—and I'm not sure what that means.

19 *In Search of Aliens*

A man can understand astronomy only by being an astronomer; he can
understand entomology only by being an entomologist (or, perhaps, an
insect); but he can understand a great deal of anthropology merely by
being a man. That same suppression of sympathies, that same waving
away of intuitions or guesswork, which makes a man preternaturally
clever in dealing with the stomach of a spider, will make him preternaturally stupid in dealing with the heart of man.

G. K. Chesterton

In the early years of the Reagan Administration, an old friend, an
eminent criminologist, telephoned me. He had recently attended a
meeting of well-known and respected experts. The impresario of the
event was management professor James Q. Wilson, guru of supply-
side criminology. The researchers had been brought together to discuss
violent crime and its prediction and by inference to mold social policy
with regard to this difficult problem. The meeting was held at the
National Academy of Science in Washington, though it had no particular relationship to the academy. The meeting room was reserved by
Justice Department sponsors. This was a harbinger of the now-familiar
practice of the Bureau of Justice Statistics and the National Institute of
Justice—that of routinely putting a "spin" on convocations, research
findings, and policy studies, imputing credibility to those that fit current ideology and disregarding or discarding the ones that don't.

But those were the halcyon days of conservatism in the saddle at last,
when it was national policy to believe we had finally turned from the
bleeding-heart and mollycoddling theories and practices of the past
and entered a new, more disciplined approach to law and order. We
were within reach of exposing the criminal mind by clinically weeding
out the psychopaths and sociopaths from among us; incapacitating the
criminal body through predictive models based in large part on whether
our correctional system had gotten its hands on the offender at an

earlier age; purging the criminal soul through a curious secular puritanism called "just deserts"; and excising the "wicked" through electrocution, firing squads, and gas chambers, occasionally feeding our fascination for death with antiseptic lethal injections given in a quasi-medical ritual.

My friend, not a cynical man, was depressed. On the plane home he had mulled over the Washington meeting. As he put it, "It was as though there were no history to the field." Important studies, theories, and research findings from the past were not known, were selectively ignored, or were cast aside. Everyone seemed to be starting from scratch in this brave new world.

Here it was, academic criminology caught in the very cycle which had characterized the practice of corrections for the past century. It was a vision of criminologists as neglectful of their own traditions and history as corrections professionals who ignore their own past practices. As far as corrections goes, this is understandable. The history of corrections is not a history of which to be particularly proud—a canon of failed variations on a theme of pain and suffering. Twenty years' experience as a corrections professional usually amounts to one year's experience twenty times over. Research and theory are judged on the basis of their potential as more management and control techniques. Ideas, debate, and creativity are mostly foreign. In the organization which claims to represent American corrections professionals, the American Correctional Association, it is gauche to discuss such things as the death penalty, since 80 percent of the membership supports it. Instead, the focus is on how to manage the execution of an inmate professionally—how to do it efficiently, how to cool the body, how to stuff the rectum of the condemned with cotton, how to kill successfully. Who would wish to dwell on a history like that? But criminologists are another matter. They have every reason to heed their own history and traditions. Surely they should see themselves as providing something beyond technologies for management and control.

Those conservative researchers who found themselves in the ascendant in Edwin Meese's ideology-driven Justice Department seemed optimistic, if not giddy, at the prospects their handiwork presented for the administration's agenda on crime and corrections. But beneath the optimism moved a familiar cynicism, though not the cynicism of the dogged researcher inured to personal disappointment at unpromising results, poor replicability, or misuses of his or her theories. No, the cynicism which gripped those called to the front of the class by the ideologues who dispensed federal funds was grounded in something else entirely.

The administration in Washington had made it acceptable to proclaim openly a heretofore well-kept secret among both academic criminologists and corrections practitioners. All were now encouraged to trumpet an old theme loudly: offenders, adult and juvenile, are indeed different from the rest of us, and those differences are what matter most. Though the same theme had been the pedal point to most criminal justice research and theory even during the so-called heyday of rehabilitation, it had now become a full-blown dirge to which liberals and conservatives dutifully trudged.

The "we-them" dichotomy has always been at the heart of American corrections. Its classification systems confirm it. Its institutional traditions set it in concrete. Woe betide him who dares, even ever so faintly, to blur this elemental distinction. But this obsessed dualism has not come on the scene in just the last few years. It was there from the beginnings of such great liberal experiments as the juvenile justice system.

A few years ago I came across a 1917 report of the Cook County Civil Service Commission about the Juvenile Detention Home. After noting that neither the plans nor the ideals of the originators of the detention home were being fulfilled, and after calling the facility more a jail than a home, the commission recommended the removal of dependent and minor delinquents.

But in an aside which strikes to the heart of the matter, the report said: "For the remaining children,—the immoral girls, the incorrigible and unruly boys and girls, the present Juvenile Detention Home and the present custodial care are none too severe." "In Detroit," the report added "individual separation rooms are installed for and occupied by the incorrigibles who deserve complete isolation, which we also recommend."[1] Among those contributing to the report were such twentieth-century reformers as Jane Addams of Chicago, Julia Lathrop of Detroit, and William Healy of Boston. Such distinctions are upheld even by the "do-gooders."

Why is this? How can we prescribe for others what we would not consider for our own? I presume that we feel a continuing need to confirm our own identity and security by telling us who we are not. Durkheim pointed to this when he said that, if we were a society of saints, we would probably invent new rules someone would be obliged to break so that the rest of us could relax, secure in the judgment that there are deviant outsiders at the gates.[2]

But why do academics and researchers rush down the same mean streets? One might excuse a Lombroso or an E. A. Hooton his elitism or racism as symptomatic of another time in history.[3] But such justifications are more elusive in contemporary criminology. I learned long ago that these diagnoses are more than anything else social prescriptions. I judge labels by the treatments they demand, and current preoccupations with issues like the criminal personality, the criminal mind, and the career criminal are more ominous than hopeful.

Though we all tend to separate ourselves from those who offend us or offend against us—and though it may take an extraordinary, perhaps even spiritual, effort to see beyond these distinctions—it is clear that in recent years many in academic criminology have given up that effort. As the theories have grown more "realistic" and the methodology more complicated, criminologists have grown more detached and disconnected from the stuff of their studies—offenders, their families, their children, their neighborhoods, their lives. As a result, our prisons and reform schools are filled with fabricated aliens made yet more alien by those who should know better, but who insufficiently understand the subjects of their research beyond narrow methodological parameters or highly controlled settings which demean and impoverish human experience.

There continues to be a plethora of studies of offenders, but most are quite different from those of the not-so-distant past. Something important is being lost. What was the lifeblood of academic criminology is leaving its veins. Researchers have found an escape in the detachment their techniques offer. Their findings are increasingly narrow, eliciting interest primarily from those in politics or government who search for smooth management of brutal systems.

As a result, current academic criminology has contributed greatly to the further deterioration of the corrections system, causing (or at least not hindering) overcrowding, programless prisons, more executions, incapacitation of much of the young black male population at one time or another, and abuse and neglect of historic proportions. Of course, these conditions have always plagued the intellectually arid and morally bereft field of corrections; but in the past there was at least some distant recognition that what was being done was not right.

These days, corrections practitioners sin boldly, with little compunction, as they go about their destructive tasks: So what if we warehouse people? Nothing works. So what if we drag juveniles and adults to the electric chair? It's a form of social poetry. So what if we lock up so many blacks, Hispanics and poor white trash? It's in their genes or their elongated third toe. So what if those rehabilitative programs we do allow are the psychological equivalent of aggravated assault? Compassion has no place in modern correctional management. Give us more razor wire, more prisons, more buildings, more staff, more uniforms, more Mace, more modern holes, more managers; and, if you do send us any helpers, make sure they are the psychojusters of an H. G. Wells fantasy—"experts" who do their business without disturbing or questioning anything we might do. A decade of models of deterrence, incapacitation grids, mandatory sentences, justice models, and "nothing works" cynicism has found an increasingly warmer home among corrections professionals. The disposition has been there for a century, and now, a banner of scientific validation is being hung from the prison flagpole.

The interesting econometric models which have been of limited use in predicting economic behavior or molding sound fiscal policy are apparently expected to produce something better in our pursuit of law and order through a mainframe. Maybe such models do hold promise, but too heavy a reliance on them in dealing with populations of individuals who are captives has grave implications for the future.

Subjects who fit ideologically driven research models well are in relatively short supply, but captive subjects can be sorted, defined, and sifted with relative ease. As the Reagan Justice Department successfully demonstrated, well-controlled research can shift a policy focus or maim the very realities we study.

Not long ago, criminologists valued personal contact, participant observation, interchange, and argument with those they studied. I think of what has been lost with the disappearance of the giants of the Chicago School—Clifford Shaw, W. I. Thomas, George Herbert Mead—great researchers, theoreticians, and philosophers who, in their studies, contributed something to the evolution of human values. They knew the persons they studied—in settlement houses, in their neighborhoods, in the prisons, and on the streets. Their research enriched society. Thorsten Sellin, Nils Christie, Michel Foucault, Lloyd Ohlin, Donald Cressey, Simon Dinitz, Bill Chambliss, and Erving Goffman never lost touch with persons, faces, stories, and lives in their pursuit of theory.

As we run thousands of adult and juvenile offenders and inmates through statistical models with little regard for how individuals might suffer in the game, we have little recognition that what we are doing is undoubtedly poor science as well. The stuff of this field, as with most, if not all, human activity, *should* be messy, frequently unpredictable, usually difficult, and always exasperating. It should cause us to question ourselves continually about what we do, our society, our values, and our goals. Beware of anyone who comes with a "solution." Finality in this field is inevitably ominous.

Criminologists cannot engage in "cut-outs"—a process spelled out by Michael Lesy in his series of essays, *Forbidden Zone.* In this professional correctional practice used in executing a prisoner, "Procedures are so fragmented that no single person remains responsible. . . . By the time a death sentence is carried out, it's impossible to accuse any particular person of anything."[4]

Criminologists must be connected to the people they study, and must assume at least *some* personal responsibility for the policy implications of their theories and findings. I am sure there are many researchers and practitioners who would not share my views about what might be a better approach to handling adult or juvenile offenders. That's all right. But unless they are willing to be held as personally responsible for their model and their suggestions as I have been held for my actions, I cannot take them seriously.

I've attended funerals and met with the families of victims of youngsters in the care of the state agencies I have run, and I have wondered whether, if we had been more stringent, the tragedy would have occurred. I have also stood with and supported those troubled and troubling juveniles we returned to the streets as a result of my policy decision to close reform schools. It wasn't particularly easy or pleasant— the slander, sarcasm, cynicism, death threats, and all those other factors added up to what the American psychiatrist Harry Stack Sullivan used to call a lack of consensual validation (a precursor of paranoia). But having experienced both the isolation and the paranoia, I don't think that others who have influenced the field far more than I should get a free ride.

Those whose models tell the Supreme Court the death penalty is a deterrent have every right to that view. I presume they will defend their views in the scholarly literature. When their research becomes the rationale for executions, however, it seems to me that they should go immediately to a death row. They should know well the person who will next be executed—meet his family, his parents, his children—come to understand him well, and then attend the execution and watch as his hands clench and his head smokes and his soul departs. That is human responsibility.

Those who compile computerized sentencing grids, adding five years here or ten years there with the touch of a button or the mark of a pencil, might spend some time in the prisons of the systems they have prescribed—not in the warden's office or on the guided tour, but sitting in a cellblock among strangers and hostile staff, or stripped nude in the hole. They might spend a week, or a month, and they might contemplate what a year, or ten years, means. Those who so glibly construct hurtful and defeating labels—"psychopath," "sociopath," "criminal personality," all diagnoses which ensure neglect, hostility, mishandling, and brutality—might first thoroughly know and respect another's life history. It takes unusual arrogance to dismiss a fellow human being's lost journey as irrelevant. It takes a pathological compulsiveness to disregard personal experience in pursuit of categories.

What I miss most in contemporary criminology is human passion—frustrating, pigheaded, wrongheaded, but always compelling and authentic. Mistakes will be made, but sins of passion are more easily forgiven than sins of the intellect. As Jacques Barzun put it in his marvelous book *A Stroll with William James*, "The mind works to serve wants, ideas are the product of desire. James did not discover this truth; Plato admitted it with regret; Hume asserted it with vehemence: 'The mind is and ought to be the slave of the passions.' But it was James who showed that desire, taking the form of interest, pursues not simply practical ends but also theoretical and aesthetic."

As psychiatrists and psychologists forsake insight and understanding in pursuit of insurance reimbursement–generated nosologies, and as sociologists pursue models fit for federal funding requirements, someone must say something about the individual. Otherwise, we will be our own undoing.

Having been raised in a Catholic tradition long since forsaken, I recall St. Thomas Aquinas, one of the great thinkers and grand theorists of Western civilization, who, on his deathbed, surrounded by his fellow monks, was reminded of his many written works. He responded that finally, his work was no more than straw. Finally, it is one's wrestling with life that matters.

As I finished writing this postscript, which was originally delivered in accepting an award from the American Society of Criminology, the latest issue of *The Criminologist*, the official newsletter of the society, arrived. In it was a moving obituary of the eminent American criminologist Don Cressey by Lloyd Ohlin. Lloyd recalled an interview John Laub had with Cressey. Asked about his dreams for the future, Cressey replied, "I dream of writing a criminal code for the U.S. . . . that doesn't have any punishment in it . . . a book telling how to run a society on the basis of a reward system. Although I know I can't do it, I know that sociologists as a gang can do it. Skinner had provided a frame. 'Beyond the punitive society,' clearly must be the goal of the next generation of sociologists and criminologists."[5]

And there, side-by-side with this blessedly out-of-sync aspiration of a pioneer in American criminology, was an almost full-page notice from the National Institute of Justice, outlining its 1988 Research Program Plan priorities—"Apprehension and Prosecution of Criminal Offenders; Public Safety and Security; Punishment and Control of Offenders; Offender Classification and Prediction of Criminal Behavior; Violent Criminal Behavior; Forensic and Criminal Justice Technology; and Criminal Careers and the Control of Crime."

Aldous Huxley, in his book *Ends and Means*, written in those dark days just before World War II began, noted that advance in civilization has not been characterized by progress in justice, but rather by progress in charity.[6] In criminology today, "charity" has become a dirty word. It is time for criminologists to recognize the other responsibilities inherent in their efforts, to lift their work to the level of a truly human act.

Notes

Preface

1. Jack A. Brizius, "People, Institutions and Public Policy: A Prospectus." Unpublished background paper prepared for *National Governors' Association,* 1976.

2. David Rothman, "Can De-Institutionalization Succeed?" *New York University Education Quarterly* (Fall 1979); see also "Report on New York Hospital De-Institutionalization," prepared by New York City councilwoman Carole Bellamy, 1979.

3. Barbara Allen-Hagen, *Children in Custody, 1987* (Washington: Office of Juvenile Justice and Delinquency Prevention, 1988).

4. As I have traveled around the country over the past fifteen years, I have grown inured to being met by corrections and mental health professionals, clippings in hand, reciting a familiar (and untrue) litany as to how the Massachusetts Experiment had failed: rising crime rates, more adolescents in adult prisons, and most commonly, the secret reopening of the reform schools.

5. Eugene Doleshal, "The Dangers of Criminal Justice Reform," *Criminal Justice Abstracts* 14 (March 1982): 135.

6. S. Gould, J. Tillem, and P. Heymann, "Jerome Miller and the Department of Youth Services," C 14–76–101,102,102s, Kennedy School of Government, President and Fellows of Harvard College, 1976.

Chapter 1

1. *In re* Gault, 387 U.S. 1 (1967).

2. Barry Krisberg, "The Juvenile Court: Reclaiming the Vision" (San Francisco: National Council on Crime and Delinquency, 1988), 12.

3. Letter of New England abolitionist Samuel Howe, 1844, supplied by Lou Brin, Marblehead, Massachusetts.

4. Quoted in Frederick H. Wines, *Punishment and Reformation: A Study of the Penitentiary System* (New York: Thomas Crowell, 1910), 379.

5. Ibid., 376.

6. Quoted in Anthony M. Platt, *The Child Savers: The Invention of Delinquency* (Chicago: University of Chicago Press, 1969), 150.

7. Julian Mack, "The Juvenile Court," *Harvard Law Review* 23 (1909): 104.

8. Cook County Civil Service Commission, "Report on Investigation of Juvenile Detention Home" (Chicago: Clohesy and Co., 1917), 5.

9. Ibid., 6.

10. Roscoe Pound, address to annual meeting of the National Council of Juvenile Court Judges, 1950.

11. George H. Mead, "The Psychology of Punitive Justice," in *Theories of Society,* ed. Talcott Parsons (Glencoe, Ill.: Free Press, 1961), 2:876–86.

12. Francis M. Rush, Jr., "Social and Historical Factors in the Development of Total Institutions: Their Relevance for the Discipline of Public Administration" (unpublished manuscript, George Washington University, 1978), 42.

13. Mary E. Richmond, *Social Diagnosis* (New York: Russell Sage Foundation, 1917).

14. D. Willard, "Form, Function, and Objectives," in Howard W. Odum and D. Willard, *Systems of Public Welfare* (Chapel Hill: University of North Carolina Press, 1925), 55–56.

15. L. Trilling, *Doing Good: The Limits of Benevolence,* eds. Gaylin, Glasser, Marcus, and Rothman (New York: Pantheon Books, 1978).

16. Richard J. Lundman and Frank R. Scarpitti, "Delinquency Prevention: Recommendations for Future Projects," *Crime and Delinquency* (San Francisco: National Council on Crime and Delinquency, April 1978).

17. Robert J. Gemignani, "Diversion of Juvenile Offenders from the Juvenile Justice System," in *New Approaches to Diversion and Treatment of Juvenile Offenders* (Washington: U.S. Department of Justice, Law Enforcement Assistance Administration, June 1973).

18. Paul Nejelski, "Diversion of Juvenile Offenders in the Criminal Justice System," in *New Approaches to Diversion and Treatment of Juvenile Offenders,* 83.

19. *Institutions, Etc.,* 1:8, National Center on Institutions and Alternatives, Washington, 1978.

20. *Hidden Closets* (Sacramento: California Youth Authority, 1975).

21. Paul DeMuro, A. DeMuro, and S. Lerner, *Reforming the California Youth Authority* (Commonwealth Research Institute, 1988).

22. Jack Brizius, "People, Institutions and Public Policy."

23. Kenneth Carlson, *Population Trends and Projections of American Prisons and Jails,* vol. 2 (Washington: National Institute of Justice, 1980); see also William Nagel, *The New Red Barn: A Critical Look at the Modern Prison* (New York: Walker and Co., 1973). The idea that we fill prisons according to the number of available cells received severe criticism. The Panel on Sentencing Research of the National Research Council, along with neoconservative writer James Q. Wilson, suggested that there is little evidence for this hypothesis in the 1971 to 1975 prison populations upon which the Nagel and ABT studies were based. The data since 1980 however, tend to support the "cells available" hypothesis.

24. The Twentieth Century Fund, *Confronting Youth Crime: Report of the*

Twentieth Century Fund Task Force on Sentencing Policy toward Young Offenders (New York: Holmes and Meier, 1978), 6.

25. Edmund Leach, *A Runaway World: The BBC Reith Lectures* (London: British Broadcasting Company, 1967).

Chapter 2

1. Charles Dickens, *American Notes* (New York: St. Martins, 1985), 45.

2. Governor's Anti-Crime Council, L. Swartz, project manager, *History of Massachusetts Statutes Relating to Delinquent Youth* (Boston: State of Massachusetts, 1985).

> The enactment of St. 1906, Chapter 413, of the Massachusetts Acts and Resolves, is generally regarded as the birth of the delinquency code in Massachusetts. Though these statutes first deemed the proceedings against juvenile offenders to be civil in nature, the pattern of treating juvenile offenders differently than their adult counterparts began in 1836. One solitary enactment of the Revised Laws of 1836 provides that certain boys and girls convicted of an offense punishable by incarceration in the state prison will serve any sentence in a house of correction, county jail or house of reformation. This was the Commonwealth's initial response to the acknowledgement of the distinctions between juvenile and adult offenders. . . .
>
> The General Statutes of 1860 carry over the 1836 prohibition on incarceration of juveniles in state prison and in Chapters 75 and 76 provide for the following additional dispositional alternatives. If the offense alleged does not call for punishment of life imprisonment and the juvenile is deemed a proper subject, he or she may be committed to either the State Reform School for Boys (Lyman) or State Industrial School for Girls (Lancaster). . . .
>
> Any girl committed, by a judge or commissioner, to the Industrial School is kept, disciplined, instructed, employed and governed under the direction of the trustees until one of three things happens: (1) she is "bound" out, (2) she arrives at age 18, or (3) she is otherwise legally discharged. The term "bound" out refers to a form of indenture where a child serves a master as an apprentice or servant. . . .
>
> [In addition to being assigned to clipper ships,] Boys could also be "bound" out or they could remain committed until the age of 21.

3. Maxwell Jones, *The Therapeutic Community* (New York: Basic Books, 1953). Jones extended his conception of the therapeutic community as practiced in Scotland's Dingleton Hospital to a facility for the "criminally insane" outside London.

4. Harry H. Vorrath and L. Brendtro, *Positive Peer Culture* (Chicago: Aldine, 1974). Vorrath's work began in the mid-1960s at the Red Wing Reform School in Minnesota and continued at the Training Institute of Central Ohio (reform school) in Columbus under the rubric "Guided Group Interaction."

5. Albert Trieschman and L. Brendtro, *The Other 23 Hours: Child Care Work with Emotionally Disturbed Children in a Therapeutic Milieu* (Chicago: Aldine, 1969).

6. Barry Feld, *Neutralizing Inmate Violence: Juvenile Offenders in Institutions* (Cambridge, Mass.: Ballinger, 1977).

7. As reported in *Impact* (Raleigh, N.C.) and in the *Criminal Justice Newsletter* (Hackensack, N. J.: National Council on Crime and Delinquency, 1973).

8. Robert Coates, Alden Miller, and Lloyd Ohlin, *Diversity in a Youth Correctional System* (Cambridge, Mass.: Ballinger, 1978). The Harvard studies eventually included seven books and thirty-five professional articles.

9. In 1986, at Illich's invitation, I was a presenter on the Massachusetts Experiment at the Institute for Higher Learning, University of Berlin. Foucault, through his biographer Colin Gordon, expressed his wish to discuss the Massachusetts model, but he died before the meeting could take place.

Chapter 3

1. August Aichhorn, *Wayward Youth* (New York: Viking Press, 1966; first published 1925).

2. Michael Burn, *Mr. Lyward's Answer* (Boston: Beacon Press, 1956).

3. A. S. Neill, *Summerhill: A Radical Approach to Child Rearing* (New York: Hart, 1960).

4. H. J. Eysenck, *Crime and Personality*, rev. ed. (London: Routledge and Kegan Paul, 1977).

5. F. J. Roethlisberger and W. J. Dickson, *Management and the Worker* (Cambridge: Harvard University Press, 1939).

6. Karl R. Popper, *The Open Society and Its Enemies* (Princeton: Princeton University Press, 1950).

Chapter 4

1. *U.S. Children's Bureau Report on Massachusetts Youth Service Board* (Washington: U.S. Department of Health, Education, and Welfare, 1968).

2. Carol Liston, "Youth Board Booted Again," editorial, *Boston Globe*, Sept. 25, 1969.

3. *Boston Herald*, Sept. 20, 1969.

4. *Boston Herald*, March 12, 1969.

Chapter 5

1. Dickens, *American Notes*, 45.

2. Wines, *Punishment and Reformation*, 376–80.

3. Ruth Richardson, *Death, Dissection and the Destitute* (London: Routledge and Kegan Paul, 1987).

4. Intake logbooks for State Training School for Boys (Lyman), 1842–1910.

5. "If under 14 years of age, a boy could be committed, by a judge, to either the State Reform School or its Nautical Branch. The Nautical Branch instructs the boys in navigation and the duties of seamen. If the trustees contract to send a boy to sea then such a voyage operates as a discharge from the institution." *History of Massachusetts Statutes*, 4.

6. Howe noted that there were already 30,000 "institutions" in Massachusetts that should be considered for wayward girls—"they are called families." Letter of Samuel Howe supplied by Lou Brin, Marblehead, Massachusetts.

7. Harriet Ritvo, *The Animal Estate: The English and Other Creatures in the Victorian Age* (Cambridge: Harvard University Press, 1987).

8. *History of Massachusetts Statutes*, 6.

9. *Boston Globe*, Dec. 17, 1970.

10. Robert Vinter, *Time Out: A National Study of Juvenile Correctional Programs* (Ann Arbor: University of Michigan Press, 1976).

11. DeMuro, DeMuro, and Lerner, *Reforming the California Youth Authority*.

12. Barry Krisberg, *The Watershed of Juvenile Justice Reform* (San Francisco: National Council on Crime and Delinquency, 1985).

13. The overlap of the child welfare, mental health, and youth corrections systems has been well documented by Paul Lerman in *Deinstitutionalization and the Welfare State* (New Brunswick, N.J.: Rutgers University Press, 1982).

Chapter 6

1. Clifford Shaw, *The Natural History of a Delinquent Career* (Chicago: University of Chicago Press, 1931).

2. The first federal funds were made available under the Juvenile Delinquency and Control Act of 1968. The initial act provided only $5 million in federal funds.

3. Decision by the California Supreme Court in 1988 upholding the redefining of a status offender as a bona fide "delinquent" when in violation of a court order. (*In re* Michael G., 44 Cal 3283, 1988).

4. This was also the impression of Howard James, correspondent for the *Christian Science Monitor*, who interviewed hundreds of youngsters in institutions in the late 1960s. His series was published as *Children in Trouble: A National Scandal* (Boston: Christian Science Publishing, 1969).

Chapter 7

1. *Boston Globe*, Oct. 11, 1954. "The unit was designed to separate those boys considered too dangerous to the community and themselves to be rehabilitated under the open school program. These boys are, according to John D. Coughlan, chairman of the Massachusetts Youth Service Board, 'that small

minority of boys who persistently rebelled at efforts to help them and became serious runaway problems'."

2. Irving Kaufman, E. S. MacKay, and J. Zilbach, "The Impact of Adolescence on Girls with Delinquent Character Formation," *American Journal of Orthopsychiatry* 29 (1959): 130–43. It was Kaufman's view that most delinquents suffer from chronic depression, which tends to get worse when they develop close interpersonal relationships. Kaufman attributed this to inadequate mothering.

3. David Rothman, *The Discovery of the Asylum: Social Order and Disorder in the New Republic* (Boston: Little, Brown, 1971).

4. *A Report of the Labors of John Augustus: First Probation Officer, 1784–1859* (American Probation and Parole Association, 1984; first published 1852).

5. *U.S. Children's Bureau Report,* 4:14.

6. *History of Massachusetts Statutes.*

7. *Boston Globe,* Nov. 10, 1971.

8. *U.S. Children's Bureau Report,* "Report on Administrative Organization of Division of Youth Services," Raymond Manella, 1966, Part I, Section C, p. IV, 4–85.

9. G. Frank, *The Boston Strangler* (New York: New American Library, 1966), 227. I was told by an older employee at Lyman School that when the thirteen-year-old Albert was in the discipline cottage there he was assigned the task of feeding a matron's cat. On an occasion when he forgot these duties, he was forced for a number of days to eat his food and drink his milk out of saucers placed on the floor while the matron stood over him. Whether one can draw a connection to his later compulsive hunt for matronly victims is, of course, a matter of conjecture.

10. John Lennon and Paul McCartney, "Here Comes the Sun."

11. *Boston Globe,* Nov. 30, 1953.

12. Usually these are more remote communities plagued by unemployment and in need of a steady income from a relatively enduring and long-lived state institution. In 1987, when Virginia announced its intention to build a new prison, a number of towns in the economically depressed coal belt competed for the institution. Illinois had a similar scenario complete with videos taped by the town fathers presented to legislative committees and correctional authorities.

13. *Boston Globe,* Nov. 7, 1970.

14. George Cadwalader, *Castaways: The Penikese Island Experiment* (Chelsea, Vt.: Chelsea Green Publishing, 1988).

Chapter 8

1. Robert Hitt, in conversation with the author.

2. *U.S. Children's Bureau Report,* 4:6.

3. Ibid., 40.

4. Robert Theobald, presentation at the Academy for Contemporary Problems, Columbus, Ohio, 1972.

5. Popper, *The Open Society and Its Enemies,* 154.

6. Ibid., 155.

7. Ibid., 159.

8. Neil J. Smelser, *Theory of Collective Behavior* (New York: Free Press of Glencoe, 1963), 24.

9. Ibid., 33.

10. An example of this can be seen in the brutal but well-managed Texas prisons of the 1970s. S. Martin and S. Ekland-Olson, *Texas Prisons: The Walls Came Tumbling Down* (Austin: Texas Monthly Press, 1987).

11. American Correctional Association, *Standards for Training Schools,* 2d ed., (U.S. Department of Justice, NIC Grant EC-7, January 1983).

12. Erving Goffman, "Characteristics of Total Institutions," in *Deviance: Studies in the Process of Stigmatization and Societal Reaction,* eds. Dinitz, Dynes, and Clarke (New York: Oxford University Press), 472–85.

Chapter 10

1. Barry Feld, *Neutralizing Inmate Violence* (Cambridge, Mass: Ballinger, 1977).

2. A particularly interesting narrative of this process from beginning to end can be found in E. Stotland and A. Kobler, *Life and Death of a Mental Hospital* (Seattle: University of Washington Press, 1965).

3. The length of stay had less to do with a young person's offense or dangerousness than with his or her ability to adjust to the demands of the institution, i.e., whether or not he or she was a management problem. Indeed, those who presented the most nagging problems in institutional control were more often with us for lesser or minor offenses. The more sophisticated delinquents had fewer problems in adjusting to institutional regimens.

4. Ohlin, Coates, and Miller, unpublished report, Harvard Center for Criminal Justice, 1970.

5. *Boston Globe,* Dec. 12, 1970.

Chapter 11

1. George H. Mead, "The Psychology of Punitive Justice," 876.

2. Roscoe Pound, 1950 address.

3. J. Rubin, *Do It!* (New York: Simon and Schuster, 1970).

4. The *Boston Globe* of April 29, 1982, in a feature article on the Bouncer program, headlined it as a "shock sentence" for juveniles. The article noted the barbed wire, floodlights, lock boxes, and general jail-like atmosphere. Department of Youth Services Commissioner Edward Murphy, "who devised what is

officially called the crisis intervention program, admits it is a slight retreat from the state's 10 year old commitment to keep most juvenile offenders out of jail." The program was closed a month later.

5. Radon eventually went on to head a halfway house for juveniles funded by the philanthropist William Coolidge. He continues in that work at this writing.

6. *Boston Globe,* Jan. 12, 1971.

7. *Boston Globe.*

8. Robert Coates, unpublished study done at the Harvard Center for Criminal Justice on detention practices in Boston, 1971.

9. Coates, Miller, and Ohlin, unpublished reports on the first year's progress in the Massachusetts Department of Youth Services research project.

10. Ibid., 12.

Chapter 12

1. *New York Times,* Sept. 4, 1988, p. 4E.

2. Richard Lamb, "Deinstitutionalization at the Crossroads," *Journal of Hospital and Community Psychiatry* 39 (1988).

3. Burton Blatt, "From Institution to Community: A Conversion Model," in *Educational Programming for the Severely/Profoundly Handicapped* (Syracuse: University Center for Human Policy, 1988).

4. Massachusetts Department of Youth Services, planning document, December 1970.

5. Massachusetts Legislature Committee on State Administration, "Report on Department of Youth Services," 1972.

6. E. Mulvey, "Amenability to Treatment in Juvenile Offenders: A Contextual Judgement" (unpublished paper, University of Pittsburgh, Western Psychiatric Institute, 1983).

7. *Diagnostic and Statistical Manual,* American Psychiatric Association, rev. 1989.

8. Massachusetts Department of Youth Services, "A Strategy for Youth in Trouble," unpublished mimeograph, 1972.

9. Commonwealth of Massachusetts, Massachusetts Legislature Joint Committee on Post-Audit, "Management Audit of Department of Youth Services" (1975), 109.

10. 1969 Mass. Acts, sec. 40, chap. 838.

11. "Management Audit," 112.

Chapter 13

1. Charles Murray and L. Cox, *Beyond Probation: Juvenile Corrections and the Chronic Offender* (Beverly Hills: Sage, 1979).

2. Elliott Currie, *Confronting Crime: An American Challenge* (New York: Pantheon, 1985).

3. Donna Hamparian, R. Schuster, S. Dinitz, and J. Conrad, *The Violent Few: A Study of Dangerous Juvenile Offenders* (Lexington, Mass.: D.C. Health, 1979).

4. P. Greenwood and S. Turner, *Selective Incapacitation Revisited: Why High Rate Offenders Are Hard to Predict* (Washington: National Institute of Justice, 1987).

5. Erving Goffman, "On Cooling the Mark Out: Some Aspects of Adaptation to Failure," in *Symbolic Interaction*, ed. Arnold Rose.

6. Ibid.

7. I think of the work of Robert Lindner, August Aichhorn, George Lyward, William Healy, Gisela Konopka, Fritz Redl, David Wineman, Melitta Schmidberg, Erik Erikson, Edward Glover, Adelaide Johnson, Kate Friedlander, Muriel Gardner, Alice Miller, Jerome Bruner, and K. R. Eissler, all of whom stressed the importance of child and adolescent development and maintain an ultimate respect for the integrity of the individual life history. Had most post-Parsons sociologists not had so much antipathy toward psychodynamic models, theories like symbolic interactionism might have been more closely allied with the generally ignored experience of the more thoughtful among clinicians. Such an alliance, I believe, would have led us in productive directions in understanding the roots of crime and delinquency.

8. Lewis Yablonsky, *The Violent Gang*, 1968.

9. The Libra program was proposed by a young adult ex-offender, an alumnus of Bridgewater's Institute for Juvenile Guidance. He set up a fine program for half a dozen youngsters in Cambridge. But the fact that a large state contract went to Libra was apparently too much of a source of conflict within the fledgling organization. A few months before I left the state, one of the officers of Libra began threatening the director of the program, apparently with an eye to controlling the funds. It culminated in his showing up in my office late one afternoon. I had put a hold on the Libra funds, and he apparently came in to kill me. As it happened, the only others working late that afternoon were two older ex-offenders I had hired. They were quick to see the bulge in the young man's coat pocket and correctly took it to be a gun. Uninvited, they sidled into my office on each side of my upset (and high) visitor. After a few minutes of his threats and shouts, things calmed down and the young man was quietly walked to the door. On a visit to Boston a few years later, I noticed his name in the newspaper. He had been convicted of murdering an acquaintance.

10. Trieschman, Whittaker, and Brendtro, *The Other 23 Hours.*

Chapter 14

1. Dane Archer and Rosemary Gartner, *Violence and Crime in Cross-National Perspective* (New Haven: Yale University Press, 1984), 177ff.

2. Donna Hamparian, "Youth in Adult Courts: Introduction," in *Major Issues in Juvenile Justice Information Training: Readings in Public Policy* (Columbus, Ohio: Academy for Contemporary Problems, 1981).

3. M. Joan McDermott and Michael Hindelang, "Analysis of National Crime Victimization Survey Data to Study Serious Delinquent Behavior," in *Juvenile Criminal Behavior in the United States: Its Trends and Patterns*, eds. M. Joan McDermott and Michael J. Hindelang (Albany, N.Y.: Criminal Justice Research Center, 1981).

4. Daniel Popeo, "Executing Juveniles Is a Social Necessity," *USA Today*, June 30, 1988.

5. Archer and Gartner, *Violence and Crime*, 177ff.

6. U.S. Justice Department, Federal Bureau of Investigation, *Uniform Crime Reports*, 1990.

7. Alabama, Alaska, Arizona, Arkansas, California, Colorado, Delaware, District of Columbia, Florida, Hawaii, Idaho, Indiana, Iowa, Kansas, Kentucky, Maine, Maryland, Minnesota, Mississippi, Montana, Nebraska, Nevada, New Hampshire, New Jersey, New Mexico, North Dakota, Ohio, Oklahoma, Oregon, Pennsylvania, Rhode Island, South Dakota, Tennessee, Utah, Virginia, Washington, West Virginia, Wisconsin, and Wyoming.

8. Georgia, Illinois, Louisiana, Massachusetts, Michigan, Missouri, South Carolina, and Texas.

9. Connecticut, New York, North Carolina, and Vermont.

10. City of Boston Police Department (1980), *Juvenile Arrest Statistics, 1975–1979*.

11. Breaking and entering offenses ranked first in frequency (33%) followed by use of a motor vehicle without authority (14%), larceny (12.5%), other property crimes (8.7%), assault and battery with a dangerous weapon (7.3%), assault and battery (6%), and robbery (5.5%). When the relationship between sex and offense was examined, it was found that juvenile boys committed different kinds of crimes from those of juvenile girls; over 58 percent of the boys, compared to 48 percent of the girls, were sentenced to the Department of Youth Services for property offenses, while a higher proportion of juvenile girls (16%) than juvenile boys (3%) was sentenced for public order crimes. Also see Marjorie Brown et al., *A Study of Juveniles Committed to the Massachusetts Department of Youth Services in 1978* (research report, Massachusetts Trial Court, Commission of Probation, Feb. 25, 1983).

12. McDermott and Hindelang, *Juvenile Criminal Behavior in the United States*, 27. (Research monograph prepared for U.S. National Institute for Juvenile Justice and Delinquency Prevention, Criminal Justice Research Center, Albany, New York, 1981).

13. Hamparian et al., *The Violent Few*.

14. M. Wolfgang, R. Figlio, and T. Sellin, *Delinquency in a Birth Cohort* (Chicago: University of Chicago Press, 1972).

15. Paul Strasburg, *Violent Delinquents* (New York: Monarch, 1978).

16. McDermott and Hindelang, *Juvenile Criminal Behavior in the United States*, 27.

17. C. Whitaker, *Teenage Victims: A National Crime Survey Report* (Bulletin NCJ 103138) (Washington: U.S. Department of Justice, 1986), 1. See also *Elderly Victims* (Bulletin NCJ 107676) (Washington: U.S. Department of Justice, 1987), 1.

18. In 1979, when the Federal Office of Juvenile Justice and Delinquency Prevention wanted to encourage treatment initiatives directed toward young inmates committed to state reform schools for crimes of personal violence, the definition had to be widened from "violent" to "serious delinquent behavior" (burglary) due to the fact that most state youth corrections systems did not have enough juveniles in the systems convicted of crimes of personal violence to justify the federal initiative.

19. He is now a lawyer and a successful crime novelist.

Chapter 15

1. Letter received from Commissioner Donovan upon the announcement of my resignation, December 1972.

2. *Boston Globe*, "Youth Services on the Mat," February 1972.

Chapter 17

1. Primarily the work of W. H. Sheldon and Eleanor Glueck at Harvard University: *Unraveling Juvenile Delinquency* (Cambridge: Harvard University Press, 1950); *Delinquents and Non-Delinquents in Perspective* (Cambridge: Harvard University Press, 1969); and W. Sheldon's work on somatotyping delinquents, *Varieties of Delinquent Youth* (New York: Harper, 1949).

2. William McCord and J. Sanchez compared the criminal careers of 1950s Lyman School alumni with graduates of New York's private, intensive, non-punitive Wiltwyck School. Five years after their release from Wiltwyck, only 9 percent of the predominantly black graduates had been convicted of a felony, while 67 percent of the mostly white Lyman alumni had been. Looking to the more serious young offenders among the overall groups, McCord and Sanchez concluded, "Wiltwyck seemed to have a dramatic impact upon the youngsters diagnosed as psychopathic (judged potentially dangerous or violent). During the first five years after their release, only 11 percent of the psychopathic men from Wiltwyck committed grave offenses—murder, rape, armed robbery—compared with 79 percent of Lyman's psychopathic inmates."

But after five years, the pattern changed. The Wiltwyck boys got progressively worse, while the Lyman graduates improved. By age twenty-five, recidivism lines had crossed, and by the time the men reached their mid-thirties, 32 percent of the Wiltwyck alumni were getting into trouble as opposed to only 8 percent of the men from Lyman.

An overwhelming difference emerged—ethnicity. Virtually all the recidivists from Wiltwyck were black and Hispanic, and even among the fewer Lyman recidivists, a disproportionate number were black or French Canadian.

The therapeutic effects of Wiltwyck grew less relevant as its inner-city alumni came up against discrimination in education, employment, and housing, and as they lived over time in socially disorganized communities. As the researchers put it, "The ex-Wiltwyck men we interviewed remembered the school fondly—in one sense, perhaps, too fondly. For most of these young men Wiltwyck offered a welcome relief from the 'real world'." The "real world" undid the therapy (W. McCord and J. Sanchez, "Curing Criminal Negligence," *Psychology Today* [April 1982]).

3. LaMar Empey and Steven Lubeck, *The Silverlake Experiment: Testing Delinquency Theory and Community Intervention* (Chicago: Aldine, 1971); LaMar Empey and Maynard L. Erickson, *The Provo Experiment: Evaluating Community Control of Delinquency* (Lexington, Mass.: D. C. Heath, 1972).

4. Lloyd Ohlin, Robert Coates, and Alden Miller, *Report on Massachusetts Department of Youth Services, 1975* (Cambridge: Center for Criminal Justice; Harvard University Law School).

5. Ibid.

6. R. Robinson, *Juvenile Cases in Massachusetts Courts* (Boston: Massachusetts Committee on Children and Youth, 1968). See also L. Williams, *Youthful Offenders Evaluation*, Vol. 2, "Bind Overs Committed to Massachusetts Department of Corrections, 1968–1979" (Boston: Massachusetts Department of Corrections, Publication #12672, January 1982); M. Brown and R. Sagan, *Juvenile Bindover in Massachusetts: 1979* (Boston: Office of Commissioner of Probation, 1980); L. Williams, *Youthful Offenders Evaluation*, Vol. I, "Youthful Offenders Committed to the Massachusetts Department of Corrections 1968 to 1979" (Boston: Massachusetts Department of Corrections, Publication #12564, September 1981).

7. Barry Krisberg, James Austin, and Patricia Steele, *Working Juvenile Corrections: Evaluating the Massachusetts Department of Youth Services* (San Francisco: National Council on Crime and Delinquency, November 1989).

8. Ibid., 26.

9. Howard N. Snyder, *Court Careers of Juvenile Offenders* (Pittsburgh: National Center for Juvenile Justice, March 1988), 10.

10. "Secure care" means something quite different in the Massachusetts Department of Youth Services than in other states. It refers usually to highly supervised settings such as group homes which are secure in terms of high staff-boy or staff-girl ratios. This is often referred to as "eyeball security"—one not reliant on hardware, locks, and walls.

However, the number of juveniles in these settings had grown to over two hundred by early 1990. This is far too large a number and carries ominous implications, since it is precisely this category (too often arbitrarily defined) of the "most dangerous" or "violent" youth which sustains the whole system. The reader should understand that greater labeling of juveniles as "dangerous" or "violent" and the consequent increase of secure care is virtually unrelated to rises in violent or serious crime rates, incidents, or numbers of violent youths. In large part the escalation of labels marks the beginnings of a bureaucratic response to political pressures and rhetoric of the times.

Chapter 18

1. M. Forsyth, *Buildings for Music: The Architect, the Musician, and the Listener from the 17th Century to the Present Day* (Cambridge: Massachusetts Institute of Technology Press, 1985).

2. Edward P. Mulvey, "Amenability to Treatment."

3. Denis Chapman, *Sociology and the Stereotype of the Criminal* (London: Tavistock Publications, 1968).

4. Edmund Leach, *A Runaway World*.

5. Hervey Cleckley, *The Mask of Sanity* (St. Louis: C. V. Mosby, 1941).

6. Alan A. Stone, *Law, Psychiatry and Morality: Essays and Analysis* (Washington: American Psychiatric Press, 1984).

7. James Q. Wilson, *Thinking about Crime* (New York: Basic Books, 1975), xiv-xv.

8. Cesare Lombroso, *The Criminal Man* (Montclair, N.J.: Patterson Smith, 1972; first published 1890); and James Q. Wilson and Richard Herrnstein, *Crime and Human Nature* (New York: Simon and Schuster, 1985).

9. A good example of this can be found in Ann Jones's book *Women Who Kill* (New York: Holt, Rinehart and Winston, 1980).

Chapter 19

1. Cook County Civil Service Commission, "Report on Investigation of Juvenile Detention Home" (Chicago: Clohesy & Co., 1917), 6.

2. Emile Durkheim, *The Rules of Sociological Method* (New York: Free Press, 1964; first published 1938).

3. Lombroso, *The Criminal Man*. See also E. A. Hooton, *Crime and the Man* (Cambridge Mass.: Harvard University Press, 1939).

4. Michael Lesy, *Forbidden Zone* (New York: Farrar, Strauss, and Giroux, 1987), 140.

5. Lloyd Ohlin, obituary of Donald Cressey, *The Criminologist* (Fall 1987).

6. Aldous Huxley, *Ends and Means* (Westport, Conn.: Greenwood Press, 1969; first published 1937).

Bibliography

Reform of Youth Corrections in Massachusetts

1967

Massachusetts Committee on Children and Youth. *Report and Recommendations to His Excellency Governor John A. Volpe on "The Study of the Division of Youth Service and Youth Service Board, Commonwealth of Massachusetts."* Conducted by the Children's Bureau, Department of Health, Education and Welfare, Washington, April.

1972

Bakal, Yitzhak, Howard Polsky, and Joseph Fitzpatrick, eds. *The Conference Proceedings for "The Closing Down of Institutions and New Strategies in Youth Services."* Leominster, Mass.: Village Press.

Massachusetts General Court. *Report of the Joint Committee on State Administration to Evaluate the Programs and Facilities within the Department of Youth Services.* Boston, March.

Schucter, Arnold. *A Strategy for Youth in Trouble.* Boston: Department of Youth Services, Commonwealth of Massachusetts.

Vachon, Brian. "Hey Man, What Did You Learn in Reform School?" *Saturday Review* 55/38 (Sept. 16): 69–76.

1973

Bakal, Yitzhak. *Strategies for Restructuring the State Department of Youth Service.* (Washington: U.S. Department of Health, Education, and Welfare).

Bakal, Yitzhak, and Howard Polsky. *Closing Correctional Institutions: New Strategies for Youth Services.* Lexington, Mass.: D. C. Heath.

Koshel, Jeffrey. *Deinstitutionalization—Delinquent Children.* Urban Institute Paper. Washington: Urban Institute.

1974

Dorsey, Jim. "Smoke in Boston for a Chicago Fire." *Boston Magazine* 66/8: 30–33.

Finnegan, William H. *Management Audit of the Department of Youth Services.* Boston: Joint Committee on Post-Audit and Oversight Bureau.

Rutherford, Andrew. *The Dissolution of the Training Schools in Massachusetts.* Columbus, Ohio: Academy for Contemporary Problems.

1976

Behn, Robert D. "Closing the Massachusetts Public Training Schools." *Policy Sciences* 7: 151–71.

Gould, Stephanie. "Jerome Miller and the Department of Youth Services." Case #C–14–76–101 (A) and (B). Cambridge: Kennedy School of Government, Harvard University.

1977

Massachusetts Department of Youth Services. *The Issue of Security in a Community-Based System of Juvenile Corrections.* Final report of the Task Force on Secure Facilities, L. Scott Harshbarger, chairman. Boston: Commonwealth of Massachusetts, November.

1978

Eisele, Frederick, and Daniel Katkin. "Implementing Termination: Deinstitutionalizing Juvenile Corrections in Massachusetts and Pennsylvania." Paper presented at the annual meeting of the American Political Science Association, New York.

Massachusetts Committee on Criminal Justice. *Client Flow and Information Collection in the Massachusetts Juvenile System.* Belmont, Mass.: Contract Research Corporation.

Massachusetts Committee on Criminal Justice. *Massachusetts' Compliance with the Deinstitutionalization and Separation Mandates of the Juvenile Justice and Delinquency Act:* 1978 Monitoring Report. Boston: Massachusetts Committee on Criminal Justice.

Massachusetts Department of Youth Services. *Annual Report, 1977.* Boston: Commonwealth of Massachusetts.

Sprowls, James T., and Bruce Bullington. "Removing Juveniles from the State Correctional Institution at Camp Hill: A Case Study." *Juvenile Delinquency: Little Brother Grows Up,* January 1978.

1979

Massachusetts Committee on Criminal Justice. *Directory of Residential Programs for Court-Involved Youth.* Boston: MCCJ, August.

Massachusetts Department of Youth Services. *Annual Report, 1978,* Boston: Commonwealth of Massachusetts.

Massachusetts Office for Children, Institutional Advocacy Project. *Community Review of Children in Institutions Proposal.* Boston: Massachusetts Office for Children, May 24.

Vachss, Andrew H., and Yitzhak Bakal. *The Life-Style Violent Juvenile.* Lexington, Mass.: D.C. Heath.

1980

Vorenberg, Elizabeth, et al. *Delinquent Justice: Juvenile Detention Practice in Massachusetts* (Task Force on Children Out of School). Boston: Massachusetts Advocacy Center.

1981

Serrill, Michael S. "Massachusetts: A Harder Line toward Juveniles." *Corrections Magazine,* February.

1984

Rutherford, Andrew. "The Massachusetts Alternative: A Radical Approach to Juvenile Justice." *The Listener Magazine* (BBC–London), May 3.

Velie, Lester. "The State That Freed Its Young from Jail." *Readers Digest,* May.

Welch, G. Michael. "Establishing a Violence-Free Atmosphere in a Secure Treatment Unit—An Exploration of the Robert F. Kennedy School," in *Violent Juvenile Offenders: An Anthology,* ed. Robert Mathias, Paul DeMuro, and Richard Allinson. San Francisco: National Council on Crime and Delinquency.

1985

Greenwood, Peter W., and Franklin E. Zimring. "One More Chance: The Pursuit of Promising Intervention Strategies for Chronic Juvenile Offenders." Rand Corporation, May.

1986

Altshuler, Alan A. "A Comment on 'Groping Along.'" *Journal of Policy Analysis and Management* 7, 4: 664–67.

Behn, Robert, "Management by Groping Along." *Journal of Policy Analysis and Management* 7, 4: 643–63.

Bullington, Bruce, James T. Sprowls, Daniel Katkin, and Harvey Lowell. "The

Politics of Policy: Deinstitutionalization in Massachusetts, 1970–1985." *Law and Policy* 8,4 (October).

Landers, Robert K. "Juvenile Justice Inside or Out?" *Congressional Quarterly Editorial Research Reports.* Washington: Congressional Quarterly, Nov. 28.

Margolis, Richard J. *Out of Harm's Way: The Emancipation of Juvenile Justice.* New York: Edna McConnell Clark Foundation.

1990

Krisberg, Barry, James Austin, and Patricia Steele. *Unlocking Juvenile Corrections: Evaluating the Massachusetts Department of Youth Services.* Final Report. San Francisco: National Council on Crime and Delinquency.

Publications and Reports on Reform of Massachusetts Department of Youth Services: Center for Criminal Justice Harvard Law School

1973

Coates, Robert B., Alden D. Miller, and Lloyd E. Ohlin. "Strategic Innovation in the Process of Deinstitutionalization: The University of Massachusetts Conference." In *Closing Correctional Institutions,* ed. Y. Bakal and H. Polsky. Lexington, Mass.: D. C. Heath.

Coates, Robert B., and Alden D. Miller. "Neutralization of Community Resistance to Group Homes." In *Closing Correctional Institutions,* ed. Y. Bakal and H. Polsky. Lexington, Mass.: D. C. Heath.

Ohlin, Lloyd E. "Institutions for Predelinquent or Delinquent Children." In *Child Caring, Social Policy and the Institution,* ed. Donnel M. Pappenfort, Dee Morgan Kilpatrick, and Robert W. Roberts. Chicago: Aldine.

1974

Coates, Robert B., Alden D. Miller, and Lloyd E. Ohlin. "The Labeling Perspective and Innovation in Juvenile Correctional Systems." In *Issues in the Classification of Children: A Sourcebook on Categories, Labels, and Their Consequences,* ed. Nicholas Hobbs. Beverly Hills: Jossey Bass.

Ohlin, Lloyd E. "Organizational Reform in Correctional Agencies." In *Handbook of Criminology,* ed. Daniel Glaser. Rand McNally.

Ohlin, Lloyd E., Robert B. Coates, and Alden D. Miller. "Radical Correctional Reform: A Case Study of the Massachusetts Youth Correctional System." *Harvard Educational Review* 44 (February).

1975

Coates, Robert B., and Alden D. Miller. "Criminal Justice Sets, Strategies, and Component Programs: Evaluating Change in the Criminal Justice System." In *Criminal Justice Research,* ed. Emilio Viano. Lexington, Mass.: D. C. Heath.

Coates, Robert B., and Alden D. Miller. "Evaluating Large Scale Social Service Systems in Changing Environments: The Case of Correctional Agencies." *Journal of Research in Crime and Delinquency* (July).

Ohlin, Lloyd E. "Reforming Programs for Youth in Trouble." In *The Mentally Retarded and Society: A Social Science Perspective,* ed. Begab and Richardson. University Park Press.

Ohlin, Lloyd E., Robert B. Coates, and Alden D. Miller. "Evaluating the Reform of Youth Corrections in Massachusetts." *Journal of Research in Crime and Delinquency* (January).

1976

Miller, Alden D. "Knocking Heads and Solutions to Functional Problems: Components of Change." *Sociological Practice,* 1/1.

1977

Feld, Barry C. *Neutralizing Inmate Violence: Juvenile Offenders in Institutions.* Cambridge, Mass.: Ballinger.

Miller, Alden D., Lloyd E. Ohlin, and Robert B. Coates. "The Aftermath of Extreme Tactics in Juvenile Justice Reform: A Crisis Four Years Later." In *Corrections and Punishment: Structure, Function, and Process.* Sage Criminal Justice Annals, 8.

Miller, Alden D., Lloyd E. Ohlin, and Robert B. Coates. *A Theory of Social Reform: Correctional Change Processes in Two States.* Cambridge, Mass.: Ballinger.

Ohlin, Lloyd E., Alden D. Miller, and Robert B. Coates. *Juvenile Correctional Reform in Massachusetts.* A collection of articles from the project published by the Law Enforcement Assistance Administration. Washington: U.S. Government Printing Office.

1978

Coates, Robert B., Alden D. Miller, and Lloyd E. Ohlin. *Diversity in a Youth Correctional System: Handling Delinquents in Massachusetts.* Cambridge, Mass.: Ballinger.

McEwen, Craig A. *Designing Correctional Organizations for Youths: Dilemmas of Subcultural Development.* Cambridge, Mass.: Ballinger.

1979

Miller, Alden D., Lloyd E. Ohlin, and Robert B. Coates. "The Politics of Correctional Reform: An Analytical Approach to the Natural History of Social Change." Paper presented at the 1979 meeting of the Society for the Study of Social Problems, Boston. It was later used in two training conferences and can be found in the *Pennsylvania Association on Probation, Parole, and Corrections Quarterly* 26, 3 (Autumn).

1980

Harvard Center for Criminal Justice. "Report on Preliminary Feedback from the Harvard Study of Secure Care Decision Making." Cambridge, Massachusetts.

Miller, Alden D., Robert B. Coates, and Lloyd E. Ohlin. "Evaluation of Correctional Systems under Conditions of Normal Operation and Major Change." In *Handbook of Criminal Justice Evaluation,* ed. Klein and Teilmann.

Miller, Alden D., and Lloyd E. Ohlin. "Conceptualization and Measurement for Study of Change in Youth Opportunity Systems and Youth Correctional Systems." Cambridge: Harvard Center for Criminal Justice.

Miller, Alden D., and Lloyd E. Ohlin. "Decision Making about Security for Juveniles: Report of the First Two Years of the Secure Care Project." Cambridge: Harvard Center for Criminal Justice.

1981

Miller, Alden D., and Lloyd E. Ohlin. "Mobilization of Policy for Day to Day Social Control Affecting Youth Opportunities." Cambridge: Harvard Center for Criminal Justice.

Miller, Alden D., and Lloyd E. Ohlin. "The Politics of Control and Opportunity: A Background Paper on the Youth Opportunity System, the Day to Day Social Control System, and the Policy Making System." Cambridge: Harvard Center for Criminal Justice.

1982

Miller, Alden D., and Lloyd E. Ohlin. "Baseline Data on Mobilization for Day to Day Social Control Affecting Youth Opportunities in Two Communities." Cambridge: Harvard Center for Criminal Justice.

Miller, Alden D., Lloyd E. Ohlin, and Julie A. Taylor. "Community Changes, Social Control, and Juvenile Delinquency." Cambridge: Harvard Center for Criminal Justice.

Miller, Alden D., Lloyd E. Ohlin, and Julie A. Taylor. "A Method of Studying Change in Delinquency and Community." Cambridge: Harvard Center for Criminal Justice.

Miller, Alden D., Julie A. Taylor, Lloyd E. Ohlin, and Robert B. Coates. "Responding to Delinquency: The Importance of the Community." Cambridge: Harvard Center for Criminal Justice.

1983

Miller, Alden D., and Lloyd E. Ohlin. "Final Report on Correctional Reforms in the Department of Youth Services." Cambridge: Harvard Center for Criminal Justice.

Miller, Alden D., Lloyd E. Ohlin, and Julie A. Taylor. "Youth Violence and System Response." Cambridge: Harvard Center for Criminal Justice.

1985

Miller, Alden D., and Lloyd E. Ohlin. *Delinquency and Community: Creating Opportunities and Controls.* Beverly Hills: Sage.

Index

Abuse: at county training schools, 201-2; of inmates, 32, 44, 49, 56-57, 69, 71, 94-96, 97-98; inmates' hiding of, 108-9. *See also* Cottage Nine; Discipline cottages; Isolation rooms; "Tombs"; Victimization

ACA. *See* American Correctional Association

Accountability. *See* State bureaucracy: accountability in

Ackerman, Nathan, 24

Adams, Rudy, 30

Addams, Jane, 7, 242

Adolescent Remand Center (Rikers Island, NY), 213

Age: average, of inmates in MA reform schools, 50

Aichhorn, August, 26

Air conditioning: Miller's use of, 146

Alcohol: and delinquency, 50

Alternative programs: effects of, 147-48; relation to institutions, viii, 153-55. *See also* Community-based programs

American Correctional Association (ACA), 75, 85, 90, 181, 241

American Federation of State, County, and Municipal Employees, 97

American Psychiatric Association, 155, 233, 236

American Society of Criminology, 247

Andros program, 196-98

Armstrong, Chris, 34-35, 36, 74, 104

Atkins, Chester, 202

Augustus, John, 67, 110

Avery, Len, 55-56

Backman, Jack, 40, 206

Bakal, Yitzhak, 132, 147, 150

Bartley, David, 39-40, 163-64, 202, 205-6, 211

Barzun, Jacques, 246

Batterton, Dick, 30

Beal, Frank, 153

Beatings. *See* Abuse

Beaumont, Gustav Auguste de, 5-6

Bellamy, Carol, 154

Bender, Evelyn, 175

Bender-Gestalt tests, 157

Bergeron, Father, 212

Best, Eric, 139

Bettelheim, Bruno, 188

"Bill," 112-14

"Billy," 71

Blacks: numbers of, in MA reform schools, 50, 51

Blumer, Herbert, 88, 89

Bolster, Bobby, 109-10, 145

Boone, John, 117, 204

Boston Globe, 108, 130, 210; and Miller, 106, 170, 202, 207, 211; on reform schools, 48, 69, 78, 142, 147, 202

Boston Herald, 36, 209, 216

Boston Herald-Traveler, 180

Boston House of Reformation for Juvenile Offenders (MA), 6, 16, 43

Boston Legal Assistance Project, 145

Boston Magazine, 216

Boston Mental Health Foundation, 196

Boston Phoenix, 86

"Boston Smoke for a Chicago Fire" (*Boston Magazine*), 216

Boston Strangler, 63, 70

"Bouncer" program, 139

Bourque, George, 137

Bowen, Louise, 7

Boys' Industrial School at Shirley. *See* Shirley Industrial School for Boys

Brewster. *See* Forestry Camp at Brewster

Bridgewater. *See* Institute for Juvenile Guidance at Bridgewater

Bridgewater State Hospital, 72

Briggs, George, 69

Brown, Bob, 70-71, 127

Brown, Dan, 24

Bruno, Joey, 144

Brutality: in reform schools. *See* Abuse